# Education – An Anatomy the Discipline

*Education – An Anatomy of the Discipline* focuses on the development of the discipline of education, how it is understood and practised in contemporary universities, and the potential threats to its future. As the author John Furlong argues, disciplines are not only intellectually coherent fields of study; they also have a political life, they are argued for, supported, challenged and debated. Nowhere is this truer than in the discipline of education.

In this authoritative text, Furlong describes the history as well as the current state of the discipline of education in universities. He also explores the range of national and global changes that have helped to shape the discipline in recent years. Education's final 'arrival' in the university sector coincided with major changes in universities themselves. Today, universities are very diverse institutions: they no longer have a sense of essential purpose and have largely accepted their loss of autonomy, especially in education where government intervention is particularly strong. If education is now fully integrated into universities, then, like the system as a whole, it urgently needs to find a voice, set out a vision for itself and state what its purpose should be within a university in the modern world.

The book therefore brings together four vitally important topics:

- the changing nature of the university;
- the academic and scholarly study of education as a field;
- the professional education and training of teachers;
- the nature and organisation of educational research.

*Education – An Anatomy of the Discipline* will occupy a central place in contemporary literature about education; although based on evidence from British universities, its implications are important across the world. The book will be invaluable reading for all professionals working in university departments and faculties of education as well as those with an interest in the changing role of the university in contemporary society.

**John Furlong** is Emeritus Professor and former Director of the Department of Education at the University of Oxford, UK.

# Education – An Anatomy of the Discipline

## Rescuing the university project?

John Furlong

LONDON AND NEW YORK

First published 2013
by Routledge
2 Park Square, Milton Park, Abingdon, Oxon, OX14 4RN

Simultaneously published in the USA and Canada
by Routledge
711 Third Avenue, New York, NY 10017

*Routledge is an imprint of the Taylor & Francis Group, an informa business*



*British Library Cataloguing in Publication Data*
A catalogue record for this book is available from the British Library

*Library of Congress Cataloging-in-Publication Data*
Furlong, John, 1947- author.
Education : an anatomy of the discipline / John Furlong.
pages cm
1. Education--Study and teaching (Higher)--Great Britain.
2. Teachers--Training of--Great Britain. 3. Universities and colleges--Curricula--Great Britain. I. Title.
LB2173.G7.F87 2013
370.71'10941--dc23
2012033108

ISBN: 978-0-415-52005-8 (hbk)
ISBN: 978-0-415-52006-5 (pbk)
ISBN: 978-0-203-07885-3 (ebk)

Typeset in Galliard
by Saxon Graphics Ltd, Derby

Printed and bound by CPI Group (UK) Ltd, Croydon, CR0 4YY

This book is dedicated to my father

Bill Furlong

(1914–1973)

My first and most important teacher about the world of education

**Anatomy:** from the Ancient Greek ἀνατέμνειν, *anatemnein*: *ana*, 'separate, apart from' and *temnein*, 'to cut up, cut open' – Wikipedia

# Contents

# Abbreviations

| | |
|---|---|
| AARE | Australian Association for Educational Research |
| AERA | American Educational Research Association |
| BEd | Bachelor of Education |
| BERA | British Educational Research Association |
| BBC | British Broadcasting Corporation |
| CPD | Continuing Professional Development for teachers |
| CATE | Council for the Accreditation of Teacher Education |
| DCSF | Department for Children, Schools and Families |
| DfF | Department for Education |
| DfEE | Department of Education and Employment |
| DENI | Department of Education, Northern Ireland |
| DfES | Department for Education and Skills |
| DES | Department for Education and Science |
| EPPI | The Evidence for Policy and Practice Information and Co-ordinating Centre |
| EdD | Doctorate of Education |
| ESRC | Economic and Social Research Council |
| Estyn | Her Majesty's Inspectorate for Education and Training in Wales |
| EC/EU | European Community/European Union |
| EERA | European Educational Research Association |
| GTCNI | General Teaching Council for Northern Ireland |
| GTCS | General Teaching Council for Scotland |
| HMI, HMIE | Her Majesty's Inspectorate/Her Majesty's Inspectorate of Education (Scotland) |
| HESA | Higher Education Statistics Agency |
| HEFCE | Higher Education Funding Council for England |
| IOE | Institute of Education (University of London) |
| LEA | Local Education Authority |
| MEd | Masters of Education |
| MTL | Masters in Teaching and Learning |
| MOTE studies | Modes of Teacher Education research project |
| Ofsted | Office of Standards in Education (for England) |

| | |
|---|---|
| OECD | Organisation for Economic Co-operation and Development |
| PGCE, PGDE | Post Graduate Certificate of Education/Post Graduate Diploma in Education (Scotland) |
| QAA | Quality Assurance Agency for Higher Education |
| QR | Quantum for Research (funding) |
| RAE | Research Assessment Exercise |
| REF | Research Excellence Framework |
| SFRE | Strategic Forum for Research in Education |
| TLRP | Teaching and Learning Research Programme |
| TDA | Training and Development Agency for Schools |
| UCET | Universities' Council for the Education of Teachers |
| TTA | Teacher Training Agency |

# Acknowledgements

Thanks are due to the academic colleagues, too many to mention, with whom I have worked over the last 40 years; directly and indirectly they have all helped to contribute to what I have written here. More specifically, the thinking behind this book began during a visiting International Fellowship at Sydney University; I am grateful to the university and to my colleague there, Peter Goodyear, for making that possible. I would also like to acknowledge those in the 10 case study universities who so willingly gave time and thought to their participation in this project; without their willing cooperation, there would have been no project. Thanks are also due to the many colleagues who, in the last few years have discussed my ideas with me, provided references or read parts of this book in draft form. They include Marilyn Cochran-Smith, Hubert Ertl, Keri Facer, John Gardner, Bill Green, Susan Groundwater-Smith, Hazel Hagger, Harry Judge, Martin Lawn, Alison Lee, Mark Lofthouse, Sara Loosemore, Ingrid Lunt, Ian Menter, Geoff Whitty, Richard Pring, Alis Oancea, Judyth Sachs, Jason Todd and David Watson.

Finally I want to acknowledge the ongoing support of my family, especially my wife Ruth.

# Preface

I have dedicated this book to my father, Bill Furlong, because it was he, whether consciously or not, who gave me my vocation, my lifelong commitment to the field of education and to the teaching profession. He also opened my eyes – and this was definitely not conscious on his part – to some of the contradictions and tensions that constantly bedevil the teaching profession and the field of education more generally.

Many of those contradictions and tensions, I will argue, have their roots in different forms of educational knowledge, often somewhat simplistically expressed as the differences between 'knowing how' and 'knowing that', between the theory and the practice of education. Historically, those differences were expressed institutionally in distinctions between the teachers colleges and universities. Universities did research and theory, and were based on the principles of liberal education, while teachers colleges were dedicated to the world of practice.

Today, in most of the English speaking world, teachers colleges have become integrated into (a much changed) university system. As a result, those tensions are now lived out in different ways, but they still concern unresolved debates about the nature of prospective teachers' personal educations, about the role of theory and practice in professional education and training and about the relationship between research and the development of policy and professional practice in schools and elsewhere. In the modern world, therefore, all of these perennial issues are experienced in terms of debates about the relationship between our universities and the field of education. And these are the concerns of this book, concerns that I first became aware of at a personal level, through my own father, a highly successful primary school teacher and headteacher.

Although he was a successful teacher, my father did not go to university. As a child of a very poor single-parent family growing up between the wars, he was educated at the local elementary school and left at the age of 14. He then took a seven-year apprenticeship as a printer and bookbinder. It was the war that gave him the opportunity to continue his education. In the army, with the support of his commanding officer, he completed his school certificate and later, as a sergeant, he informally began tutoring some of the men in his platoon. When the war ended he was determined not to go back into the printing trade and opted instead for the Emergency Teaching Training Scheme which ran from 1945 to

1951 to deal with the teacher shortage after the war (Crook, 1997; Cunningham, 1992).

As he said quite explicitly, he wanted to 'better himself' and the Emergency Teacher Training Scheme – designed to take people like him, with comparatively modest educational backgrounds – was too good an opportunity to miss. He completed the one-year course in 1947 and there then followed a highly successful teaching career, firstly in the closing years of the elementary school system and then in primary schools in Hertfordshire. In 1961 he was appointed headteacher of Tewin JMI School, a village school of some 150 pupils near Welwyn Garden City. He died in 1973, while still in post.

But in the 1950s and 1960s, Hertfordshire was no ordinary Local Education Authority. Under the leadership of Sir John Newsom, Hertfordshire primary schools were attracting national and international acclaim for their pioneering educational practice. Primary schools in Hertfordshire captured the spirit and the letter of the Plowden Report (Plowden, 1967). They led the country in the development of open-plan schools, the 'integrated day', the 'new maths', the teaching of reading through the Initial Teaching Alphabet and, closest to my father's heart, outdoor education.

As the Plowden Report documents, each of these innovations was coming about because of the developments in psychological, pedagogical and philosophical research; research that was taking place in universities in the UK and internationally. And my father and his school at Tewin were at the forefront of every one of these new developments, taking those research-based ideas and putting them into practice. As a result, he became highly regarded across the county as one of the leading practitioners of all that was excellent in contemporary primary schooling.

Heady days, though, of course, it was precisely these 'evidence-informed' practices (evidence for the Plowden Report ran to over 600 pages) that were to become the bête noire of New Right activists of the 1970s and 1980s in their campaign against progressive education. Within a generation, all of the educational innovations that my father had championed had been swept away by the Thatcher revolution.

But that was the future. In the world in which I grew up, schools and teaching were part of everyday life. It is what was discussed around the tea table every night after school; it is what gave my father and my mother success and standing in their family (my father was the only one in our extended family who could claim to be a 'professional'); and it was the teaching profession that, despite leaving school at 14, gave him the social mobility that he and my mother so very much wanted. As a result, it was not at all surprising to me or to anyone else when I decided at the age of 22 to take up education as a career – firstly, as a teacher but with my background as a social scientist, always with the idea of becoming an educational researcher and lecturer. Education was pretty much in the blood.

And yet, even as a teenager, it became clear to me that matters were not that straightforward. As well as developing a high regard for education and the teaching profession, I also learned, subliminally at first, of the contradictions and tensions in the field. Although my father was very highly regarded locally, it was always *only* as a primary school teacher. The masters at my grammar school never gave any sign of acknowledging him or our family as being the same status as they. When he taught their children, which he did in a number of instances, there were polite and personal affirmations but never between equals. My father, as a primary school teacher was a *practitioner*; it was they who were the professionals, university men every one, most with no professional training at all.

My consciousness of these tensions eventually became explicit because of a particular incident that happened in 1963. My mother and father celebrated their silver wedding by taking a 10-day coach trip to Italy and they took me with them. On the return journey our coach stopped for the night at a hotel in Switzerland and we found ourselves seated at dinner with another couple travelling independently. The conversation soon turned to education and it emerged that the man at our table was a retired HMI. On learning that my father had recently been appointed a headteacher, he asked about his training. 'I hope', he said, 'you were not one of those 'semitrained' teachers who entered the profession through that Emergency Teacher Training Scheme!'

The family row between my parents in their bedroom after dinner was not about how awful the man had been, but about how my father did not stand up for himself and his professional training. My father, whom I respected and whom I thought everyone else respected because of his professional status, was rendered speechless by someone he did not know, by an attack from someone who was supposed to be in the same profession. In the face of this attack, he had nothing to say. I suspect that that was because this 'university man', with all of his condescension, had touched his Achilles' heel: the reality of his own educational and training background and all of its inadequacies.

These are, of course, all personal stories, some kind of explanation as to my personal interest in the subject matter of this book. But what I now recognise is that these personal stories were all examples of public issues; they have much wider significance. My father's career as a successful village schoolteacher demonstrates many of the historic tensions in the field of education: tensions between different sections of the teaching profession; debates about the nature of professional education; debates around the role of research, evidence and political ideology in the development of professional practice; and, where my father was particularly vulnerable, debates about the personal education of teachers.

Despite his very humble beginnings, my father made a huge success of his career, but he was not merely successful; he was also passionate about education probably because he was aware of how much he personally and the majority of his generation had missed out on educational opportunities as children. Whatever its origins, he passed on his passion to me. He was, of course, a teacher in a very different time, yet many of the questions raised by his career remain unanswered today.

What I hope is that through this book, I can begin to lay bare some of these underlying tensions as they are currently lived by all of us with my father's commitment to education so that we might perhaps in the future find better ways of resolving them.

Oxford
30 September 2012

# Section I

# Introduction

# Section

# Introduction

# 1 Education

## A discipline?

> When they are performing at their full potential, the professional schools of the university (that is, departments and schools of education, law, medicine and so on) are positioned in a delicate balance between the university and the society... The university protects them from becoming the vassals of the profession; the profession, in turn, protects them from becoming mere satellites of the graduate school of arts and sciences... That delicate balance puts the professional schools into their leadership position in lifelong education that is reshaping the mission of the university as a whole.
>
> Jaroslav Pelikan (1992: 183)

> Education is the second largest discipline under consideration and perhaps one of the most complex. Structural, historical and institutional factors affect all disciplines in different ways, but, in education, their impact has been quite profound.
>
> ESRC Demographic Review, Mills *et al.* (2006)

### Introduction and overview

This book is about the 'discipline' of education, particularly as it is currently understood and practised in contemporary universities. Some readers might find the use of the term discipline provocative; it is intended to be. This is because disciplines are not merely intellectually coherent fields of study; they also have a political life. They are argued for, supported, challenged and debated. Nowhere is this more true than in education and particularly in England where the role of university-based knowledge within professional education continues to be fiercely debated (DfE, 2010). But such debates are not new; nor are they confined only to England or indeed professional education. Even in Scotland, where the contribution of the universities to study of education is widely supported, there remain questions as to precisely what sort of educational knowledge is most appropriate for beginning teachers (Donaldson, 2011). And as we will see in later chapters, there are also major debates between different research traditions in education with fundamental differences in theory and in method. Epistemologically, education therefore lacks the consensus and indeed the coherence of some of the more established disciplines; nevertheless institutionally and politically, it functions very much as a discipline in its own right, even though, for most of its existence, it has not been 'master' of its own destiny.

This political weakness has come about largely because, as in the USA (Labaree, 2004) as a discipline, education has always been dominated by its involvement with teacher education. While research, the teaching of higher degrees and, increasingly today, 'nonprofessional' undergraduate degrees, while all of these are vitally important parts of education faculties today, the field as a whole has been profoundly shaped by its engagement with professional preparation. As we will document in more detail in the next chapter, the universities in the United Kingdom began their first tentative involvement with teacher education at the end of the nineteenth century; however, it was not until the last quarter of the twentieth century, a full 100 years later, that the majority of teacher education institutions (colleges, polytechnics) become firmly established as part of the university system in the UK.

What is interesting and indeed ironic about that history is that by the time education finally became fully integrated in the university sector, things had changed in universities. That final integration coincided with the massification of higher education, which, in combination with the neo-liberal turn (the pursuit of markets), has resulted in the 'multiversity,' or what some describe as the postmodern university, characterised more by difference than similarity. Universities are now highly differentiated institutions both between themselves and in themselves. Cardinal Newman (1853a), with his ideal of liberal education is dead or at least his voice is lost in a cacophony of 'difference'.

The fact that the university system has become increasingly postmodern is evidenced by the fact that even our most ancient of universities have found it possible to accept the full integration of the discipline of education; they have done this at a time when education – or at least some key parts of it – have become increasingly centrally controlled, increasingly based on a technical rationalist conception of knowledge and, especially in England, directed by central government fiat. If the teacher trainers of the early and middle twentieth century thought that moving into the university sector would give them protection from external intervention, then they were to be very much mistaken.

A central argument of this book is that as a consequence of education's final integration into the university system, the difficulties and dilemmas it faces are now no more than an extreme version of the difficulties faced by the university system as a whole. At the root of the discontents of the modern university, as Rothblatt (1997) and many others have argued, is the lack of a coherent idea or set of ideas as to what a university actually is. As Smith and Webster (1997) put it, 'When difference is so strong a factor, fragmentation is the corollary. The confidence of intellectuals in their own activities has been reduced and there is no one available to speak for the university' (p. 4). The result is an apparent passivity of higher education in the face of the massive changes that have overcome it. 'There is a marked reluctance to articulate a motivating purpose, to address questions about the *raison d'être* of higher education… The university seems resigned to a preset agenda which is narrowly instrumental, one can say passive... No alterative vision seems to be available' (Smith and Webster, 1997: 4).

If education as a field of study is therefore now fully integrated into the university system, then, like the system as a whole, it urgently needs to find a voice; it needs to set out a vision for itself; it needs to state what its purpose or purposes should be within a university in the modern world.

That modern world, though, is different from the past; it is not the nineteenth century world of Newman and the pursuit of knowledge for its own sake, nor is it the world of 1960s, when Paul Hirst found certainty in disciplinary-based knowledge (Hirst, 1966); nor is it the world of the early 2000s, with the search for evidence-based practice that could be 'rolled out' across the educational system as a whole. It is a world where universities are increasingly only one of many authoritative 'voices' craving attention in our society; it is a world where sophisticated organisations run by highly educated workforces and where new technologies are combining increasingly to 'decentre' the university, encouraging new forms of knowledge production and participation; it is a world where the social problems we face are increasingly complex, increasingly interconnected. The challenges of educating the next generation for this world of hypercomplexity are huge. But, in addition, many of the educational problems we face take us well beyond traditional school populations. The environment, our aging population, migration, economic recession, global competitiveness, all of these issues have important educational dimensions that raise powerfully important questions that educationalists, in collaboration with others, need to respond to.

And this brings us to the purpose of this book. It is to contribute to the political project that is education; to stimulate and contribute to the debate about the nature of education, what it is and, most importantly, what it should be as a university-based discipline. Hence the subtitle, *Rescuing the University Project?* The book's aims are fourfold, reflected in its structure. Chapters 2 and 3 consider the history of the discipline and examine the century-long struggle to establish the study of education in universities in the UK. It is argued that, in the end, the victory was a pyrrhic one given the extension of government control to the universities in the late twentieth century.

The next section of the book is concerned to take stock; drawing on primary and secondary data, the aim is to characterise the current practice of university-based education in terms of teaching and research. Section III provides an analysis of the current situation. Drawing on debates about the nature of globalisation and its impact on both universities and the teaching profession, this section asks how education has come to be shaped as it is. The final section looks to the future and asks what the discipline of education should aspire to be in a modern university. A range of implications for research, professional education and institutional structures are outlined.

For the most part, the evidence on which the book is based is drawn from across the UK; where appropriate, I have also drawn on evidence from elsewhere internationally. The focus on the UK is for two reasons. Firstly, because policy histories are specific; to write a more generalised story would risk the danger of not recognising the complexities of a particular policy context. But at the same time, it is clear that the UK provides a very important 'case'; some of the messages from the UK experience have been widely influential, particularly in the English speaking world, though, as with all 'policy borrowing', those ideas and practices have been changed as they entered other specific policy contexts. Although much of the empirical evidence that I draw on is therefore from the UK, I do believe that the analysis that the book provides has a much wider significance, touching on changes that, though differently interpreted internationally, have implications for all of those who work in the discipline that is education.

## But what is a discipline?

But before we consider some of these arguments in more detail, it is important to ask again what a discipline is. As I said, using the term *discipline* to refer to the university-based study of education will be seen by some readers as inappropriate. The most common term used to characterise education is as a 'field'. Because the study of education covers so many different educational contexts (from early years to lifelong learning), so many different topics (from the teaching of reading to the management of higher education), because it draws on so many other disciplinary perspectives (from neuroscience to economics and philosophy) and because it is studied by using so many different approaches to research and scholarship (from history or literary studies to ethnography or randomised control trials), because of all of this diversity, how could it be anything else but a 'field'? By definition, it must fail the first test of a discipline, which demands some coherence, distinctiveness and rigour in terms of epistemology – what Bridges (2006) calls 'the discipline' of disciplines.

And, of course, these objections are all true. In order to find the rigour that Bridges seeks, one has to go to the subdisciplines of education: the sociology, psychology and history of education, etc. (Furlong and Lawn, 2010). But why is education so epistemologically weak? Keiner (2010) has argued that its weakness arises from the fact that its answers to epistemological questions – about theory, about method, about the nature of evidence – these answers have, throughout the English speaking world, been largely pragmatic and professionally oriented. Becher (1989), in his classic study of academic tribes and territories, reaches a similar conclusion: knowledge in education, he argues (as in social administration and the social aspects of medicine) is 'soft', being mainly derived from reinterpretations of the humanities and social sciences and the primary outcomes are 'protocols and procedures, whose functions are judged mainly in pragmatic and utilitarian terms' (p. 16).

Wagner *et al.* (1993), in their study of different national traditions of social science, argue that this pragmatic approach arose in the nineteenth century as different professional groups in the USA and the UK tried to define themselves in terms of their access to specialised bodies of knowledge and strove to develop universities as institutions devoted to the development and reproduction of this professionally oriented knowledge. This phenomenon, Wagner *et al.* suggest, has come to shape the very understanding of what a profession is in these countries in a way that is hardly transferrable to other societies. In the French and German traditions, social scientific disciplines emerged with very little reference to the professions at all. As a result, while educational enquiry in the French and German traditions is understood primarily as a science, focusing on theory and basic research, in the Anglophone world it is built on an enduring but unstable pragmatic compromise, a compromise between theory and practice, between knowing that and knowing how, in the commitment of the academy to make both an intellectual *and* a practical contribution to the advancement of the field.

As we will see throughout this book, debates and disagreements over the form, content and control of educational knowledge are central to understanding the discipline; it was these debates that fundamentally shaped the development of the field historically and they continue to be of significance today. Even more importantly, in the last section of this book, it will be argued that rethinking questions about the nature of educational knowledge is essential in re-imagining a future for the discipline of education.

But, actually, Wagner et al.'s (1993) formulation of the epistemological difficulties facing the field of education is somewhat oversimplified. Certainly, Gilbert Ryle's (1949) distinction between knowing that and knowing how is an important one, but a closer examination of what Green (2011) calls 'the knowledge problem in education' reveals that there are at least four different approaches taken in debates about knowledge in education – debates about what it is and what its role should be in research, in professional education and in practice. Given this diversity, it is not surprising that education at an epistemological level often feels incoherent.

## Epistemological debates: knowledge and education

Perhaps the most appropriate place to start a discussion of knowledge in a book that focuses on the university is with Newman and his conception of knowledge as an end it itself. As he puts it in his Discourse 5 entitled 'Knowledge its Own End':

> When, then, we speak of the communication of Knowledge as being Education, we thereby really imply that that Knowledge is a state or condition of mind; and since cultivation of mind is surely worth seeking for its own sake, we are thus brought once more to the conclusion… that there is a Knowledge, which is desirable, though nothing come of it, as being of itself a treasure and a sufficient remuneration of years of labour.
>
> (Newman, 1853a: 6)

Not only was knowledge an end in itself, for Newman it was also the best form of professional preparation. As he explained in his Discourse 7 'Knowledge Viewed in Relation to Professional Skill':

> (The) general culture of mind is the best aid to professional and scientific study and educated men can do what illiterate cannot; and the man who has learned to think and to reason and to compare and to discriminate and to analyze, who has refined his taste and formed his judgment and sharpened his mental vision, will not indeed at once be a lawyer... but he will be placed in that state of intellect in which he can take up any one of the sciences or callings I have referred to...with an ease, a grace, a versatility and a success, to which another is a stranger.
>
> (Newman, 1853b: 6)

Liberal education, undertaking prolonged and intensive involvement with an area of academic life, where one is introduced to what Matthew Arnold described as 'the best that has been thought and said' (Arnold, 1869), it is this that is important in education because of its ability to civilise, to educate and to refine 'the man'. Of course, what exactly a society or, indeed, a university defines as important educational knowledge at any one time is, in the end, culturally arbitrary, but that does not mean that it is without huge significance. As many commentators have noted, it represents what powerful groups in society define as important knowledge (Young, 2008).

As we will see in the next chapter, it was this line of argument – the need to educate and refine prospective teachers through liberal education – that first encouraged the universities to open their doors to teachers at the end of the nineteenth century through the establishment of the Day Training Colleges. A very similar conception of knowledge also underlay the proposals of the Robbins Report of 1963, which recommended that all teacher education be moved into higher education proper. And it is still this conception of the role of liberal education that underlies contemporary initiatives to encourage the 'brightest and the best' into teaching through schemes such as Teach First and Teach for America. In a move that Newman would have fully appreciated, these schemes argue that professional preparation is far less important for prospective teachers than their own personal education; it is their own highly successful engagement with academic knowledge that gives them 'an ease, a grace, a versatility' that will ensure their success.

But Newman's conception of liberal education and its role in professional education is very different from three other interpretations of the role of knowledge in education. Directly and indirectly derived from the work of Aristotle, these are all concerned with some kind of engagement with the world. Firstly and perhaps most obviously, there is a disciplinary conception of knowledge. This, as Deng and Luke (2008) remind us, is associated with Aristotle's notion of 'episteme', that is formal knowledge for understanding and explaining the world. Disciplinary knowledge of this sort is made up of facts, concepts and ideas that have been developed through logical and formal procedures. As we will see in the next chapter, such knowledge began to be developed in education at the end of the nineteenth century, when the principles of science first began to be applied. Initially primarily psychologically oriented, such knowledge was then developed and elaborated from the 1960s onwards with the addition of philosophy, sociology and history – the so-called 'foundation disciplines' of education (Tibble, 1966). For a brief period following the Robbins Report (1963), it came to dominate professional education in what Bell (1981) described as the development of 'specialized expert training' of the day.

Arguably, we can also see this approach underpinning the evidence-based policy-and-practice movement of today. Formal, disciplinary knowledge, as I and Martin Lawn have argued (Furlong and Lawn, 2010), still remains a vitally important ingredient in education research; it is also the stuff of numerous learned societies, special interest groups, conferences and journals. Where its position has been weakened in recent years, especially in England and Wales, is in its contribution to professional education, particularly initial teacher education.

Then there is a practical conception of knowledge: knowing what to do in practice rather than in theory. This is a rich and complex area of debate, but its importance has been observed by many. We have already noted Ryle's (1949) distinction between knowing that and knowing how. Others, such as Polanyi (1966), capture more of the complexity in relation to knowing how through reference to tacit knowledge, a special kind of knowing embedded in practice. Schön (1983) makes a somewhat similar point when talking about the importance of knowing-in-action within 'the swampy lowlands of professional life'.

All of these characterisations of practical knowledge perhaps owe at least part of their genesis to the work of Aristotle. Aristotle talked about two forms of practice, both of which imply different notions of excellence. The first was *techne*, technical skill or the trained ability to produce an agreed outcome with clearly definable standards of success. As Oancea (2006) argues, excellence here 'may well be assessed using sets of external indicators and criteria; it consists of... 'extrinsic goods' of expertise e.g. fitness to purpose, effectiveness, efficacy, etc' (p. 7). In the contemporary world of education, the competency movement would perhaps be the purest example of this conception of practice, but in somewhat softer form, it underlies the notion of 'standards' that now dominate large swathes of educational policy.

But Aristotle also talked of a different form of practical excellence: *phronesis* or practical wisdom. Here Aristotle is arguing that practice is more than a space for the application of skills; it involves deliberation about ends and reflective choice. As Oancea explains, practical wisdom is derived from experience; it is not a discrete skill, but is embedded in who we are, individually and as a community.

> Its judgment is ethical and professional and ultimately human, which is why it is so difficult to achieve: it is the practically wise person who chooses the salient issues and sets the implicit standards through the very act of her judgment and in the concreteness of her situation.
>
> (Oancea, 2006: 8)

This suggestion that there is an ethical or *moral* dimension to some forms of educational knowledge, that educational knowledge can sometimes be concerned not only with what to do but also with what is right to do has interesting links with Confucian principles of education. Hayhoe and Li (2010) argue that in the Confucian tradition, both the moral as well as the practical dimensions of learning are emphasised; they are largely achieved through the educative (in its broadest sense) relationship between teacher and student.

But while in the Confucian tradition, the moral has always been seen as a key ingredient in education; in the West it is now less visible. As we will discuss in the next chapter, moral education in the form of religious instruction was the defining characteristic of nineteenth century teachers' colleges. But a richer version also became established in the 'normal college' tradition that dominated the English speaking world for much of the twentieth century and is still visible in China today. As Hayhoe and Li (2010) make clear, the term *normal* in English can only be properly understood with reference to its French roots, where it means 'setting a moral standard or pattern'. And as Bell (1981) vividly documents, in England, teacher education institutions were primarily moral institutions right up until the 1950s.

Today there may be little evidence of such an institutionalised approach to the moral in educational knowledge, but many educationalists would individually recognise the processes referred to here. One of the reasons that the supervision of students in initial teacher education programmes is so demanding, especially when students are undertaking school experience, is precisely because they are going through a learning process that is so context-based, that is so personal to them and who they are and that is ultimately 'moral'. Teacher educators are doing more than 'educating' them in an intellectual sense; they are also helping them to find 'the right way' to act – right for them and right as a member of a moral community.

There is also a strong moral dimension to much of the research undertaken in education; the moral commitment to making a difference that is still a hugely important force in defining the field. It is that commitment that underlies the difference between what Whitty (2006) called education research, where social scientists study educational processes in and for their own sake and education***al*** research which is concerned to 'make a difference'. The fact that it is this latter definition of research that is dominant throughout the English speaking world today (see, for example, the titles of all of the major national educational research associations – the British Education*al* Research Association, the American Education*al* Research Association, etc.) makes it clear that the moral within educational knowledge remains a vitally important if seldom spoken-of dimension.

As we will see in the remainder of this book, it is epistemological debates and tensions between these different forms of educational knowledge that explain much of the complexity in the field, both its strengths and its weaknesses.

## Sociological issues

But as important as epistemology is, a central argument of this book is that disciplines are not only defined at an epistemological level. As Barnett (1990) suggests, it is valuable to distinguish between a discipline's epistemological and its sociological dimensions. While the epistemological dimensions of disciplines focus on questions of theory, of method, debates about the nature of evidence and how it should be represented and defended, their sociological dimension examines the means through which they are established within the field. A discipline, whether it is physics, theology or education, has to be realised in some way; it needs an existence in terms of courses and qualifications, in lectureships and professorships, in specialist journals, in learned societies and in a whole range of other institutionalised practices.

Education may lack the epistemological coherence of some other disciplines, but at the same time, it has a strong institutional reality. In the UK today there are some 5,000 academics who are employed in university education departments; it is the UK's second largest social science and is equally large in other English speaking countries: the US, Australia, Canada, Malaysia, Hong Kong, New Zealand, etc. In addition, there are many academics working in other faculties – psychology, history, sociology – who might be considered educationalists as well. According to the Australian Research Council (2010), there are over 600 academic journals in the English language in the field of education and there is any number of learned societies, professional associations and specialist and nonspecialist conferences. In these terms, if not on epistemological grounds, education does have some claim to the title of a 'discipline'.

More importantly, the recognition that disciplines have a sociological as well as an epistemological dimension brings to the fore the political aspect of disciplines: the recognition that if disciplines are to advance sociologically, then they need to be seen as a political 'project'. However epistemologically distinctive and coherent, in reality they will not progress unless they are championed by powerful groups, unless they are argued for, unless they are 'managed'. The idea that disciplines are a political project rather than some pregiven intellectual entity is particularly well illustrated by the politics of teacher education. Over the past 120 years or so, teacher education has constantly been fought over by a range of different interested parties; its history is one of struggle for recognition as it slowly moved out of the old teacher colleges of the nineteenth century and into the university sector.

But why has the study of teacher education – which has been and remains so important in defining 'the discipline' – been so politically charged? The answer is not hard to find. It is because behind debates about the form and content of educational knowledge in teacher education lie debates about teachers, what it is they know and what it is they do. In short, they are debates about the nature of teacher professionalism. The significance of this link between knowledge in teacher education and the management of the teaching profession in contemporary policy is an issue that is explored in some detail in Chapter 8.

Historically, politics about teacher education has involved a number of different parties, all of them concerned to advance their own particular conception of educational knowledge. The first and, by far, the most important party has been the government. Unlike the USA, where Labaree (2004) argues it is the market that has defined the nature of teacher education and teacher professionalism, in the UK, as in many other English speaking countries, the urge to control the nature of teacher professionalism by governments has always been strong. From the earliest days, governments of every political hue have insisted on maintaining a tight control of the numbers of those in training. Unlike other countries that take a more laissez-faire approach to human resource management, where being trained does not necessarily equate with getting a job in the teaching profession, entry into teacher training throughout the UK has always been seen as central to the management of teacher supply; governments have always directly controlled the flow of students and, therefore, the main funding stream of education faculties.

More controversial and indeed more variable over time have been government concerns over the 'quality' of training. As we will see in the next chapter, at times governments have been content to delegate issues of quality to the universities themselves; at other times, in the nineteenth and early twentieth century as well as today, that is an issue that they have wished to control themselves – through inspection, through validation processes and through specification of the curriculum. Under the guise of 'quality', governments have therefore had the ability to interfere directly in the detail of teacher education and to define the nature of educational knowledge. When they have done this, they have almost always promoted practical and reductively utilitarian forms of knowledge – what Aristotle would call *techne*.

The second party with an interest has been the universities. They have long been suspicious about the nature of knowledge in teacher education, about the extent to which its pragmatic focus will compromise their commitment to *episteme*: fundamental research and scholarship. They have also been extremely cautious of the ways in which any entanglement with teacher education, with its strong external governmental control, might compromise their independence. It is these epistemological and political concerns that historically explain much of the universities' reluctance to embrace the discipline of education.

A third group to engage in debate about the nature of knowledge in teacher education is practitioners and students. In the English speaking world, practising teachers, as well as student teachers, have long been suspicious of forms of professional education that are overly theoretical. Their critical views were particularly influential in the 1970s and 1980, the high point of a theoretically led curriculum.

The final party has been teacher educators themselves. On occasions during education's history, teacher educators have formally been ceded responsibility to direct the nature of professional knowledge, but for most of the discipline's history, this has not been the case. Rather they have had to work within a variety of different governmental technologies – curriculum documents, certification, inspections – that have attempted to define the form and content of the knowledge they profess. In recent years, most particularly in England, the scale of these interventions has been unprecedented.

But, of course, that does not mean that in the privacy of their own colleges and classrooms, in their own professional associations, journals and conferences, they have no autonomy. In what Bowe and Ball (1992) characterise as 'the context of practice', there is always an opportunity for doing something different. Some policies are more tightly defined and more tightly policed than others. But even the most strongly framed policies have a 'potential of meanings' (Fiske, 1987); they can be read in different ways. In looking at contemporary practice in Section II of this book, we will be particularly concerned to take into account of what contemporary practitioners – teacher educators and researchers – actually do to advance their discipline, how they attempt to work within government frameworks while at the same time realising their own vision of educational knowledge.

If it is the politics of teacher education that have significantly shaped what one part of what education has become as a discipline, then it becomes important to take into account how those politics have differed in key ways in different parts of the UK. It is also important to recognise how other dimensions of the discipline have been affected by other national, regional and institutional drivers – through policies on research, on entrepreneurialism and the need for institutions to differentiate themselves in the higher education market. As we will document in Section III of this book, all of these are issues that help to shape what education has become in the contemporary university.

## Conclusion

As would be true of any discipline, trying to understand the discipline of education means taking into account its epistemological as well as its sociological dimensions. As will become evident throughout this book, education presents a contradictory picture here. Sociologically, it is and always has been strong in key respects. It is large, complex and strategically important and despite recent policy challenges, particularly in England, it remains relatively well embedded in the university system. At the same time, it is epistemologically weak, largely because of important and unresolved questions about the nature of educational knowledge. It is these difficulties that, despite its size, have served constantly to undermine its position within the academy.

Significantly, Kuhn (1962) argues that for intellectual progress to be made in any discipline, both dimensions – sociological and epistemological – are necessary. Progress requires a context where there is relatively close agreement on theories and methods of enquiry and where there is sufficient institutional certainty so that newcomers can be inducted into the discipline. Despite the size of the discipline of education, these conditions have never been present throughout education's history and they are not present even today; this perhaps helps explain why historical progress to full integration in the university system was so slow. It also helps to explain why the final and full arrival of education in the university sector was, in the end, a pyrrhic and short-lived victory. It is to the history of that arrival that we now turn in the next chapter.

# 2 The universities and education

## The first 100 years

### Introduction

The history of education as a discipline within our universities is a complex one; it is a play (a comedy, even) with two main storylines. Sometimes the players work hand in hand, heroically struggling together to establish legitimacy in the hierarchical world of the university; more often than not, they fight amongst themselves or live in uneasy compromise. As we will see in this and the next chapter, each storyline has its own history, carried by different players and different institutions even today.

One story concerns the education and training of teachers – a movement that, in Europe, began at least 300 years ago, though it was not until the latter part of the twentieth century that the majority of teacher education slowly, falteringly, moved out of a college-based system and into the university proper. The other much smaller and much more recent story concerns the development of educational research; it finds its beginnings at the end of the nineteenth century, when the principles of the enlightenment first began to be applied, initially in Scotland, then reaching out across the whole world.

As we will see, while both stories had become tentatively established in British universities by the end of the nineteenth century, the journey to university status for the majority of the system took over 100 years to complete. It was a long march and, although, with the benefit of historical distance, it might look like a straightforward line of progress, in reality, it was anything but (Gardner, 1998). And, like so many classical dramas, it also turned out to be something of a pyrrhic victory. The full and final arrival of the discipline of education in the university sector coincided with major changes that were overtaking the university system as a whole in the closing decades of the twentieth century; changes that would undermine much of the independence and status of the discipline that successive generations of educationalists had aspired to achieve.

Given the complexity of the discipline's history, these two chapters can only give a brief overview; their aim is to provide sufficient historical background to serve as a basis for the analysis of the current position of education as a university-based discipline that is the focus of the rest of the book. Between them, these two chapters are organised into three main historical periods.

This first chapter is in two parts. It begins by looking at the development of the field from the nineteenth century up until 1963, when the Robbins Report (Robbins, 1963) recommended the full integration of initial teacher education into higher education – a move that also had major implications for the development of educational research. The second part looks at developments in the 1960s and 1970s, when the position of the universities was strong. The next chapter examines the Conservative years, 1979–1997, under Margaret Thatcher and John Major, when the role of universities in the field of education began to be challenged. As we will see, education's story is one of constant struggle – with governments and their various agencies, with universities themselves and with the teaching profession. Central to these debates, as we noted in the last chapter, have been struggles about knowledge – what knowledge is in an applied field like education and who should control it.

## Universities and education: an uncertain beginning

### *From teacher training college to institute of education*

Today most university faculties and departments of education have a broad remit: they provide professional education – both initial and in-service; they undertake research; they teach advanced courses; and they train the next generation of researchers. But, in reality, it is teacher education that is the most important factor in defining their character. In the vast majority of cases, even today, as we will see in the next section of this book, teacher education is their core business; it defines the majority of the courses that they offer and, perhaps more importantly, the staff that they recruit. This, in turn, affects in important ways the research that they undertake. In this regard (if not in others), the discipline of education in the UK is strongly paralleled in the US. As Labaree (2004) says in his book on the American 'Ed Schools': 'The roots of the American education school are in teacher education. Preparing teachers was the Ed Schools' original function and this function has continued to the present day as the primary focus of its institutional effort and its primary identity in the eyes of the public' (p. 17).

Formal teacher education in Europe has at least a 300-year history. Jean Baptiste de la Salle established the first *école normale* at Reims at the end of the seventeenth century; in Germany the first training seminars (*Lehrerseminar*) were established in Gotha in 1698 (Moon, 1998), while in England, formal training dates back to 1798, with the establishment of a teacher training college in Southwark based on the monitorial system. In 1836 David Stow of Glasgow established the first 'normal school' for teacher training in the UK. A 'normal school' was a school created to train (and *train* is the right word) older pupils to be teachers; as we noted in the last chapter, the term *normal* in English can only be properly understood with reference to its French roots, where it means 'setting a moral standard or pattern'. Such institutions were therefore markedly different from universities that grew out of the European tradition with the core values of autonomy and academic freedom. Stow's initiative – to develop a form of teacher training based on training in strong moral principles – attracted considerable attention from across the UK. In the USA a similar institution was established in 1839 in Lexington, Massachusetts.

As Moon (1998) explains, expansion in the USA was more haphazard than in Europe, with more rapid development in the northern than southern states. In England and Wales teacher education took a more strategic path when, in 1840, James Kay Shuttleworth, who had visited Stow's school in Glasgow, set up his training college in Battersea, London. However, by 1843 the college had run into financial difficulties and had to be taken over by the Church of England National Society. The Anglicans apparently found his methods, based on religious belief and rote learning, simple and cheap to apply and the system was rapidly expanded; it was also copied by other dominations (Lofthouse, 2009).

Spurred by the religious enthusiasms of the day, residential denominational 'normal' colleges very quickly came to enjoy a monopoly of institutionalised teacher training and they did so for the rest of the century. But even then they only provided a minority of teachers. For much of the nineteenth century, the dominant route into teaching was via the 'pupil-teacher' system where at the age of 13, more academically successful pupils were 'apprenticed' to their 'master' for five years before taking an examination in order to become qualified. In sharp contrast to those attending the colleges, most teacher training was therefore largely based on a practical apprenticeship; only the most successful pupil-teachers could apply for a Queens' Scholarship, to enter a training college (Judge *et al.*, 1994). The colleges themselves were austere institutions and, in sharp contrast to the aspirations of American normal schools that were emerging at the same time (Labaree, 2004), their approach to knowledge was narrow. They saw their job as producing disciplined, utilitarian, reliable and, of course, religiously based instructors adept in implementing the government-imposed Revised Code of 1862 for the mass of the population; this they did largely alone, with only modest state support. It was this hegemony that, after 1890, was challenged by the universities.

The first university to become involved in the education of teachers was Manchester, which provided evening classes for working elementary school teachers as early as 1852. Other universities – Aberystwyth, Nottingham, Leeds and Oxford – followed suit a few years later. However, it was not until 1888 that the Cross Commission (1888), a Royal Commission set up to enquire into the consequences of the 1870 Education Act, which had established universal (though not compulsory) elementary education in England and Wales, proposed a more formal role for universities in teacher education.

In order to deal with substantial shortfall in teacher numbers, the Cross Commission proposed an experiment to allow a small number of universities to establish Day Training Colleges. In marked contrast to the normal school tradition, the Day Training Colleges offered courses for prospective teachers based on notions of liberal academic education. Interestingly, once announced, 'the idea caught fire' (Lofthouse, 2009: xiv). Large numbers of students applied, taking the universities by surprise, and within just a few short years, the field of education was established in the English and Welsh university systems. Growing numbers of students recognised that they could study for a degree and become qualified as a teacher through membership of the same institution. Universities, for their part, recognised that even if this work was low status, it was a reliable and profitable source of student-fee income paid for out of public funds (Dent, 1977).

Yet despite the success of this 'experiment', university-based teacher education was always only for the minority of teachers. The Day Training Colleges, which, within a generation, were becoming full-fledged university departments of education, were, in most cases, small. They were also often marginal to their parent universities. Viewed with suspicion and even condescension, they were mostly kept physically as well as politically distant from the more established faculties. Again, as Lofthouse notes, linking the teaching profession to the university system in this way did little to overcome the traditional tendency of the English (though not the Welsh or the Scots) to look down on its teachers, especially the teachers of 'the masses'.

In spite of their marginal status and the fact that they were relatively small in size, the long-term challenge, which the Day Training colleges represented for the conventional training college model, was well understood by their contemporaries (Gardner and Cunningham, 1998). With growing expectations from elementary schools, particularly in the urban areas, the new form of professional education challenged and intended to challenge the twin pillars of the traditional system: the pupil-teacher system, which was criticised as narrow and mechanical; and the centrality of religiously based training, seen as denominationally and intellectually narrow. Instead, they used their freedom from government control to adopt a liberal education perspective. 'Education of the man' took precedence over the practical skills of teaching. As we will see below, they also, for the first time, provided an institutional home for the establishment of educational scholarship, theory and research that was already emerging in Scotland and on the continent (Gardner, 1998).

A further challenge to the denominational colleges in England and Wales came in 1902, with the passing of the Balfour Education Act, which allowed the newly established Local Education Authorities (LEAs) to set up teacher education colleges of their own. From the opening of the twentieth century, therefore, the tripartate system of teacher education – the religious colleges, the local educational authority colleges and the (much smaller) university system – was put in place. At a sociological level, it was the distinctions, challenges and tensions between these three sorts of institutions and especially between the colleges on the one hand and the university-based system on the other, with their markedly different conceptions of professional knowledge, that were to shape the field of education for much of the next 70 years.

But what were these two very different systems of preparing teachers actually like in reality? We can gain some insight from this commentary by Margaret Phillips, who, by 1926, had been a lecturer in both sectors. Through her comments, one can see clearly the differences between a 'normal' college tradition based on the idea of a moral community and the more liberal educational ideals of a traditional university.

> Coming to work in a two-year college after experience of two different university education departments and trying to account for the contrast with which I am faced, I find the … University says, in effect, 'You want to teach? Then your first business is to become a fully developed person and, as far as possible, a finished student.' The policy of the two-year college, on the other hand, may be expressed somewhat thus: 'The teacher's work is immensely significant. Therefore, it is important that he should make as few mistakes as possible; however good a person he may be in general, teaching demands a special technique, without which he will not be able to bring his general qualities to bear. *This technique we propose to give him.*'
>
> (Phillips, 1926: 39–40, quoted in Gardner and Cunningham, 1998: 239; emphasis added)

Initially, it was not anticipated that the new university-based system would lead to permanent divisions; indeed, it was intended that the benefits of a more liberally based education and training system would permeate the colleges too. However, this was not to be the case. From 1911 onward a 'consecutive' model of training was permitted in the universities: three years personal education followed by one year professional preparation. The colleges by contrast stuck to their two or three year combined programmes (Judge *et al.*, 1994). Once the new system was in place, the universities, with their class-based recruitment and prestigious status, rapidly came to focus their attention on the expanding secondary school system of the early and mid-twentieth century (Patrick, 1986). Almost all of their graduates went on to teach in public and private secondary schools and there was little appetite to engage with the working-class elementary school system. By contrast, those from the colleges – both the local authority colleges and the increasingly impoverished religious colleges – were left to focus, much as they had always done, on preparing teachers of the working classes.

Gender as well as class also came to influence the differences between the two systems. From the late nineteenth century, women had come to dominate elementary school teaching, though they were paid considerably less than men, had fewer promotion opportunities and were required to resign on marriage (Gardner, 1998). Not surprisingly, given that men dominated universities at the time, it was men who to came to dominate the new higher status Day Training Colleges. Gender divisions, therefore, came to reinforce powerful class divisions between the two systems and they, together with their very different conception of professional education, strongly discouraged universities from entangling themselves with the colleges. Though a fuller engagement with the university system was something that was occasionally whispered of in the colleges (Lofthouse, 2009), it was a vision that was treated with condescension by universities themselves. As vulnerable departments in their own institutions, it was simply not in their interests to engage seriously with the feminised, lower-class college sector.

Instead, the new university departments focused on becoming more conventionally academic. Chairs of education were established from the 1890s, with important contributions made by historians and psychologists (Patrick, 1986). In addition, most departments began to offer higher degrees in education and, as a result, by the early 1920s, teacher education in the universities was taking on quite a different complexion from the much larger teacher training system in the colleges. That system remained largely unchanged from the nineteenth century; its conception of educational knowledge centred on instruction and rote learning rather than research and the principles of liberal education.

### *Lost opportunities*

Moving into the twentieth century, Lofthouse's study of the church-training colleges in England and Wales identifies two key moments – after the First World War and after the Second World War – when there was a serious possibility of creating a unified system; in each case, though, these opportunities were deliberately passed by.

In the period immediately following the First World War, both the National Union of Teachers and the Labour Party adopted policies advocating moving initial teacher education into the university system lock, stock and barrel. R.H. Tawney, for example, in a joint TUC/Labour Party document, insisted that the effective training of teachers demanded the highest academic as well as professional standards (Patrick, 1986). The universities would take over the colleges which would become halls of residence and there would be a move for all teachers to the consecutive model – one year of professional training following a three-year degree. And although he did not articulate a particular model, the idea that somehow the universities were to be 'saviours' of the discredited and inferior college-training system was also known to have the support of H.A.L. Fisher, president of the Board of Education.

The idea of a university solution provoked alarm in Conservative quarters. As Simon (1974) documents, there was growing concern in that party about increasing support for Labour. A teachers' Labour League had been established and attracted the support of socialist luminaries such as Bertrand Russell, Sidney Webb, H.G. Wells and R.H. Tawney. In the early 1920s the National Union of Teachers (NUT) conducted a series of bitter strikes as the government tried to reduce teachers' pay and encouraged the employment of unqualified teachers as a way of dealing with its financial crisis.

In Conservative eyes the alignment of teachers with the Labour movement was seen as nothing less than a breach of trust, 'which might have incalculable effects on national morality and stability' (Simon, 1974: 71). In these circumstances, handing the colleges to the universities, which, in effect, would put teacher training beyond the Board of Education's control, could not be countenanced. A change of government and a new minister allowed the idea to be skillfully sidelined by senior civil servants. Instead, the universities were persuaded to take part in a Joint Board scheme in collaboration with their local colleges overseeing the final examinations of college students, but Her Majesty's Inspectorate (HMI) maintained their grip of the assessment of teaching practice and, of course, funding. At an institutional level, the colleges and the universities therefore remained at arm's length and the divided system remained largely unchanged (Patrick, 1986).

A second opportunity to integrate the two systems occurred after the Second World War, but on this occasion, the procrastinators were not civil servants or, indeed, the government, but the university vice chancellors. Gardner (1998) argues that at the end of the war, after fighting German state fascism, there was no longer an appetite in the country for central government and its bureaucracies to control bodies such as the teaching profession. With this change of mood, one of the major obstacles to integrating the two systems – the fact that it would make teacher education independent of the government – withered away. The opportunity for integration arose with the McNair Report (McNair, 1944), set up to examine the implications for teacher education of the 1944 Education Act, which established free secondary education for all.

As Lofthouse (2009) documents, there was a great deal of politics behind the appointment of McNair, vice chancellor of Liverpool University, as chair of the commission. McNair, like many vice chancellors, was against integration from the start. Opposition was particularly strong in Scotland and Northern Ireland Richardson (2002). Not surprisingly, the McNair Committee became hopelessly divided. Some members proposed integration; others, led by McNair himself, played the epistemological card: training should not be confused with education and training had no place in a proper university (Crook, 1995).

Instead, McNair proposed a loose federation of colleges that would work together under the purview of their local university. These Area Training Organisations, which oversaw newly established Institutes of Education, emerged some two years later after lengthy negotiations with the university system (Patrick, 1986) and gave the appearance of a unified system of higher education. In reality, they demanded little of the universities themselves. What these regional Institutes of Education did do, though, was break the control of central government over the detailed specification of the teacher training curriculum in the colleges. While the Ministry of Education still controlled numbers and (after considerable negotiation and compromise (Taylor, 1988)) HMI continued to inspect courses in a generalised way, it was the Institutes, dominated by university representatives, that oversaw the curriculum and the final assessment of students.

Despite this tentative coming together, at an institutional level, the two systems remained very different. During the 1950s, teacher education in the universities remained a highly academic affair, far removed from the world of practice. Life in the colleges was very different; it was based on what Bell (1981) describes as 'charismatic education'. Typically, the colleges were small, they were single-sex and physically and intellectually isolated – all factors, Bell argues, that enhanced their capacity for creating a moral community. At the heart of their morality was the conviction that teaching had to be seen as a diffuse, child-centred process of socialisation rather than as an act of functionally specific instruction.

Taylor (1969) supports this view, in his analysis of the system, arguing that in the colleges of the time, there was a suspicion of intellect: experiential knowledge, particularly classroom experience, was held to be of prime importance based upon the stock of teaching skills personally accumulated by the education tutor. Education tutors regularly accompanied 'their' students into schools where their demonstration lessons enabled them to reveal their prime expertise and claim to authority before their students. In sharp contrast to education as it was practised in the universities, there was very little reference to research evidence or theory; the overriding emphasis was on the value of personal experience. In this regard, colleges of education had more in common with the nineteenth century normal colleges than the contemporary university. All this was set to change after the intervention of the Robbins Report of 1963. But before looking at those developments, we need to return to the development of the other dimension of the discipline of education: research.

## *The beginnings of educational research*

Finding the right name for this second dimension of the discipline of education is not straightforward. I have chosen to call it *educational research*: others, particularly European academics, use terms such as *pedagogical* or *educational science* (Hofstetter and Schneuwly, 2002). But for me, educational research seems a more appropriate term because it is neutral, embracing a whole range of different traditions, both in terms of epistemology and topic. As we will see below, not everything that we would recognise as educational research is or tries to be a science and, substantively, its interests go much broader than a focus on pedagogy. Why a consideration of educational research is important, of course, is because it is research that helps to provide the content of education as a university-based discipline. Understanding what constitutes research in education and how it developed and changed over time is, therefore, central to an understanding of the discipline.

Up until the end of the nineteenth century, as John Nisbet (2002, 2005) reminds us, educational thought and practice throughout Europe was based on tradition and authority – whether from God or classical figures such as Aristotle – rather than science. And in some parts of Europe (France, German-speaking Switzerland), one can still see the outworking of that tradition, where academic discussion of education is primarily philosophically based, exploring general and abstract principles intended to guide educational thought but explicitly seen as quite distinct from the world of practice (Hofstetter and Schneuwly, 2002). However, in other parts of the world, especially Scotland, Germany and the US, a radically different approach began to emerge at the end of the nineteenth century. It was at this point that the principles of the Enlightenment, which had spread rapidly to medicine, agriculture, engineering and science more generally in the early part of that century, began to influence the world of education.

But as Nisbet (2005) also makes clear, since that time, what educational research actually *is* has changed substantially. He suggests that it has gone through a number of stages of development, but, actually, the truth is more complex. Over the past 130 years, dominant discourses of educational research have certainly changed, but rather than one approach being succeeded by another, with old traditions withering away, the reality is that new ones have simply added to previous traditions. As a result, today educational research is multivocal, embracing a range of different traditions each of which might claim different historical roots.

So educational research has certainly changed and diversified over time. But in writing its history, how can it be captured? How can we 'see' the history of something as ephemeral as a research tradition? The answer I will suggest is to examine its sociological dimensions – the different ways in which educational research has been institutionalised: in professorships and qualifications; through the establishment of journals and learned societies; through the writing of textbooks and the development of publicly available research instruments; and, indeed, through the development of personal and professional networks (Lawn *et al.*, 2010).

Of these, one of the most important is the establishment of chairs, for as Hofstetter and Schneuwly (2002) argue, the establishment of chairs, which, until the very recent past, were only rarely created, marks an important degree of institutional recognition often only coming about after a period of internal institutional struggle. Chairs also lay the foundation for the reproduction of a discipline; they help to establish a space where new knowledge and new ways of thinking can be passed on to successive generations of scholars.

Despite being a relatively small country, Scotland has an important role on the international stage in the history of educational research. The first British university chairs in education were established in Scotland in 1876 at Edinburgh and St Andrews. And at about the same time (1879), the philosopher Alexander Bain of Aberdeen published his book *Education as a Science*, suggesting that scientific principles might be applied to the art of teaching; from that point on, educational research as we know it in the English speaking world began to take root. Bain's ideas particularly caught the imagination of the teachers' trade union, the Educational Institute of Scotland (EIS), which saw a potential advantage to the teaching profession of allying itself closely with experimental research. In 1917 the EIS set up its own research committee and this, in turn, had a central role in the establishment of the Scottish Council for Research in Education (SCRE), set up in 1929 as the first national body of its kind.

Virtually all of this early 'science' was psychologically oriented (for a detailed discussion, see Tibble, 1966). In England, Francis Galton's early work on the relationship between body types and intelligence proved to be a blind alley and was not followed up, but in continental Europe, laboratories to study different aspects of intelligence were established in Germany, Switzerland and France. These laboratories attracted the interest of American (and Scottish) scholars, many of whom studied at them for their doctorates. In 1905 Binet and Simon, in Paris, developed the first intelligence test and in 1908 Thorndike, in the US, developed the first standardised test of achievement. The idea of using standardised tests spread rapidly in the US and by 1917, 900,000 copies of Thorndike's most popular test had been sold (Nisbet, 2005).

At about the same time, 1900, the London County Council established its own inspection service and its inspectors, including Cyril Burt, began to develop tests of their own in the decades that followed (Tibble, 1966). By 1929, when Scotland established SCRE, it immediately began research programmes on intelligence and the environment and pupil progress and attainment levels; it also began to develop a library of tests and instruments imported from Germany and the US (Lawn *et al.*, 2010). As a result of all of this activity, by the end of the first decades of the twentieth century, sufficient experimental work had been conducted in Germany, France, Switzerland and Scotland for the first textbooks to be published and the first academic journals to be established. The textbooks in particular, which were overwhelmingly psychologically oriented, had an important influence in the shaping of the field for the next 30 years.

A further push to the establishment of the discipline of education came in 1918, when four of the universities in Scotland established a new degree in education: the EdB/BEd. The degree was a second degree, intended for qualified teachers with ideas of 'experimental education' at its core. A similar degree was launched in 1948 in Queens Belfast but not in England and Wales. In Scotland the numbers on the new degree were small; but it was very powerful in feeding the new discipline. Lawn *et al.* (2010) report that during the interwar period, 84 per cent of its graduates left teaching and moved into educational administration, teacher training and psychology; in this way, the messages of educational science became embedded within key parts of the educational system in Scotland.

Interestingly, the tradition in England and Wales was somewhat different in that the first chairs of education were established within the University Day Training Colleges, which were focused on teacher training. As Patrick (1986) points out, it was their contribution to the study of education that helped to mark out the difference between the UDEs in England and Wales and the much larger college sector. Aberystwyth and Bangor appointed their first professors of education in 1893 and 1894 respectively, while the first English chair was established at Newcastle in 1895 (Crook, 2002).

Research degrees also began to be established across the UK, particularly in London, so much so that by the 1930s, educational research had established a certain degree of respectability and acceptance. But as Nisbet (2002: 33) notes, it was only 'a certain degree', because very few teachers in schools or educational administrators regarded it seriously. But it did slowly develop acceptance within senior levels of educational service. By the interwar period, educational researchers were regarded and indeed regarded themselves the specialist experts, the 'backroom boys' of the educational service, providing intelligence on the school system. Co-opted, particularly in the development and running of the 11-plus examination, which was used to select a minority of 11-year-olds for a selective grammar school education, educational researchers found themselves increasingly accepted as part of the educational establishment.

In reviewing the early development educational research, it is clear that the pattern that was established in the early decades – from 1890 to 1910 – then went on to dominate the whole of the first half of the twentieth century. Educational research, right up until the 1950s, was specialist activity, primarily psychological and statistical, a laboratory activity distant from practice. And, as Nisbet (2002: 44) notes:

> it was not until the 1950s and 1960s that other paradigms for educational research began to challenge – in particular, sociological studies, curriculum development, evaluation, case studies and the teacher-researcher movement.

These challenges were stimulated by the Robbins Report of 1963, which recommended integrating teacher education firmly within higher education. As we will see below, this, in turn, had major implications for the nature of educational research.

## Universities and education: confidence and control

### *The Robbins Report and teacher education*

Despite the constitutional (if not epistemological) changes brought about by the establishment of McNair's Institutes of Education in the 1950s, it was not until the 1960s, with the publication of the Robbins Report (Robbins 1963), into the future of higher education that teacher training changed to become a full and integral part of the higher education in the UK. With this integration also came the first full flowering of educational theory and research in the university system.

The Robbins Report was based on social democratic ideals of the day, arguing 'The good society desires equality of opportunity for its citizens to become not merely good producers but also good men and women'. Higher education qualifications 'should be available for all those who are qualified by ability and attainment to pursue them and who wish to do so' (Robbins, 1963: para. 31). It should, therefore, aim to develop learners as rationally autonomous individuals; if it was to achieve that aim, then higher education had to be centrally concerned with learning, which was both fundamental and general, for only in this way could autonomy be promoted and the learner freed from the constraints of the 'present and the particular' (Bailey, 1984).

This social democratic ideal had an influence on the Robbins Committee's conception of teacher education too. The Committee's vision of a professional teacher was of someone who was themselves 'rationally autonomous'. How else could they develop rationally autonomous children? Teachers, therefore, needed a strong personal education; courses should be 'liberal in content and approach', with academic work taking priority over practical training. Courses were lengthened from two to three years and the four-year BEd degree was introduced for the academically more successful students. With the extended courses, there was a dramatic increase in student numbers and new staff had to be recruited. Because of the expansion, residence of staff and students was no longer a requirement, which profoundly altered the character of the colleges and the student experience. No longer could they be a moral community; as a result, the links with the nineteenth-century 'normal college' tradition became increasingly challenged.

The main vehicles for ensuring that the new courses were degree worthy were main subject study, which was to be pursued 'to as high a pitch as can be attained throughout the whole duration of the course' (Eason, 1971) and 'education', reinterpreted as the study of the four -ologies: sociology, history, psychology and philosophy. Overall, the aim was to produce the well-rounded 'scholar who happened to want to be a teacher' (Bell, 1981: 13).

During this period, then, when academics themselves first came to control of the curriculum, educational knowledge became much more academically focused; theory and research assumed a far greater significance than in the past. However, as Bell (1981) notes, the new knowledge, which underpinned the courses, especially in the sub-disciplines of education – sociology, psychology, history and philosophy of education – this knowledge was almost entirely generated outside the colleges, in the universities and particularly in their schools of education. In other words, the arrival of the college system in higher education created a whole new market for the consumption of educational research and theory and had the effect of substantially stimulating the academic research culture of university departments of education. The established universities also benefited from growing demand for higher degrees for those employed in the colleges; for the first time there were now academic career opportunities for their most able graduates.

In the 1960s, therefore, teacher education courses started to look much more like university degrees; but even then the universities themselves continued to hold the colleges as institutions at arm's length. Robbins himself recognised this problem and was personally concerned about it (Taylor, 1988). He argued that to associate the colleges with the universities for academic purposes but to deny them the autonomy that was appropriate in higher education would deny them the proper conditions for development. Here there were important differences between the situation in Scotland as opposed to England and Wales. In Scotland there were only seven, proudly autonomous colleges of education; they were of substantial size and entirely independent of their local universities. In England and Wales, by contrast, there were 144 colleges, with half of them having less than 250 students and they were academically overseen by their local universities.

In Scotland, Robbins therefore recommended the development of a partnership between the colleges and their local university to oversee the move to degree-level work. In England and Wales the position was more complex. The colleges were already preparing most of their students almost to degree level and were pressing to be recognised. As Robbins argued:

> we do not believe that the colleges can develop in the ways we have advocated and achieve their full standing in higher education unless they are accorded collectively within the university orbit a sufficient degree of autonomy. This being so, it is highly desirable that academic and administrative responsibility should go hand in hand.
>
> (Robbins, 1963: para. 353).

Some form of institutional integration was going to be essential if teacher education was to become a proper part of higher education. The final report, therefore, hoped that in the future, some colleges might broaden their scope and become constituent parts of a university; others might combine with leading technical colleges to form new universities (Robbins, 1963: para. 314, p. 108). And from the 1970s onwards, this is indeed what started to happen in England and Wales, though the process was much slower and more traumatic for the colleges than Robbins could possibly have imagined.

### *University status at last*

The Labour government of the day accepted Robbins' main proposals for the expansion of higher education though rather than expand the universities, they developed an alternative system, based on the polytechnics. A new national award-bearing body, the Council for National Academic Awards (CNAA), was also established to validate their courses and award their degrees.

However in relation to the teachers colleges, the government rejected Robbins' suggestion that they should be given the same autonomy as universities. Like so many before him, the Minister of Education at the time, Sir Edward Boyle, was highly nervous of losing control of teacher education. As a result, throughout the 1960s the colleges remained in an anomalous situation – increasingly part of higher education in terms of the courses they offered but not institutionally part of it. This, as Judge *et al.* (1994) noted, left them in a vulnerable position.

That vulnerability became of paramount importance in the 1970s when there was a sudden and unexpected downturn in the demand for new teachers. Between 1973 and 1978, student teacher numbers were reduced from 114,000 to 45,000; the result was a massive programme of college closures and amalgamations.

> After successive waves of contraction, by the late 1970s, many of the colleges had been closed and nearly all of the rest had been transformed in some fashion; even the survivors resented and were shaken by the process that they were forced to endure.
>
> (Judge *et al.*, 1994: 192)

And over the next 20 years, even those colleges that did survive began to amalgamate either with their local polytechnics or their local universities. Some of these amalgamations were a success, particularly the amalgamations with the polytechnics; there were expanded faculties, new buildings and new and more diverse populations of student teachers entering the profession. Those joining established universities had a more varied experience. While some amalgamations were also successful – particularly those in Scotland, where between 1993 and 2000, all of the established colleges were integrated into old, new and 'ancient' universities – in many other instances, the expansion of courses and student numbers foundered after a few years. When that happened all that was left was the very substantial real estate the old colleges brought with them to their universities as their dowries.

But not all colleges followed this route. As Robbins had predicted, others chose a different, more autonomous pathway. In the 1990s many joined with other types of local colleges to become autonomous Higher Education Institutes. In these smaller institutions, unlike the polytechnics and universities, education faculties were often amongst the largest and they consequently had greater influence on the institution's future direction. Initially working under the aegis of the CNAA or a local university, they then applied for degree-awarding powers and eventually university status in their own right. All of the teacher colleges in Wales followed this route, as did many in England. Today only a very small number of mainly denominational colleges, including two in Northern Ireland, remain as independent institutions.

At an institutional level, therefore, the changes that were set in motion by the Robbins Report did eventually mean that teacher education became part of a unified higher education system. And with the abolition of the binary line between universities and polytechnics in 1992, all teacher education became formally part of the university system. The journey had been a long one, taking over 100 years since the Cross Commission (1888) first suggested an 'experiment' with university-based teacher education, but today virtually all of the old colleges of education are now fully integrated into the university sector; they are fully part of a self-governing institution that can award its own degrees.

### *Robbins and the new dawn for educational research*

The Robbins Report did not only have a major impact on teacher education, it also profoundly affected educational research as well. After the war the teacher training system throughout the UK experienced a massive rush of demand. The country not only had to respond to the postwar baby boom and the fact that few teachers had been trained during the war – equally important were the consequences of the 1944 Education Act – the development of universal secondary education and the consequent raising of the school-leaving age to 15. As we have discussed earlier, the government's response was the establishment of the McNair Inquiry (McNair 1944); and as we know, McNair rejected the idea of integrating the college system with the universities from the very beginning. McNair's view was, it seems, considerably influenced by the standing of educational research at the time.

The universities in Scotland and Northern Ireland, which had developed some research capacity, had steadfastly refused to engage with teacher training. In England, where UDEs were mainly focused on teacher training, academic standing was low and they were regarded as largely marginal, barely tolerated by their universities (Richardson, 2002). Only in Wales did McNair consider there to be sufficient academic capacity in the UDEs for the idea of integration with the college system to be entertained. The failure to integrate initial teacher education properly into the university system held back the development of research for another ten years or so.

But opportunities for research and scholarship in education did begin to grow, if somewhat slowly, in the postwar years. That growth is reflected in the numbers of journals that began to appear. The *British Journal of Educational Psychology* had been established in 1931, though then, as today, it was dominated as much by psychologists as those who would consider themselves educationalists. But, as Richardson (2002) documents, other more educationally oriented journals began to appear at some of the newly established university institutes of education that grew up as a consequence of McNair's recommendations: Hull University began *Studies in Education* in 1947; Birmingham established *Educational Review* in 1948; and Durham University founded *Research Review* in 1950. Particularly significant was the establishment in 1951 of the Standing Conference on Studies in Education and its associated journal, the *British Journal of Educational Studies.*

But despite this activity, the actual research capacity at the time was still profoundly limited. Nisbet (2002) estimates that in Scotland in the late 1950s, there were probably only five full-time educational researchers. In England and Wales things were not much better; there was no research capacity whatsoever in the colleges and in the universities, such capacity as there was was almost entirely focused on large-scale measurement surveys.

The real impetus to the development of educational research came not with the foundation of more journals but with the Robbins Report of 1963. As a result of the report's recommendations on teacher education, across the UK, the number of academic staff and students in the colleges dramatically expanded in the 1960s and many of the new universities that were created – Sussex, Exeter, Dundee, Ulster – included new departments of education. Even in Scotland and Northern Ireland, where university resistance to involvement in teacher education had been the strongest, there was now an acceptance that the universities would need to become involved in the validation of the new college-based BEd degree.

All of this activity stimulated debate about the nature of advanced study in education at undergraduate and at Master's level, where demand increased dramatically with the expansion of the college system. The question that was constantly posed was: how could the study of education be considered degree-worthy? The answer was to be found in the development of the 'foundations' of education.

In that search for degree worthiness and the subsequent domination of the 'foundation disciplines', R.S. Peters had a key role to play. Just six weeks after the publication of the Robbins Report, Peters used his inaugural lecture as professor of philosophy of education at the University of London Institute of Education to stress the urgent necessity for conceptual clarity in the field of education; conceptual clarity, which he argued, only philosophers could bring.

And, as Richardson (2002) documents, the result of this intervention was the immediate convening by the government's Department of Education of a closed seminar held in Hull in March 1964, at which selected professors of education from England, led by Peters, hammered out the structure within which educational studies in England and Wales would expand and develop over the coming two decades.

The new foundation disciplines, which the conference endorsed, were to include philosophy, psychology, sociology and history (rather than Peters' original proposal of economics). And it was these four disciplines that were set out in what became the core educational textbook of the 1960s, J.W. Tibble's *The Study of Education* (Tibble, 1966). The book also included a seminal paper from the philosopher Paul Hirst, justifying the position of educational theory (understood in terms of the foundation disciplines) as the essential background to the development of rational educational practice (Hirst, 1966).

In reality, the initial numbers on the new BEd degree were small; however, its significance lay in the fact that it was a new degree that was agreed across the whole of the UK, including Scotland and Northern Ireland. Not only did the new degree help to establish the hegemony of the foundation disciplines of education, it also helped to challenge the supremacy of psychology and psychometric testing.

During the 1960s and 1970s, governments increasingly came to be interested in what this more broadly based conception of educational research might provide. As a consequence, between 1964 and 1969, expenditure on educational research in Britain multiplied tenfold. An Educational and Research Board was appointed within the Social Science Research Council with funds for projects throughout Britain; and in the Scottish Education Department, a Research and Intelligence Unit initiated research programmes and funded research in universities and colleges.

Governments were particularly interested in the contribution of research to key policy initiatives; the Newsom Report (Newsom, 1963) on secondary schooling and the Plowden Report (Plowden, 1967) on primary schooling both commissioned and drew on substantial bodies of research, as did the Educational Priority Areas scheme that developed in the 1970s. In addition, the new BEd degree, with a strengthened 'main subject study', stimulated the development of research in the many areas of the school curriculum: in science, mathematics, English, history and geography. And, indeed, these initiatives were strongly supported, if indirectly, by governments of the day via the Schools Council that was established in 1964, working closely with the Nuffield Foundation. However, as Richardson (2002) argues, the study of pedagogy and curriculum were specifically excluded from the Hull conference and from Tibble's book and this had long-term consequences.

> The consequences were serious in the long run, regarding the ability of educational studies to create common cause between educationists in higher education and those in teacher organisations, HMI and government who looked to the field for theoretical insight into how central problems in education might practically be addressed.
>
> (Richardson, 2002: 19)

With the establishment of the Schools Council in 1964, curriculum and pedagogical work did begin to flourish in the 1960s, 1970s and early 1980s, but following on from the Hull conference, it was never institutionalised in the way that the foundation disciplines were. Outside of the University of London Institute of Education, there were very few designated chairs or lectureships established in science education or English education or, indeed, in any other area of teaching; as a result, this line of research rapidly withered in the turn to the practical in teacher education after the mid 1980s. Today, while the foundation disciplines do continue, if in reduced form (Furlong and Lawn, 2010), only mathematics education and science education survive as strong curriculum-based areas of enquiry in the UK.

## Conclusion

The first 100 years therefore – from the Cross Commission of 1888 to the abolition of the distinction between polytechnics and universities in 1992 – saw education slowly and often falteringly enter the university world. Education was now a significant part of the greatly expanded university system – in size if not in status. It had very large numbers of students studying for first and second degrees and had an increasingly rich and diverse research culture. And as part of higher education, it had become used to being largely autonomous, defining the structure and content of its courses, choosing what research it pursued. But the irony was that at the very moment that education formally and fully joined the university world, its autonomy was already being profoundly challenged. That is the story to which we turn in the next chapter.

# 3 The universities and education

## The reassertion of control

### Introduction

The last chapter explored the first 100 years of the discipline of education. This chapter continues that story up until the end of the twentieth century. It looks first at developments in teacher education and then at research.

As we saw in the last chapter, throughout the first 100 years the system of provision for teacher education was divided. The majority of teacher education took place outside of the university system – in the teachers colleges run by religious authorities and, from the early twentieth century, by local authority colleges as well. Research, such as it was, was located in the much smaller university sector. But successive generations of college-based teacher educators, from time to time supported by politicians and leading intellectuals, always aspired for something more, aspired to see teacher education if not taken over, then at least working on an equal footing with the university sector. And after 100 years of experiment, politics and sometimes betrayal, that ambition began to be finally realised.

The amalgamations of the 1970s and 1980s saw many colleges of education join newly formed polytechnics. The subsequent ending of the binary line in 1992 meant that from that point in time, the majority of departments and faculties of education were based in or at least linked to, institutions that were designated as universities. They were autonomous in terms of their financial management and had independent degree-awarding powers. And since then, other amalgamations and changes of status have seen that process complete as the remainder of the old colleges of education became integrated into the university sector as well.

All of this can be interpreted as the working out of the original recommendation of the Robbins Report (Robbins, 1963), which argued that teacher education should become fully part of higher education. In Scotland, Robbins noted that the teachers colleges already had a higher status than many of their counterparts in England and Wales. However, the report argued that in the future, *all* teacher training colleges should have the same autonomy in defining academic and professional education as was enjoyed by the much smaller university-based system of teacher education. But as we will see in this chapter, in the end, that long journey to university status was a pyrrhic victory; autonomy from government control was relatively short-lived, particularly in England and Wales.

Once teacher education became firmly established within higher education, universities were – at least for a while – in charge of defining what professional education should be. What Lord Robbins recommended and what universities quickly accepted was a highly academic, highly theoretical model of teacher education. With a vision that Cardinal Newman himself might have applauded, Robbins advocated that the first aim of professional education was the liberal education of the young man or woman who happened to want to be a teacher. Practical preparation in the skills of actually teaching was very much a second-order activity. And, as we noted in the previous chapter, this vision had significant implications for the development of research and higher degrees within the existing university departments of education.

However, once it was put into operation, it fairly soon became clear that the Robbins conception of professional education was untenable. There were significant unresolved epistemological difficulties concerning the relationship between 'theory' – based on 'scientific' knowledge derived from psychology, sociology, philosophy, etc. – and 'practical knowledge' derived from experience in classrooms; the majority of lecturers and students remained sceptical about the value of an overly academic approach to professional preparation. Once the 'degree worthiness' of the new BEd had been accepted, the Robbins conception of the liberally educated professional started to be challenged and the search for a professionally oriented degree gained momentum. But despite its obvious weaknesses, the academic approach to teacher education, led by higher education, remains an important dimension of the policy debate even today; if nothing else, it serves as a very useful shibboleth for those intent on reform (see, for example, the 2010 English White Paper, *The Importance of Teaching* (DfE, 2010)).

## From Robbins to Thatcher – intervention in teacher education begins

The critique of the Robbins academic model of professional education began with the establishment of the James Committee (James, 1972). Its proposals were radical, strongly emphasising the role of universities in professional education. It proposed three cycles of linked education and training (personal, initial training and in-service), with statutory rights for teachers to have one term's study leave every seven years. While the report's proposals on in-service education were not followed up systematically, the distinction between personal and initial training was increasingly recognised in national policy. Teaching moved to become an all-graduate profession during the 1970s, though, at the same time, there was a progressive move away from the four-year BEd route into teaching towards the PGCE. For a growing number of students, therefore, their personal education was something that was important, but that was completed before they entered a department or faculty of education.

But, actually, far more significant than the James Report at this time were the radical changes brought about by demography. In England and Wales a downturn in the birth rate resulted in a severe reduction in the demand for new teachers. As a result, between 1972 and 1983 numbers of students in colleges of education were reduced by a massive 85 per cent, forcing large-scale closures and amalgamations (Richardson, 2002; Pratt, 1997). Significant reductions were also experienced in Northern Ireland, but in Scotland, where there was less concern over issues of supply, there was greater stability in the system.

But these were changes in the structure of provision for teacher education. What about its content? Interestingly, the 1970s saw very little government intervention here; the content of courses was something that was left to the professionals: university teacher educators, the Council for National Academic Awards (CNAA), philosophers of education, the teaching unions and Her Majesty's Inspectorate (HMI). The result was increasing fragmentation; older universities stuck to their more academic model, while newer universities and polytechnics began to explore more professionally oriented programmes (Wilkin, 1996).

By contrast, in Scotland, as Menter and Hulme (2008) argue, there developed a strong policy community, including civil servants (at that time working within the Scottish Office), members of the Schools' Inspectorate (HMI), local authority education officials, teacher union officers (notably those leading the dominant union, the Educational Institute for Scotland) and college principals. These different groups came together institutionally in the General Teaching Council for Scotland (GTCS), which, from 1965 onwards, assumed a key role in validating all professional courses for teachers. This body, drawing as it did on a core group of people who 'understood each other' and who shared a common set of beliefs about the traditions, purposes and virtues of Scottish education, was critical in Scotland's resistance to many of the changes pursued by the London-based Thatcher government and, indeed, those who followed have followed since.

When Margaret Thatcher came to power in 1979, she inherited a system of initial teacher education in England and Wales that had, in recent years, rapidly expanded and then contracted as projections of teacher supply had changed. The need to maintain a flexible system of supply therefore remained a high priority for successive Conservative Secretaries of State. The system was also highly diverse. There were three different types of institutional providers – universities, polytechnics and colleges – each with their own histories, commitments and professional associations; course content and structure varied widely too.

Interestingly, the incoming Conservative government of 1979 was, at first, slow to develop any significant policies in initial teacher education. In fact, it was not until its second term of office – when both neo-conservative and neo-liberal critiques of teacher education started to come to the fore in the public policy debate – that it made any significant moves.

For neo-conservatives, schooling is first and foremost about the induction of the young into established bodies of knowledge. From this point of view, the primary task for initial teacher education is to develop professionals who are xperts in their own subject area. Such preparation, it is argued, recedence over training in research-based knowledge of pedagogy; O'Hear (1988) and Lawlor (1990) – two prominent neo-ritics of the day – argued that university teacher education courses on pedagogical theory actually *diminished* the effectiveness of teachers because they focused on *how* to teach rather than *what* to teach.

If, for neo-conservatives, higher education's focus on pedagogy rather than content was the problem in teacher education, then the answer was to be found in a different political belief system that was sweeping the Conservative Party at the time: neo-liberalism. In the field of initial teacher education, there was an assertion amongst neo-liberals that initial training needed to be opened up to the market in two different ways, both of which would lead to improvements. Firstly, courses needed to be opened up as much as possible to the market of schools so that practical work would take precedence over university-based training; this would, in turn, challenge the liberal educational establishment and their obsession with research-based knowledge of pedagogy. Secondly, there needed to be the development of alternative forms of teacher education led by schools themselves; market competition would raise the quality of training and progressively help to challenge the dominance of higher education's control of the system. Both of these lines of thought have remained key parts of teacher education policy in England to this day and, despite devolution in 1999, they are still to be felt in Wales.

Specific intervention first began in 1984, with the issuing of DES Circular 3/84 (DES, 1984). It was this circular that established the Council for the Accreditation of Teacher Education (CATE), which was charged with the responsibility of overseeing initial teacher education in England and Wales on behalf of the Secretary of State. New regulations were put in place that defined, for the first time, the length of courses and the time student teachers must spend in school.

The circular instituted two other very important changes as well. First, it insisted that those employed in universities and colleges to teach pedagogy should themselves have recent and relevant classroom experience. In a move that had more in common with the Chinese cultural revolution than British higher education, during the 1980s, lecturers were sent back to the classroom on regular basis to refresh their practical teaching experience. In the event, the strategy of sending existing lecturers back to the classroom was relatively short-lived; instead, universities and colleges increasingly began to recruit staff directly from schools. Some of these new staff members were permanent, bringing with them their own strongly professional rather than academic forms of expertise; others were temporary and part-time, opening the door to the future casualisation of university staff. The second change was that the establishment of CATE was to be supported by government inspection. For the first time, even the oldest universities had to allow HMI to inspect their provision for teacher training. Richardson (2002) reports that when the first inspections were carried out in 1985, eight of the first nine institutions inspected in England, Wales and Northern Ireland failed to meet the required standards.

So, despite the fact that most teacher education was now provided through formally autonomous universities, through this circular, the Secretary of State was able to reassert his right to have a say in the detailed content and structure of initial teacher education in England and Wales; he also had a say in who was employed to teach on those courses. Even the oldest universities in England, Wales and Northern Ireland lost their autonomy. In establishing the mechanism of increased accountability and central control, the Circular was, therefore, hugely important. The position in Scotland was now fundamentally different. With the General Teaching Council for Scotland 'holding the ring' between government, local education authorities, the unions and higher education, the relative autonomy of the universities was protected and a strong university-led dimension to professional education was maintained.

In England and Wales, by opening up training courses to the realities of the market of schools, the government and its agencies progressively introduced a more practically focused professionalism. Yet despite the challenges to their autonomy, universities were still seen as making a very important contribution to professional education. Their contribution was now defined by government; educational knowledge had to be practically oriented, focusing sharply on the realities of school life. Nevertheless, there was little doubt that those in universities still had an important contribution to make.

The aim of teacher education courses in the 1980s was to produce an 'expert teacher', someone who had access to the specialised, research-based and theoretical knowledge that was sharply practically focused and someone who was also highly practically competent. And a national study of teacher education undertaken at the time (the MOTE study, Furlong *et al.*, 2000) demonstrated that this was the form of teacher education that was established in the majority of institutions in England and Wales in the late 1980s and early 1990s.

## Enter the TTA

However, in England and Wales, the changes that were introduced in the 1980s did nothing to stem the tide of criticism within the policy debates that surrounded the Conservative government at the time; neo-conservative critics were particularly influential (Hillgate Group, 1989). In the autumn of 1991, a new Secretary of State for Education was appointed: Kenneth Clarke. His appointment marked the beginning of a very different and much more confrontational period of reform. Much of the confrontation was with those in the universities. Over the next three years, new policies came thick and fast, each of them seeming more radical than the last. The most significant came in 1994, with the establishment of the Teacher Training Agency (TTA), later renamed the Training and Development Agency for Schools (TDA). With the establishment of this new agency, funding for teacher education in England was separated from all other funding in higher education. But the TTA was not just a funding body; it was also a policy body, regulating student numbers and defining the shape and content of teacher education programmes.

With the post-1992 reforms, there was a much more concerted attempt than before to establish a more practically based form of professional education in England and Wales: the amount of time student teachers had to spend in school was increased; the option of a three- rather than four-year undergraduate route was introduced (the assumption was that the student 'market' would drive down the length of courses to three years); and, in a measure that significantly undermined the stability of many university departments and faculties of education, all teacher education programmes had to enter into formal partnership agreements with their local schools and pay up to 25 per cent of their fee income over to them to cover the cost of supervision.

Almost equally important, however, was the concern to use a newly devised competency framework in order to increase direct control of the curriculum and the assessment process, whoever was responsible for delivering them – either schools or those in higher education. Students were required to focus on the competences of teaching throughout the whole period of initial training and in order to ensure conformity to the new competency framework, the remit of Her Majesty's Inspectorate HMI (later to become Ofsted) in teacher education was extended to include the inspection of schools where students were based for their training.

This period also saw the challenge to the role of English and Welsh universities taken a stage further with the launching of a range of employment-based routes into teaching. In principle, such routes are based primarily on practically based knowledge and do not demand the involvement of universities at all. Early versions were the Articled and Licensed Teacher Schemes, which have, today, evolved into the Graduate Teacher Programme and Teach First. Today some 22 per cent of new teachers in England enter the profession in this way, their training being undertaken almost entirely on the job.

Importantly, all of these developments were resisted in both Scotland and Northern Ireland. In these countries teacher education has remained largely led by those in higher education and there has been no move from a four-year to a three-year undergraduate degree. Wales, by contrast, moved entirely to a three-year undergraduate degree in 1996. In Scotland, under pressure from England, a brief experiment was made in the development of a partnership model of initial teacher education, with the transfer of significant responsibilities to schools (McIntyre, 2006); however, it remained just a pilot scheme and was eventually dropped. As Menter and Hulme (2008) comment: 'This can be seen as another example of the Scottish education policy community resisting what was seen by many as an English idea that was being imported.' When a similar scheme was proposed in Northern Ireland, it was resisted by the combined might of Catholic and Protestant bishops, probably keen to maintain the autonomy of their denominational teachers colleges.

In England and Wales, though, the mid- and late 1990s was a period of considerable influence for neo-conservative thinkers in relation to initial teacher education. Their stated aim was the suppression of 'lengthy, doctrinaire and demoralising' training courses (Lawlor, 1990) and the creation of a 'neutral' system in which teachers, rather than teacher educators, prepared trainee of predefined practically based competences. And evidence from tł round of MOTE studies (Furlong *et al.*, 2000) confirmed that, on tł this aspiration was largely achieved.

Despite the hope on the part of those in the university sector that they would be able to maintain a vision of the reflective practitioner by collaborating with teachers in schools, thereby ensuring that students were offered more than mere practical training, in reality, this proved hard to achieve. Students spent a significant part of their time in schools, away from the influence of those in higher education. Reduced funding, because so much was now passed to schools, and increasing pressures from Ofsted meant that what was offered to students inevitably became a narrower, more practical form of training. If 1984 saw the introduction of the possibility of government control over teacher education programmes in England, 1992 saw that become a reality. Any semblance of university autonomy evaporated without trace; in teacher education, it has not been reasserted.

## Research: from relativity to evidence-based practice

And, finally, what was happening to educational research in these closing years of the twentieth century? For much of the Conservative period, educational research was an irrelevance. Margaret Thatcher was not someone who needed research or educational experts to tell her how to run schools, colleges or universities. As a self-avowedly conviction politician, she knew exactly what was needed. And what was not needed was that prospective teachers should study the fruits of educational research – irrelevant theory. In England and Wales in particular, theory and research were therefore progressively marginalised from initial teacher education. Increasingly taught only at graduate level, they were left, for a period at least, like any other social science: driven by the academy itself with its own internal methodological and theoretical debates and disputes.

A key turning point in those theoretical debates came only five years after the publication of Tibble's confident book on *The Study of Education*, with Michael Young's *Knowledge and Control* (Young, 1971). Mirroring the relativist intellectual currents of the day, Young argued that all educational knowledge, including research knowledge, is socially constructed; as such, his work fundamentally challenged the positivist principles on which the majority of educational research at the time was based. Similar challenges appeared the following year with Parlett and Hamilton's (1972) attack on psychometrics as the dominant model for evaluating the effectiveness of educational innovation. Taken together, these interventions had a number of major implications for the field. Firstly, their work supported the growing interest in qualitative research in education, some of which was relativist in inspiration. As Nisbet (2005: 35) puts it:

> Quantitative research could show that there were wide ranges of individual differences in every kind of measure but seldom was able to explain the

> meaning or implications of the findings for everyday contexts: its aim was generalisation for the purposes of prediction and management. Qualitative research in contrast aimed at understanding and insight into the complexities of learning and human behaviour.

As such, qualitative research had a much wider appeal to the growing numbers of teacher educators who were both practitioners and budding researchers.

A second consequence was that if educational research was socially constructed, then there was no reason why it should be only pursued by specialist experts in universities. The teacher-researcher movement argued for the democratisation of the research process. Championed by the philosopher Lawrence Stenhouse (1970, 1981), it involved teachers studying and reflecting on their own classrooms with a view to improving their practice. Born in England in the 1970s and strongly supported by BERA (the British Educational Research Association), which was established in 1974, the teacher-researcher movement spread rapidly round the English speaking world and remains a vibrant strand of the educational research scene to this day, though it is still viewed with suspicion by many more traditional researchers.

A third consequence of these relativist arguments was that they helped to open up the theoretical framing of research in new and important ways. If knowledge was socially constructed, then rather than providing a blueprint for educational research, positivism was only one way of interpreting the world. And from the 1980s onwards, a much wider repertoire of methodologies and theories started to come into education. Literary theory, cultural studies, activity theory, feminism, postcolonial theory – all of these and many more began to make their claims for a space in the analysis of educational questions. In a very short period of time, they began to undermine (or 'enrich', as some might put it (Bridges, 2006)) the theoretical hegemony of sociology, psychology, history and philosophy. Taken together, this richness of theoretical resources served to reinforce relativism. In the words of Maclure, such approaches 'reject the idea of universal truth and objective knowledge, delivered through the proper use of reason and assert that truths are always partial and knowledge is always "situated"' (Maclure, 2003: 174–175).

And it was this challenge to positivism – the consequent proliferation of different theoretical frameworks and the postmodern turn – that was perhaps of the most lasting significance from this challenge. Indeed, it was this line of thinking that eventually contributed to the collapse of certainty in educational knowledge that is the hallmark of the contemporary period. But that is an issue to which we return in more detail in Chapter 7.

Driven by the growing need for those involved in degree-level teaching to engage in research themselves, the 1980s therefore saw the volume of educational research begin to grow. And this was a trend that became all the more significant as the first Research Assessment Exercises of 1986, 1989 and 1992 began to make an impact. When colleges of education were amalgamated into existing universities or, after 1992, when all existing polytechnics became universities, with the expectation that education academics had to perform in research terms like any other academics, this idea began to take root. But with the diversity of intellectual frameworks available, with the strong emphasis on qualitative research and with the lack of a strong research tradition in many departments and faculties, this rapid growth in educational research laid it open to criticism, criticism that it was a 'cottage industry', small-scale, unsystematic and largely noncumulative. And, indeed, these were precisely the criticisms that were levelled at educational research in the late 1990s. It was a public debate that was to be highly significant in shaping the future of educational research in the coming decade.

This critical ball was set rolling by David Hargreaves in a widely reported public lecture to the Teacher Training Agency in 1996 (Hargreaves, 1996), where he argued that much of educational research was 'frankly, second-rate' and 'bad value for money'.

His lecture attracted a great deal of attention amongst educational researchers and spilled over into the press. Chris Woodhead, the then controversial Chief Inspector for Schools in England, in an article in the *New Statesman* entitled 'Academia Gone to Seed', claimed that he never read educational research:

> I have given up. Life is too short. There is too much to do in the real world with real teachers in real schools to worry about methodological quarrels or to waste time decoding unintelligible, jargon-ridden prose to reach (if one is lucky) a conclusion that is often so transparently partisan as to be worthless.
> (Woodhead, 1998: 51)

Anthea Millett (Millett, 1997), the then Chief Executive of the Teacher Training Agency (TTA), attacked educational research too, but in her case the issue was not so much the quality as the focus. Far too little research, she argued, has actually focused on the central issue of how we can improve the quality of teaching or pedagogy, the very topics that had been explicitly excluded from the famous Hull conference of 1964. And despite the rebuttals made by educational researchers themselves, (Hammersley, 1997; Edwards, 1997), the criticisms were so trenchant and so frequently repeated that they had an effect. In 1998 the New Labour administration commissioned an enquiry into the quality of educational research. And although presented in more measured language, Hillage *et al.* (1998) largely supported Hargreaves' views.

But why was it that these criticisms had so much force at the time? Educational research has always been subject to considerable criticism, so why were these criticisms being taken up with such vigour and so publicly? The answer, as Kennedy implied at the time, is to do with the changing relationship between research and the state.

> The connection between research and practice is not one in which research influences practice, as many researchers might hope, nor one in which practice influences research as many might hope, but rather one

> in which both research and practice are influenced by and are perhaps even victims of the same shifting social and political context.
>
> (Kennedy, 1997: 9–10).

In the 1960s and 1970s, educational research was seen as having an important contribution to make to the social democratic ideals of the day. Its fundamental purpose (as the OECD suggested in 1995) was to find out about changing clients' needs and wants and then evaluate the impact of government policies in responding to those needs. Using research in this way was central to the social democratic project.

In the Conservative years of the 1980s and 1990s, there was a move away from the view that either policy makers or teachers and lecturers *needed* research-based information. In a world where policy was explicitly ideologically driven, where those in schools as well as higher education were seen as part of the problem rather than the solution, then the findings of research were an irrelevance. Given the Conservatives' educational project at the time, there was little that research could contribute that was of value.

But the role of research in the educational world was about to change. The government's view of research that was emerging at the end of 1990, a view that came to full fruition under New Labour in the decade that followed, was profoundly different. The very public critique of research that emerged in the late 1990s was part of the build-up to that change. Educational research's primary role – the reason that New Labour came to invest in it so strongly – was to influence the world of practice by finding out 'what works'. With a strong reassertion of at least a (quasi) positivist vision of research, its aim was to gather a body of research-based knowledge that could be utilised to develop a range of policies, including pedagogical guidelines or standards for teachers and thereafter to facilitate the auditing of their practice. When the New Labour government came into power in 1997, it believed that the previous Conservative administration had handed it the means of managing the educational system: through market competition and the audit culture. But it also believed that without more content, without more direction, these strategies alone could not ensure that it achieved its own key ambitions, i.e. raising standards and increasing equality of opportunity.

As Alan Luke, a leading educational researcher in Australia who, at the time, had recently moved into the world of educational government, argued (Luke, 2003), despite the creation of quasi-markets in education, despite massively increased competition between schools, colleges and universities, despite the plethora of targets and performance indicators, we still had not solved the problem of underachievement, especially amongst the most disadvantaged groups in society. We therefore, Luke argued, need to turn to the research community to help us find out what *really* works.

And as we will see in Chapter 9, under New Labour, the government invented the mechanisms to manage the educational-research system so that it did, at least in part, deliver that promise. With institutional competition driven by the RAE (RAE 2008a) and with substantially increased funding (research funding in education doubled between the 2001 and 2008 RAE reviews, with almost 60 per cent of it being from government in one form or another), the government was able to establish a new social contract for research, where it increasingly came to define the topics that were studied and the methodologies that were used to study them.

## Conclusion

What this history of the discipline of education has tried to highlight is the constant political struggle since the mid-nineteenth century as to what educational knowledge is, how it should be researched and how it should be acquired in initial teacher education and further professional development. In the field of initial teacher education, at different periods of time and for different student groups, the knowledge on which teacher education programmes has been based has ranged from the rote learning of the Revised Code in the nineteenth century religious colleges to the disciplinary-based theory of the post-Robbins period; from experiential knowledge embodied in the practice of the education tutor in the postwar colleges to the TTA-defined competences of the late 1990s; from the liberal educational principles of the early Day Training Colleges to the employment-based routes of today. What constitutes knowledge in the field of research has also changed markedly from the early days of measurement to the foundation disciplines of education; from practitioner enquiry to postmodernism and then New Labour's focus on what works. Throughout this history, it would seem that many (though, not all) of those working in higher education have had a leaning towards a more academic model of professional knowledge and education, while successive governments, teachers and students have aspired to a much more pragmatic approach, sceptical of the value of theory and research.

But what this and the previous chapter have also shown is that in the end, the struggle to advance education's cause, to become fully part of the university system proper, has been a pyrrhic victory, at least in part. At the very time that education was at long last beckoned to the university high table – the end of the twentieth century – this was the time when governments began profoundly challenging the autonomy of universities in relation to their control of teacher education and of educational research. Only 20 years after its license for autonomy from the Robbins Report (Robbins 1963), the discipline of education was faced with Circular 3/84, which, in England and Wales (if not elsewhere in the UK), reasserted right of government to control the structure and content of initial teacher education. And through the RAE and differential funding opportunities, the government has more recently found ways of progressively shaping the national educational research agenda as well.

As New Labour came to power in 1997, the mechanisms were therefore in place for the discipline of education to move out of the relative policy backwater that it had inhabited for so many years and become more and more directly involved in the national and, indeed, global politics of the day. As I will argue in Section III of this book, it is now increasingly national and global policy drivers that shape the discipline of education as it is found in our universities. But before we turn to this issue, it is necessary to look in more detail at what the current position of university departments and faculties of education in the UK actually is. That is the purpose of the next section of this book.

Chapter 4 examines what we know about the individuals who work in education departments and faculties today, their backgrounds and their qualifications; and we look at the different institutions where they work, the similarities and, in many cases, their very real differences in what remains a hierarchical system. Then Chapters 5 and 6 examine current teaching programmes and current research. After that, in Section III we return to a consideration of the increasingly global forces that shape the discipline today.

# Section II

# Where are we now?

# 4 We're all universities now

## Worlds of similarity and difference

The purpose of this section of the book (Chapters 4, 5 and 6) is to provide an overview of university departments and faculties of education as they are today in the UK. Building on the historical introduction set out in the past two chapters, this section draws on data from national data sets and from case studies of ten institutions to address four key questions: Who are education academics today? What sort of institutions do they work in? What do they teach? And what research do they undertake? Questions as to why the discipline of education is shaped in the way that it is are then addressed in Section III.

### Introduction

Education is big business for British universities. In 2010–11 there were over 223,000 full- and part-time students recorded as studying education in the UK (HESA, 2011). As such, education was the second largest of all higher education disciplines, representing about 9 per cent of all registered students; only business and administration was larger.

But education is not only large; it is also widely distributed. Typically, universities in the UK are seen as falling into one of a number of different groups. There are the ancient universities – Oxford, Cambridge, St Andrews, Lampeter, etc. – established from the medieval period onwards and the 'redbrick' or 'civic' universities – Liverpool, Leeds, etc. – mainly established in the nineteenth and early twentieth centuries. Then there are 'new' universities – e.g., Sussex, York, Stirling – established after the expansion of higher education in the 1960s.

Another group of new universities are the ex-polytechnics such as Manchester Metropolitan, Coventry, Glamorgan, established as universities in 1992. Many claim a much older history, usually back to the nineteenth century, as technical institutes of different sorts. Finally, there are the 'recent' universities (e.g., Chester, Bath Spa, the University of the West of Scotland). These are institutions that were Institutes of Higher Education or University Colleges until relatively recently but have now been granted degree-awarding powers in their own right. Once again, many claim a much longer heritage, often developing from nineteenth century schools of art, teacher training colleges, etc.

Given its size as a discipline, it is not surprising that education is available in all of these different types of universities. Of the 96 universities and university colleges offering education in 2011, 38 of them were older, pre-1992 universities, including 16 that belonged to the elite Russell Group of research-intensive universities. Of the 54 'new' universities offering education, 25 were ex-polytechnics and had therefore been fully part of the higher education system since the 1960s. The remainder, the recent universities, had been granted degree-awarding powers in the past ten years or so.

Looking at the different countries across the UK, education is currently offered as a subject in seven universities in Scotland and eight in Wales. In Northern Ireland it is available at two universities and two university colleges. The remaining 73 institutions are based in England, though provision offered by the Open University is available across the UK as a whole.

Education, then, is a huge part of the university system in the UK and is available as an area of study in virtually all of our tertiary institutions. And at first glance one might see considerable similarities amongst faculties and departments of education in these different institutions, whatever their history or status. Virtually all of them offer some kind of initial teacher education; the only exception is Lancaster University, where there is substantial teaching and research in education but where initial teacher education is not available. At the undergraduate level many departments and facilities offer a three- or four-year undergraduate route into primary school teaching – the BEd – and a growing number also offer an undergraduate degree in educational studies that is not a professional qualification. The one-year postgraduate course for prospective primary and secondary teachers (called the PGDE in Scotland and the PGCE elsewhere) is offered in some form by virtually all of these institutions. Most institutions also offer a professionally oriented master's degree: the MEd. Doctoral work includes the PhD and a professional doctorate, the EdD. Most of these institutions also engage in research; 83 of them entered the 2008 Research Assessment Exercise (RAE).

Despite these commonalities, the reality is that what it means to study education and what education *is* varies significantly across the sector as a whole. At the national level there are important differences to be recognised between education as it is offered in England, Scotland, Northern Ireland and Wales, but there are also many more subtle differences as well; differences that arise because of different institutional histories, different geographies, different degrees of research intensity, different staffing structures, etc. The result is that within its different institutional locations, what education is as a discipline is clearly differentiated. Some might argue that it is clearly stratified. If it is, then that stratification is complex and multifaceted.

In order to describe the different ways in which education is now realised in British universities, I have drawn on a number of different sources of evidence. These include national data sets – HESA, TDA and HEFCE, RAE 2008. These data are important in setting the broad scene. In addition, however, in order to provide more detail, I have made case studies of ten different faculties and departments of education from across the UK – seven from England and one each from Scotland, Northern Ireland and Wales. The sample was chosen to be broadly representative of the different types of universities described above. I chose five older 'redbrick' universities (two of them from the elite Russell Group of research-intensive universities) and five newer universities – one 'new' post-1960s university, two ex-polytechnics and two 'recent' universities. For each case study, I visited the institution on one or two occasions during the academic year 2010–2011, interviewing between four and six senior colleagues in each case.

Those interviewed typically included the dean or head of department, the director of research, the head of initial teacher education programmes, the head of higher-degree programmes and one or two other senior colleagues as seemed appropriate. The interviews, which lasted between 45 and 60 minutes, began with a discussion of the individual's personal professional history; however, the majority of the discussion focused on a descriptive account of their area of responsibility – how research was organised, what was distinctive about the courses they offered – and pressures or drivers they experienced in the shaping of their area of responsibility. In total, 46 interviews were conducted. In addition, each institution was asked to complete a short proforma, detailing staff and student numbers on the different programmes they offered for the academic year 2010–2011. Finally, some additional material was extracted from institutional websites and relevant national data sets, including each institution's 2008 RAE return (RAE 2008a).

In analysing evidence from these case studies, I have chosen to address issues thematically. This is primarily in order to preserve the anonymity of the different universities that agreed to take part in the research. The only exception is the Institute of Education in London (IOE). As the largest single institution in terms of staff, students and research (for example, in the 2008 RAE period (2001–2008), the IOE accounted for some 28 per cent of all the UK university-based research funding in education), it was not only essential to include it in the sample, but also impossible to disguise.

In trying to present a picture of education as a discipline today, it will be helpful to begin at the level of the individual, looking at who education academics are today, where they come from and what qualifications they have. After that it will be possible to turn our attention to the institutions where they work.

## Who are education academics in England today? A segmented labour force?

### *Demographic data*

In the 1960s it was possible for the vast majority of senior education academics working in the university world to know each other. Today that would be impossible. So, who are education academics today? How many are they? Where do they come from? What qualifications do they have? What sorts of contracts are they employed on?

We can gain some insights into these important questions by looking at data from the Higher Education Statistics Agency's (HESA) staffing survey for 2010–11. The figures that follow present HESA data from education and number of other social studies subjects; data from physics is also presented for comparative purposes.

There are now over 5,200 education academics working in UK universities. As such, it is the second largest social science (after business studies and administration); it is more than twice the size of economics or politics and three times as large as social policy and social work (see Figure 4.1).

Education academics also tend to be considerably older than their counterparts in other social science disciplines, with 69 per cent of staff over the age of 46 and approximately 36 per cent over 56; other comparator subjects have a much younger age profile, particularly economics and physics (see Figure 4.2).

There are also important differences in terms of the employment of academics working in education. While education employs roughly the same percentage of academic staff on full teaching and research contracts, compared with other subjects, it has far more staff on teaching-only contracts (35 per cent) and a much lower percentage of contract research staff (4 per cent) (see Figure 4.3).

HESA data also give an interesting insight into a number of other features about academic staff employed within education. For example, it is a largely feminised professional group, with over 66 per cent of lecturers being women, higher than any of the other social sciences. Given this gender profile, it is perhaps depressing but unsurprising that education also has the lowest proportion of staff on middle to higher salaries, with only 19 per cent of staff reporting salaries over £50,000.

HESA data also demonstrates that since the mid-1990s, social sciences as a whole have experienced significant increases in the recruitment of overseas staff, particularly from Europe. However, this has not happened in education, which

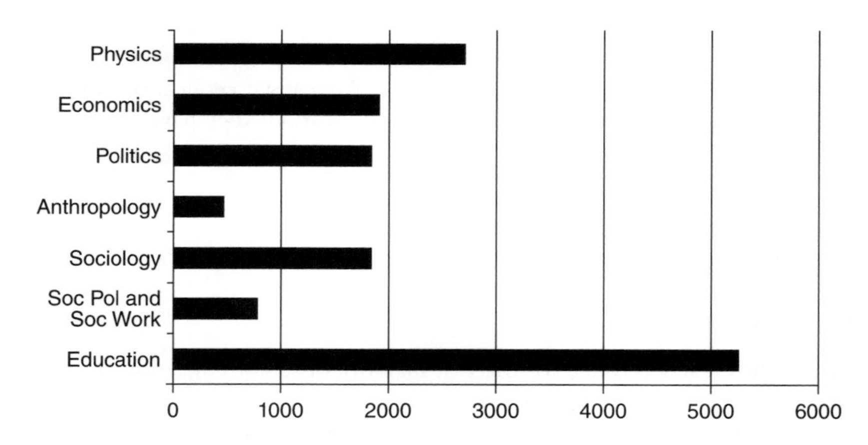


*Figure 4.1* Numbers of UK academic staff in education, social studies and physics.

Source: HESA Staff Record 2010–11

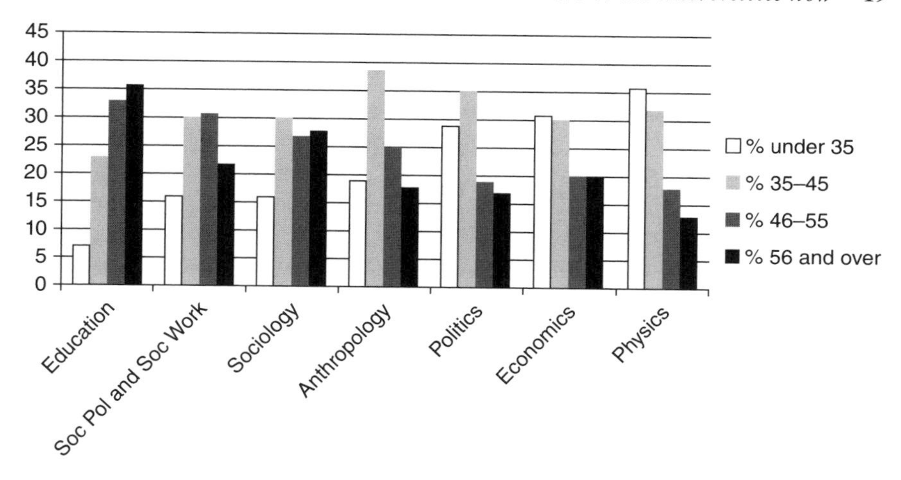


*Figure 4.2* Percentage of UK academic staff in education, social studies and physics by age.

Source: HESA Staff Record 2010–11

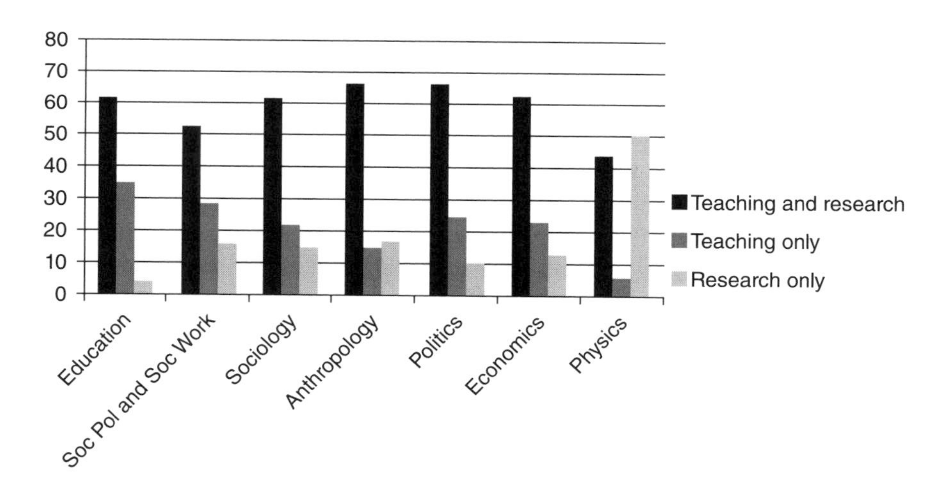


*Figure 4.3* Percentage of UK academic staff by terms of employment in education, social studies and physics.

Source: HESA Staff Record 2010–11

has, by far, the lowest recruitment levels of non-UK nationals amongst the comparator subjects (7 per cent). As Figure 4.4 demonstrates, education as a field also has the smallest proportion of black and minority ethnic employees (4 per cent).

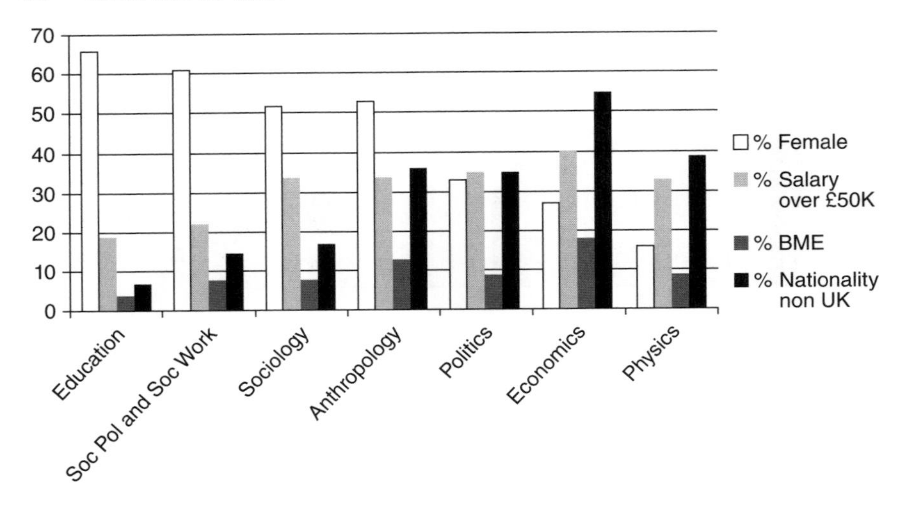


*Figure 4.4* Percentage of UK academic staff in education, social studies and physics by gender, salary, ethnicity and nationality.

Source: HESA Staff Record 2010–11

The view of education academics that emerges from this demographic data therefore is that overall, they are older than other social scientists and have shorter higher education careers because they start later; they are less likely to be recruited from ethnic minorities and non-UK nationals than other social scientists; they are more likely to be female; they are relatively low-paid; and a greater proportion are on teaching-only or casualised contracts.

And what of their qualifications? As Figure 4.5 shows, only 23 per cent of education academics had a doctorate as their highest academic qualification. As such, education had the lowest proportion of staff with doctorates across the subjects surveyed here. On the other hand, in absolute terms, it employed roughly the same number of staff with doctorates as economics, politics and sociology and many more than anthropology or social policy and social work. There is also evidence from the earlier ESRC demographic review of the social sciences (Mills *et al.*, 2006) that education is a 'net importer' of staff from other disciplines. While subjects such as anthropology or economics are relatively pure, with most academic staff having studied their highest qualification within their own discipline, only about 60 per cent of education academics have their highest qualification from the discipline itself. Others enter education from a range of different disciplines, particularly psychology and sociology.

We can also ask, whatever their background, what proportion of academics in education are research-active. HEFCE data suggest that only roughly 36 per cent of education academics were entered for the 2008 RAE, a smaller proportion than in most other social sciences. As we will discuss below, this does not mean that the other 64 per cent were not undertaking of research of any kind. It does, however, mean that they were not undertaking it in a manner and at a level that

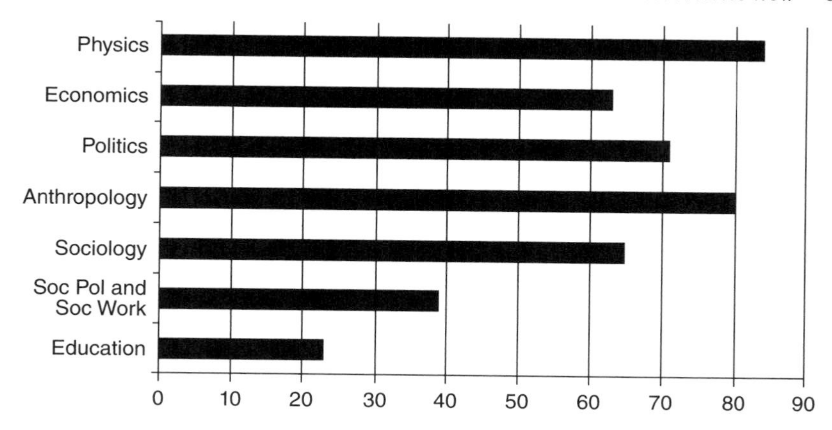


*Figure 4.5* Percentage of UK academic staff in education, social studies and physics with a doctorate as highest qualification.

Source: HESA Staff Record 2010–11

would be recognised by the wider university system. However, despite this low entry rate, in terms of absolute numbers, education, with 1,696 staff entered, constituted the second largest group of research-active social scientists in the UK (again, business and management was the largest). The education numbers were roughly similar in size to psychology and almost twice the size of economics or sociology.

Taken together, what these figures hint at, therefore, is a segmented labour force (a view corroborated in Scottish universities by Menter, 2011). While the majority of education academics may have shorter research careers, lower qualifications, are more likely to be on teaching-only contracts and are less likely to be entered into research assessment exercises than their colleagues in other social science disciplines, it is also true that very significant numbers of education academics have a quite different profile. Very large numbers overall have high-level academic qualifications, are employed on full-time teaching and research contracts and are engaged in high quality research, much of which is recognised as internationally significant.

### *Adding more colour*

The difficulty with this type of demographic evidence, of course, is that it does not give any detail about individuals or subgroups within the population as a whole, for this one needs a different source of evidence. Some further insights into who education academics are can be gained from the sample of 46 teacher educators interviewed during the fieldwork. While the sample selected was not representative of the entire population (they were deliberately chosen as senior academics – deans, directors of research and senior programme leaders), their personal stories do provide some insights into the different types of biographies to be found in contemporary faculties and departments of education.

Those biographies can be broadly classified into three groups. The first two groups of respondents – by far the largest in number – had begun their careers as teachers, in primary schools, secondary schools or further education colleges. However, there appeared to be important differences amongst them in the extent to which the teaching profession had been a 'primary' identity during their early careers.

Some had substantial schoolteaching careers. For example, one PGCE programme leader had been employed in her university for just five years prior to which she had a 30-year career as a secondary school teacher; another respondent, who was currently a dean, had spent ten years teaching in primary schools. 'Then I realised I could either start applying for headships at a relatively young age or go into teacher education and there was then an interest in people with recent and relevant experience and I got a job in X College in 1986.' For some, this personal history as a teacher was still seen as a key part of their professional identity even though they now worked in a university.

What is interesting about this group of academics is that many of them had been unusual teachers. Two had been publishing school textbooks while teaching ('I did anthologies of short stories and books for schools.'); two others had Cambridge doctorates before going into teaching (they both talked about deliberately choosing teaching instead of postdoctoral work). Several others had studied for a PhD whilst teaching and most had some experience of working with student teachers placed in their schools. As one respondent explained:

> I was a primary teacher. I did BEd honours, then did a master's at (X University) and then there was a long gap before I decided that this was what I was going to do, go into teacher education. It kind of happened from working with students in school ... For my masters' degree I was released a few hours early on Thursday evening. I did it over two years, but then when I wanted to start doctoral work, contractually, it would have been hard to sustain, so I went part-time and did some contract work here for a bit.

For some of this group, the transition to higher education was relatively straightforward; they came directly from school on secondments or temporary contracts. For others, though, as in the case of the respondent above, it was much more difficult and involved a period of part-time work while studying at the same time. But what characterises this group was their initial commitment to teaching as a career. As one of them said: 'I loved school. I was a primary deputy head within five years; I was headteacher within eight.'

A second group of respondents had also been teachers; however, they appeared to have had a somewhat weaker identity as teachers during their early careers. Although they had spent time teaching in schools or FE colleges, in many cases this was only of relatively short duration. Some had taught for a year or so overseas, while others had begun in British schools but had typically made a rapid transition into higher education, either as a researcher or as a lecturer.

As one Dean explained:

> For my first degree I did chemistry and chemical engineering, then did a PGCE in chemistry and, while teaching, did part-time PhD in chemical engineering at home in the weekends. Then the School of Education offered me a research-assistant post on a project on science education …

Another senior colleague told her story.

> My first degree was in politics. I got a third because I did not do any work, so I did a PGCE and got a job teaching in an all-boys secondary modern school in London. And while I was doing that, I did another degree in psychology and got a first and went on to do a PhD. That was at a point when teacher education was moving to degree level and they wanted teachers to have high quality theoretical input.

All of these education academics were different from the third group in terms of biography – those who had not come into education through teaching. Rather they had more conventional academic careers, often with doctorates and postdoctoral research experience before becoming a university lecturer either in education or in a related discipline.

As one current director of research explained:

> I did my first degree in anthropology, looking at schools; then I got a job as a research officer looking at communications with our district councils here. Then I was offered a lectureship in the University of X and then I came here. Education had always been a theme in what I had done, but I was much more about community relations generally.

Another programme leader for graduate studies explained:

> Okay, well, I did an undergraduate degree in sociology and psychology at (University A) and then a master's degree in sociology at (University B). And then I worked at (University of C) for three years as a research assistant … and then I started a PhD in (University D). And when I finished the PhD in the sociology department, I then got a job at (University E) in research and I was there for about just under two years and then got the job here at (University F), so I've been here for eight years. Time flies.

Although smaller in number, these types of senior academics were a significant group, especially in research-intensive universities.

These biographies therefore illustrate many of the demographic features described earlier: the fact that many but not all education academics come into the university system as second careers and the fact that, in important ways, education is a net importer of academic staff who have qualified in other disciplines. But these stories also illustrate other differences too. There is a clear sense of different generations of staff moving into universities. The oldest group – those currently moving into retirement – are the disciplinary specialists (sociologists, psychologists, etc.) who were recruited up until the mid-1980s to teach 'the disciplines of education' in the post-Robbins era. As the psychologist quoted above put it, 'That was at a point when teaching was moving to a degree and they wanted teachers to have high quality theoretical input'.

Then, in accounts from a slightly younger generation, there are references to recent and relevant school teaching experience. This was a requirement for virtually all new staff recruited to education faculties in England and Wales in the middle to late 1980s; for this group, the transition into higher education was relatively straightforward in that universities at the time were required by the government of the day to recruit staff straight from school if they were to be allowed to continue offering initial teacher education courses. Then there are the more recent appointments where university agenda have been increasingly influenced by the pursuit of research priorities. On the one hand, this has led to the appointment of academics with backgrounds in social science rather than school teaching – all of them strongly research-active. And on the other hand and significantly underrepresented in this particular sample, have been the growing number of teaching-only staff, many of them on hourly paid contracts, appointed directly from school in order to allow others to focus on research.

What these accounts don't illustrate, however, is that these groups of different lecturers, even in the same institution, often have significantly different responsibilities and working conditions. The differences between hourly paid staff and those in tenured positions are obvious. But there are also differences between those staff whose main teaching is associated with initial teacher education (where university terms are longer and teaching more intensive) and those whose work is primarily focused on master's and doctoral teaching or on research. (Some of these differences have recently been explored in a study of 'The Work of Teacher Education,' by Ellis *et al.*, forthcoming).

## Institutions: worlds of difference and stratification

So much for individuals. What about the institutions where they work? As we have already indicated, there are currently 96 universities and university colleges in the UK offering education as a subject (courses of initial teacher education in England are offered in a further 127 institutions of different sorts, ranging from individual schools to Local Authority Consortia). What are those institutions like? In what ways are they similar and in what ways are they different?

### *Size and shape*

The first thing to note is that departments and faculties of education differ in terms of their size and in the courses they offer. As part of the fieldwork, all ten case study institutions were asked to complete a proforma outlining staff and student numbers for the academic year 2010–2011. Tables derived from this data are presented in the Appendix.

Firstly, data on staffing. As Table 4.1 illustrates, there were significant differences in the size of these ten faculties and departments. One 'recent' university (Institution 9) had only 23 full-time teaching staff compared with the two ex-polytechnics that had 74 and 75 and 159 at the Institute of Education (IOE) (Institution 3). The table also shows the very considerable variations in the numbers of contracted research staff employed full- and part-time. The IOE had a total headcount of 142 contracted research staff, reflecting their very substantial research income. Another Russell Group institution (Institution 2) reported 17 research staff, whereas several others had very few or no research staff at all.

Institutions also differed considerably in the degree to which they employed teaching-only staff. Some institutions, for example, had a considerable proportion of staff on teaching-only contracts (Institutions 1, 2, 4 and 5); interestingly, all of these were part of universities that considered themselves to be research-intensive. Other departments and faculties, including many of those that were not research-intensive, did not make this distinction. Table 4.1 also shows considerable differences in the extent to which institutions were making use of hourly paid teaching staff. While all institutions employed some hourly paid staff, some institutions seemed particularly dependent on it as a staffing strategy. In most of the institutions visited, it emerged that such staff were seen as particularly important in supporting professional programmes.

It is also instructive to look at the proportion of staff entered into the last RAE in order to gain some insight into the character of different faculties and departments and their focus on research. In Table 4.2, a research-intensity ratio for each of the case study institutions has been calculated by dividing the number of staff entered to the RAE in 2008 by the number of FTE academic staff employed at the time. A ratio of 1.0 would indicate that all staff were entered for the RAE; a ratio of 0.0 would indicate that no staff were entered. As Table 4.2 demonstrates, ratios for these ten institutions ranged from 0.12 to 1.22.

Considerable care needs to be taken in interpreting these data for two reasons. Firstly, institutions may well have changed substantially between 2007, when staff were entered to the RAE, and 2010–2011. Indeed, during that period, the Scottish institution included in the sample had seen significant staff reductions, but there may well have been important changes in other institutions too. In addition, under the rules of the 2008 RAE exercise, not everyone entered was necessarily currently employed by the submitting department. Some of those entered might have been retired and some might have been conducting educational research but based in a different department; that is why two institutions – 2 and 3 – had a research-intensity ratio of higher than 1.0. Despite these caveats, the table does illustrate, if only in broad-brush terms, substantial differences between these ten faculties or departments of education in terms of staff involved in research defined according to the RAE. Three of the institutions, for example, would appear to have a very high level of research intensity – between 0.77 and 1.22 – suggesting that a high proportion of eligible staff was entered.

By contrast, four others would appear to have had a much smaller proportion of staff entered (0.12 or 0.25). As one might expect, history is key here: all of the more research-intensive departments were in 'older' universities; they were part of universities that saw themselves to be research-intensive. All but one of those with lower scores were in newer universities. One case study department (Institution 4), however, challenged this 'rule' with relatively few members of staff being entered (hence a low research-intensity ratio) despite the fact that it was in an older university, one that considered itself to be research-intensive.

Data gathered on student enrolments on different programmes also reveals key differences between institutions. Tables 4.3, 4.4 and 4.5 set out student numbers for enrolments of new students for the academic year 2010–2011 on the most commonly occurring teaching programmes within the ten institutions. In reality, most institutions offered a range of other types of courses as well. Some of these additional courses were in the field of education – diplomas, non award-bearing course; others were in a range of related fields such as youth work, medical education, counselling, etc.

Table 4.3 shows student enrolments on Foundation and undergraduate programmes. Seven of the ten institutions reported figures for two-year Foundation Degree programmes, typically for teaching assistants wishing to upgrade their qualifications; however, in most cases, the numbers were relatively small, with 49 being the largest intake for the year and many programmes being much smaller. Foundation Degree teaching therefore represents only a relatively small part of departments' and faculties' teaching activities. By contrast, most of the newer universities now offer a BA in education studies, a degree that does not lead to a professional qualification as a teacher. While the traditional BEd degree for primary school teachers was still strong, in two of the institutions visited, it was being reduced in length from a four-year to a three-year degree and in one of the 'recent' universities, it had been phased out entirely.

Table 4.4 presents enrolments of students on one-year postgraduate teacher education courses for prospective teachers at primary, secondary and postcompulsory levels. All ten institutions offered these types of programmes, though the size of individual courses varied substantially. For example, the IOE (Institution 3) reported 822 full-time secondary PGCE students. As the head of initial teacher education at the IOE explained, this had major implications for their staffing and for student experience:

> So, what makes it distinctive is the size of teams. We have fifty historians (on the programme) and a team of three tutors and that creates a particular kind of experience for students having a team of tutors and it is a lot healthier. At (my last university) it was just me with sixteen students; it was a very intensive relationship.

The next largest secondary PGCE programme (Institution 9) number was 335, while another (Institution 10) had only 17 students in just one subject area. Institution 9 also had the third highest number of primary PGCE students (156) and the second largest undergraduate education studies programme, with 95 new full-time students on a three-year programme. All this despite the fact that this institution reported one of the smallest numbers of full-time teaching staff – just 23.

Table 4.5 presents enrolments of students on higher degrees, including different types of master's and doctoral programmes. Most institutions reported substantial professional master's programmes, with much of this provision being part-time; for example, one institution (Institution 5) reported 450 part-time master's students. Only three institutions reported significant full-time programmes. Numbers on other research-based master's courses were, in most cases, small except at the Institute of Education, which reported very significant numbers, as did two other institutions.

At doctoral level, important differences emerge between these ten institutions. Although all formally offered PhD programmes and eight offered a taught doctorate, the EdD, the numbers registering for the PhD programme in particular varied considerably, with some institutions recruiting new full- and part-time students in double figures, while others recruited only modest numbers. In the newer universities a major constraint was the available capacity to supervise at doctoral level.

Similar variations were revealed in relation to international students. While all institutions reported some international students, for example, on PGCE programmes, in most cases these numbers were relatively small. In this sample international students in any significant numbers were confined to the IOE and one other Russell Group institution (Institution 2), which reported a particularly strong international profile at master's and doctoral levels.

In looking at this evidence, what emerges, then, are the considerable differences between institutions. While all of these ten institutions offered a similar *range* of programmes (BA, PGCE, MSc, PhD, EdD), there were important differences between them. Only a small number of institutions had attracted significant numbers of international students or doctoral students and only a small number were able to offer research-based master's degrees. And behind this variation lurks history, the history of differentiation. With some minor exceptions, it is mainly only the older universities that currently offer well-staffed higher-degree programmes; it is mainly the older universities that have strong research profiles; it is mainly the older universities that have been able to draw in substantial numbers of international students.

### *Other distinguishing features: focus*

But today's departments and faculties of education are not only distinguishable in terms of their size and shape, they also differ on a range of other dimensions as well. For example, the substantive focus of departments varies. As Tables 4.3, 4.4 and 4.5 demonstrate, the Institute of Education (Institution 3) offers courses focusing on all stages of learning, from early years to lifelong learning and at all levels – from Foundation Degrees to doctoral programmes. The only area where they do not currently have significant provision is in the undergraduate route into teaching. And their provision is not confined to university-led teacher education. They are also significantly involved in supporting employment-based routes into teaching – the Graduate Teacher Programme, the assessment-only route and Teach First. As the director of the IOE explained:

> So, in relation to teacher education, we want to make sure that we are wholly engaged with innovation and development across the piece and we need to be. The London educational scene is extraordinarily diverse … there are thirty-two boroughs, but they are of decreasing significance as schools develop greater autonomy. We have a very fractured system, so we have got to face multiple audiences. Therefore, the IOE offers a very large mainstream PGCE – primary, secondary and postcompulsory. We also have a very large graduate-teacher programme and we are doing that because as schools diversify and they start to experiment with what they want, it is absolutely imperative that we stay close to them. If we don't, others will and we can't afford for that to happen. And we have just secured the Teach First contract for London … that is important because it means that we now do have a full range of provision and we can begin [to] think intelligently about the whole range and the links across the range and it also means that we have diversified risk.

The Institute of Education is clearly unique in the UK in offering such a breadth of provision; most other universities demonstrate particular specialties. Here institutional history is again key. Sometimes those histories were seen positively by my respondents, sometimes negatively; very often they were hardly noticed at all, just taken for granted. For example, in the two departments in Russell Group universities, no primary or undergraduate courses were offered. And what was offered in terms of initial teacher education had not changed significantly since before the Second World War. Research and higher degrees had been added to their activities, but their overwhelming focus was on secondary education, as it was before the Second World War, when they were Day Training Colleges; that legacy lived on undisturbed and unnoticed.

By contrast, those institutions that had a strong primary focus nearly all had historical links to the old college sector. This was most clearly the case amongst the 'recent' universities, where ex-teachers colleges had been a key part of the new institution; it was also true of a number of other universities, including ex-polytechnics, that had taken over teacher colleges at some stage in the past.

And the two faculties that had the strongest teaching and research profile in postcompulsory education and training were ex-polytechnics with a strong tradition of vocational education. As the dean of one of them explained:

> Historically, this faculty was a vocational teacher training college … vocational-teacher training was very much at the heart of its philosophy as well. It wasn't just what it happened to be; it shaped its culture and everything

> else. And then that's still there – in our FE training – it has, until very recently, been about half our business.

History influenced course provision and research in other ways too. Two of the case study institutions visited had evolved from amalgamations between established universities and previously independent and highly successful former colleges of education. At the time of their amalgamation, both of these colleges had begun to diversify their curricula substantially, offering courses such as autism, child guidance, deaf education, counselling, theatre education and many others as well. Interestingly, remnants of this diversification were still to be seen 20 or 30 years on in what these universities considered to be education. As the dean of one of those universities explained, compared to other universities:

> we have a broader concept of education. For a start, we have historically had more of a multidiscipline context in which to work. We always had lots of other disciplines represented in education on this site – physical education and sport, speech and language therapy. We've got a strong commitment to community education, social education, applied arts and so on ... Throughout the twentieth century, [we] have been involved in professional education for numerous disciplines as well as teachers and we retain part of that even today.

### *Epistemological differences*

Different institutions therefore express different conceptions of education in terms of 'breadth'. Some institutions, particularly the Institute of Education, demonstrate a very broad view; others are more narrowly focused. But what of the more subtle epistemological differences discussed in Chapter 1? In that chapter it was suggested that it is possible to distinguish four fundamentally different views or discourses about what it is to be knowledgeable in the field of education. These different discourses imply different conceptions of what should be involved in teaching and research within the discipline. To what extent were these differences visible within these ten institutions?

The four different discourses identified were firstly that of liberal education, making available to learners what Matthew Arnold described as 'the best that has been thought and said' (Arnold, 1869). Liberal educationalists can be sharply distinguished from those who have emphasised scientifically developed disciplinary knowledge as a basis for teaching and research. As became clear in Chapter 2, in the first half of the twentieth century, such knowledge was primarily psychologically defined. Since that time, it has been substantially elaborated to include a wide range of social, scientific and humanities-based perspectives. Processes of research have been applied to the professionally arena as well. A third discourse – and one that has dominated policy documents nationally and internationally over the last quarter of a century – has been concerned with practical knowledge. As was suggested in Chapter 1, practical knowledge is now very widely recognised as an important element in professional education; it is also very widely recognised as very difficult to pin down. A final approach to knowledge argues that it is not only important to consider what to do, but also what is right to do. In these interpretations practical knowledge is seen to have a moral dimension as well. In the UK and elsewhere, such ideas were echoed in the 'normal' school tradition with its strong emphasis on the moral community (Bell, 1981).

So, to what extent were these different conceptions of knowledge visible in these ten different institutions? To what extent might they capture and explain some of the more subtle differences in how education as a discipline is realised within them?

If one begins with a research-based conception of knowledge, it is clear that there are subtle but important differences of emphasis between these ten institutions. All institutions demonstrated a range of different interpretations of research and scholarship, ranging from a strongly disciplinary-based approach, of the sort that would be recognised within the RAE (now called the Research Excellence Framework – REF) to other conceptions of research that were more professionally oriented. As one dean put it:

> I would say there are three sorts of research. There is the REF, largely peer-reviewed in academic journals and books with national and international significance, the other sort of research that won't get into the REF because it is not national or because the journals are not considered academic enough; and then there is publication that is creative original, interesting and relevant, theorised but would not be called research under those headings – textbook writing and so on.

All institutions recognised this diversity but clearly valued it differently. The Institute of Education, for example, articulated a particularly strong social scientific conception of education. As one senior colleague put it:

> The strap line we introduced was 'Leading education and social research'. Our remit is education and related areas of social science and professional practice ... We have a breadth in embracing the social scientific study of education in a way that was, to some extent, recognised by the parent disciplines. Richard Peters came here from Birkbeck – a social philosopher – and Bernstein worked with Mary Douglas in UCL and those people saw themselves in a way that philosophers and sociologists in other university departments of education by and large did not see themselves, as peers with the parent discipline.

Social science was therefore a key dimension in what constituted research at the IOE, a fact expressed in the very large numbers of students enrolled on its research-led master's and doctoral degrees. But, as we have already seen, some other institutions only entered a very small proportion of their staff into the last research assessment exercise. That did not necessarily mean that their staff were not undertaking research and scholarship; some staff clearly were but it was conceptualised somewhat differently from that undertaken in more research-intensive intuitions. As a PGCE course leader explained:

> I came from a new university, so it is quite an interesting shift. One of the changes I saw was that in the new university, research was something that some people did, but it did not necessarily impact on their practice, whereas here people are much more engaged in research or professional scholarship and that does inform the programmes in thinking about the nature of the programme, its structure, but also those teaching sessions with partnership schools.

But even though research was taken seriously in her institution, it was not always conceptualised in social scientific terms.

> If you take the drama example, the course leader does a lot of research on the teaching of drama in schools, which is shaping how drama is taught in secondary schools, as well as ensuring his trainees here learn that. He does the sort of thing that is disseminated in professional journals, in professional training.

Differences were also visible in relation to other dimensions of educational knowledge as well. For example, as will be discussed in more detail in Chapter 8, throughout teacher education over the past 25 years, there has been strong and growing emphasis on practical professional knowledge. The policy discourse, which emphasises 'the practical turn', has been particularly strident in England and Wales but is less emphasised in Scotland and Northern Ireland (Menter and Hulme, 2008). For example, in Scotland courses of initial teacher education typically involve students spending less time in schools than is required in England and Wales. As a result, the universities' contribution remains stronger both at undergraduate and postgraduate levels. As a Scottish PGDE programme leader explained, 'We are allowed to design the course as we want to ... We are aware of the political situation, but we are not led by it.'

Scottish universities have also traditionally had a stronger role than their English counterparts in the development of national schemes for professional master's degrees. In Scotland the Chartered Teacher Scheme (though currently under treat) has lead to a master's degree, is strongly school-based but includes substantial contributions from the university as well. In England the parallel Master's in Teaching and Learning (MTL) demonstrates much greater emphasis on practical work in schools, with a consequent reduction of university-based work (Furlong, 2011a).

In protecting a role for more academic conceptions of professional education, the role of the General Teaching Council for Scotland has been key; the GTCS, on which universities themselves are strongly represented, validates and inspects all professional courses for teachers. By contrast, as we will see in Chapter 8, in England regulation and inspection have come through the TDA and Ofsted, government agencies that are themselves both closely politically managed. As a result, both agencies have driven a strong emphasis on practical knowledge. And with employment-based routes now accounting for some 20 per cent of initial teacher education provision in England, it is clear that government no longer sees university-based knowledge as essential within professional education. For many new teachers entering the profession in England, their professional preparation is now entirely practical.

So, the degree of emphasis on practical knowledge varies between different jurisdictions across the UK, but what of liberal education? To what extent do these ideas of 'the education of the man' still influence thinking within the discipline? For the most part, such ideas were no longer significant in the institutions I visited. The dominant discourse implied that whether understood practically or theoretically, teaching and research in education are primarily vocationally oriented; education is primarily an applied discipline. Interestingly, however, in Scotland the importance of liberal education in the education of prospective teachers has recently been reasserted by the Donaldson Report (2011), an official enquiry into the future of teacher education in Scotland. Using an argument that both Newman and Robbins would have applauded, Donaldson argues strongly for the importance, at undergraduate level, of a more broadly based approach to professional education. He argues that one of the weaknesses of the BEd degree is that its narrow professional focus can lead to an overemphasis on technical and craft skills at the expense of broader and more academically challenging areas of study. He goes on: 'One of the major, but as yet not fully realised, benefits of placing initial teacher education within universities was that students on teaching programmes should benefit from belonging to the wider community of academic inquiry across the university' (2011: 40).

Donaldson therefore recommends that, in line with emerging developments across Scotland's universities, the traditional BEd degree should be phased out and replaced with degrees that combine in-depth academic study in areas beyond education, with professional studies and development. He specifically recommends that these new degrees should involve staff and departments beyond those in departments or faculties of education.

Unsurprisingly, such views are deeply contested by some education academics in Scotland; nevertheless, it seems likely that in the not-too-distant future, what education means in Scottish universities will be further differentiated from what it means elsewhere in the UK.

And, finally, what of the moral? To what extent is there evidence of universities still functioning as moral communities, communities where strong personal relationships between teachers and taught help induct students into accepted moral values?

One new university visited retained the strong religious ethos that was part of its original foundation; this affected all aspects of day-to-day life.

> There is no expectation that students are Christian; it is all faiths and none. (But) the Christian background to the university is important because it sets

> the tone ... it embraces a welcome sense of community. I have taught in places where you teach hundreds of people and you only know a few of them. Here I know the students I teach personally and that relates to the quality of the teaching.

The same moral ethos was profoundly important in shaping the nature of the courses offered. As the dean explained, the courses they offered were not market-driven nor were they driven merely by the expertise and interests of their staff; rather they were driven by a sense of public commitment to their local educational community and what that community told the university it needed.

> It makes sense ethically, practically and professionally to say we have an expertise in schools' work and that are there are other areas of schools' work that schools want us to develop.

In this institution its moral mission was highly visible, built into its history, exemplified by its architecture and close proximity to the local cathedral. But, interestingly, the influence of the moral was recognisable in many other institutions as well, if in more muted ways. It was perhaps strongest amongst those academic staff teaching on initial teacher education programmes in new universities. As one senior colleague who had recently moved institutions argued, his new institution was different from his old one in this regard.

> Not in terms of philosophy, but in terms of the intensity of the process, it is quite labour-intensive here; they have hung on to a greater level of care ... People are more willing to do teaching hours than they should do. It's all to do with people's professional identities. They may be seeing themselves as teachers rather than as lecturers, pressuring themselves to take on more teaching hours and pastoral work than is strictly necessary.

A senior colleague in another university put it in more personal terms.

> I am a teaching practitioner and trained as a teacher way back. I taught for fifteen years in a range of schools and that is my passion and that is what drives me on. I have been deputy head of school and assistant dean, but I suppose that what drives me on is that passion and enthusiasm. I still teach and support students as a professional, working in schools, leading on partnerships with schools. I know how it is done. I am there in schools.

## Conclusions

In conclusion, it is important to recognise that the differences between institutions are both complex and subtle. At first sight, one might suggest that all university departments and faculties of education are pretty similar. They all teach the same sorts of courses. They all contain at least some individuals who teach and undertake research that demonstrates a commitment to disciplinary-based knowledge. At the same time, all institutions have individuals who maintain a strong commitment to practical knowledge, to the development of moral communities, to the pursuit of liberal education. Most will also have individuals who work across a wide range of different topics, from primary education to lifelong learning. Some colleagues' teaching and research will be tightly focused on teaching and learning processes; others' work will be more tangentially linked.

Faculties and departments of education do, therefore, demonstrate many things in common. But a more careful look quickly reveals real differences between them. As we have already noted, there are powerfully different policy contexts across the UK that significantly shape what education is. These are especially important in recognising differences between Scotland and England, but there are differences between the other jurisdictions as well. There are also different institutional histories and hierarchies: the secondary focus of the Russell Group universities; the strong emphasis on a disciplinary-based knowledge within most of the older universities; the greater emphasis on primary education and professional knowledge amongst the newer universities; the strong emphasis on moral in the newer universities. All of these differences are there if one looks. One only has to visit these different institutions for a short while to start to recognise them, to feel the differences.

But why does this diversity continue to exist 20 years after the majority of the system moved into the university sector? There are many reasons. Chapters 7, 8 and 9, Section III of this book, will explore some of the multiple causations that have helped to shape the discipline of education in contemporary universities. Particularly important, it will be argued, is the changing nature of the university in the modern world. The overwhelming emphasis on the marketisation of our universities has led them to become far more responsive to external pressures than in the past. They have become particularly sensitive to national policies on teacher education and on research; policies that often pull departments in different directions. Universities themselves have also become much more concerned than in the past with positioning themselves within the different markets in which they operate, differentiating themselves from other institutions that are seen as their competitors, nationally, regionally, globally and in terms of their student intake.

All three of these different 'drivers', sometimes working in complementary ways and sometimes in tension, have helped to make education as a discipline what it is today. These are drivers that continue to reproduce difference and hierarchy despite the fact that 'we are all universities now'.

But before we go on to that analysis, we need to examine two more dimensions of our current practice: our teaching and our research. They are the focus of the next two chapters.

# 5 Teaching education today

## Introduction

Trying to provide an overview of the teaching offered by UK university departments and faculties of education today is, to put it mildly, something of a challenge. This is because, at the present time, so much is in flux; nothing will stand still. The largest and most obvious challenge is the economic recession. As we will examine in more detail in Chapter 7, the massive expansion of higher education over the past 30 years has been predicted on an assumption that investment in higher education – for individuals, for their families and for society at large – will be economically beneficial. But as economic growth itself falters – and on an unprecedented scale – so, too, may that assumption; indeed, the UK government has already questioned its own historical commitment to the funding of higher education. In its response to the Browne Report (2010) on higher education funding and student finance, the UK government (BIS, 2011) accepted the broad thrust of Browne's argument that the state should no longer fund universities directly for providing teaching, except in exceptional circumstances. Instead, the cost for most university courses in England, including those in education, should be moved to students themselves, with a consequent substantial rise in fees (up to £9,000 a year for undergraduate courses in many universities). Although currently limited to universities in England, the funding changes also have major implications for devolved governments as well in that their national budgets are being reduced to reflect these changed assumptions. At the time of writing, the implications of these dramatic changes have yet to work their way through the system.

But these challenges are not the only uncertainties facing the field of education; there are other more local changes in stream, changes that will affect future provision of initial teacher education in particular. These issues are discussed more fully in Chapter 8, but it is important to introduce them now.

Reference has already been made in the last chapter to the Donaldson Report on the future of teacher education in Scotland (Donaldson, 2011) and, in particular, its recommendation that the structure of the undergraduate route into teaching is fundamentally reformed to include substantial study undertaken in faculties other than education; if this takes place, it will have major implications

; of departments and faculties of education in Scotland as well as for the the undergraduate courses they offer. In Wales and Northern Ireland, tainties are of a different kind; they are at the institutional level. In lowing the Furlong Report of 2006 (Furlong *et al.*, 2006), provision of initial teacher education has slowly been rationalised into three collaborative national centres rather than in eight independent universities. But now the universities themselves are being restructured; at the time of writing, the future shape of much of the higher education sector in Wales remains unclear. In Northern Ireland a recent ministerial statement to the Northern Ireland Assembly stated that 'the current system of teacher training is neither affordable nor sustainable' (Farry, 2011). Despite this, long-standing plans to amalgamate Stranmillis University College with the School of Education at Queens University are currently on hold, mired yet again by sectarian divisions.

But the highest degree of uncertainty is in England. In the 2010 White Paper (DfE, 2010) *The Importance of Teaching* and the subsequent discussion paper (DfE, 2011a) and implementation plan (DfE, 2011b), the government outlined a future direction of travel for teacher education policy that is profoundly radical. The government's aspiration is that the role of schools as autonomous providers of initial training should, over time, be substantially strengthened. Under the School Direct model, more and more schools will simply purchase what they need from local universities or other providers implying a progressive reduction of university-led provision. And parallel changes are also in the pipeline in relation to training for further education lecturers. In the future it is proposed that FE colleges themselves be allowed to accredit courses. As a result, university-based provision is facing a major fight for survival.

There are, therefore, major policy changes in play across all four countries of the UK. And in addition, these challenges are being played out in the face of further uncertainties brought about by demographic change. In the past five years, all four countries have seen substantial cuts in provision in response to falling demand for teachers. In Scotland reductions were particularly dramatic between 2009–2010 and 2010–2011, with new primary numbers being slashed by 57 per cent (Scottish Funding Council, 2010), though all four countries also predict increased demand in the medium term.

Given all of these uncertainties in the economy, in higher education and in teacher education itself, it is hard to write with confidence about the shape of teaching provision in the discipline of education. Within five years, the ground map may look very, very different. All that can be done is to describe the system as it is today, with the health warning that certain parts of it may change quite rapidly and perhaps quite profoundly.

In characterising current provision, this chapter focuses on only the common courses that are offered. As any cursory review of institutional websites will reveal, most departments and faculties of education also offer a range of other specialist courses as well – youth work, counselling, educational psychologist training, etc. – but given the limitations of space and, indeed, the diversity of these other courses, they are not discussed here. In characterising the most common courses, the chapter draws on a range of different sources of evidence, combining data from national data sets (HESA, TDA, HEFCE, etc.) with evidence from the ten case study institutions introduced in the last chapter. This includes evidence drawn from the fieldwork interviews (conducted in 2010–2011) and from each institution's websites, most of which refer to courses available in 2012–2013.

However, before describing current provision, it is necessary to look again at the different forms of knowledge involved in educational programmes. Firstly, we need to consider the broad discourses about knowledge that were introduced in Chapter 1, then we need to consider how these different forms of educational knowledge (different conceptions of theoretical or propositional knowledge, different conceptions of practical knowledge) are brought together in particular programmes. In an applied field like education, it is the ways in which different forms of knowledge are brought into relationship with each other that define the character of the programmes that are offered.

## Knowledge and the discipline of education

In Chapter 1, four broad discourses about what it means to be knowledgeable in education were identified. They were: personal liberal education, encapsulated in Arnold's dictum about the importance of making available to learners 'the best that has been thought and said' (Arnold, 1869); propositional knowledge developed through the application of scientific and other disciplinary-based procedures to educational phenomena; practical knowledge (knowing how as opposed to knowing that); and moral knowledge, developing the knowledge and, indeed, the disposition, to behave in the right way.

If these are fundamental building blocks of knowledge in the discipline of education, how are they instantiated in particular teaching programmes today? As we will see, some programmes continue to emphasise the importance of liberal education. Debates around the role of personal education as part of the professional education of teachers are still with us 160 years after Newman's interventions (Newman, 1853a, 1853b). So, too, are concerns with the moral. Although the amalgamation of teacher education colleges from the 1960s onwards into higher education marked the end, at least in Britain, of the 'normal' college tradition, with its strong moral commitments, it still has echoes in the day-to-day practices of many of today's departments and faculties of education.

But the more complex and, indeed, important issue to disentangle are the different ways in which the practical is understood. Education, notwithstanding arguments put forward by Whitty (2006), is, in large part, an *applied* field. Its aim is to engage with the world of policy and practice – sometimes directly, sometimes indirectly. And it is this aspiration that underpins the vast majority of teaching programmes that are offered in departments and faculties of education today. But, clearly, there are many different ways of being applied. When they are addressing issues of policy and practice, some programmes do so by emphasising propositional knowledge. They may do this in a variety of ways, for example, by drawing on the disciplines of education – sociology, philosophy, etc. – or by looking at findings from professionally based research or some combination of both of these approaches. Other programmes emphasise practical knowledge, but what practical knowledge is also varies substantially (Furlong *et al.*, 1988). In some courses it involves the development of understanding, judgement and skills through direct experience in a particular context such as school classrooms. Alternatively, those understandings, judgements and skills might be addressed indirectly through talks, books, videos, role play about practice that take place in the university. Although concerned with practice, work at this level is therefore divorced from at least some of the complexities of application in a particular context. At a further level of abstraction, the practical can also be addressed in terms of its underlying principles. Some of those principles may be well founded (justified through research or other systematic procedures); others may not.

Courses in education can therefore draw on a wide range of different types of knowledge. But university programmes in an applied field like education are seldom pure; they normally involve particular combinations of different sorts of knowledge. In characterising the nature of teaching in education, we therefore need to disentangle the ways in which different forms of knowledge are brought in relation to one another in particular programmes. We can also examine who is responsible for the selection and pacing of knowledge, the learner or the teacher. (To the sociological reader, it will be apparent that these are the questions that are asked by Bernstein (1971) in his classical formulation of the classification and framing of educational knowledge.)

## Initial teacher education

Initial teacher education (at least for the present) remains the dominant part of teaching in most departments and faculties of education in UK universities. HESA data suggest that in 2009–2010, 66 per cent of all full-time students in education were enrolled in courses of initial teacher education (HESA, 2011). However, the institutional significance of initial teacher education varies university by university. For example, a senior colleague at the London Institute of Education estimated that initial teacher education represented only about 12 per cent of their overall activity; research, consultancy and higher-degree teaching made up the remainder of their work, and indeed, their budget. In some of the other institutions visited, research and higher-degree work were relatively small in scale, making initial teacher education their largest activity by far.

University-based initial teacher education in the UK has two distinct routes. Firstly, there is an undergraduate route with three- and four-year degrees (BEd, BA/BSc Education) leading to qualified teacher status (QTS). Some of these degrees are single honours; others are combined with other subjects. The second and, today, much larger route, is the one-year postgraduate programme (PGDE in Scotland, PGCE elsewhere).

Up until the 1960s, the two-year, then three-year Certificate of Education offered by colleges of education for prospective primary and secondary teachers was the main route into teaching. Numbers on the secondary PGCE, offered only by the older universities, were relatively small. For example, in England and Wales in 1960, there were almost four times as many students studying the Certificate compared with the PGCE (Alexander, 1984). In the early 1970s, when the recommendations of the Robbins Report (Robbins, 1963) began to take effect, a fourth year was added to the certificate course and it became the BEd degree. Available throughout the UK, the BEd remained the main route into teaching for a further decade. However, by 1980 (under the influence of another report – the James Report [James, 1972]), the position had changed dramatically: a primary postgraduate route into teaching had been added and there were now more students entering teaching by the postgraduate route than by the undergraduate route. Since 1980, in England and Wales, numbers on the undergraduate route have progressively dwindled and it has become almost exclusively focused on primary teaching. In 2009–2010 there were about 6,500 prospective teachers enrolled in undergraduate primary courses in England compared with just over 8,000 enrolled in PGCE programmes. At secondary level there were only around 800 undergraduate enrolments compared with 14,000 secondary PGCE enrolments (Smithers and Robinson, 2011). Similar reductions have been experienced in Wales, though in Scotland and Northern Ireland, despite reductions in overall numbers to respond to demographic change, the comparative position of the undergraduate route has remained stronger.

But what do these programmes actually look like today? In fact, there is considerable variation across the four countries of the UK. In characterising the differences between courses, it is important to recognise that all initial teacher education courses, nationally and internationally, face a number of key dilemmas; dilemmas that take us back to the different discourses about educational knowledge referred to above. One of the most abiding dilemmas is how much of the programme should be devoted to personal as opposed to professional education. But there are major dilemmas in relation to professional education as well. A vocational course such as a PGCE or BA/BSc in education must, by definition, be professionally oriented. But how should that professional dimension be addressed? How much time should be devoted to examining professional issues theoretically by drawing on theory and research and how much devoted to learning through direct practical experience? And, finally, how should the different elements of programmes be integrated? Should there be a close integration between the world of the university and practical work in school or should there be strong demarcation?

In England and Wales debate about some of these complex concerns in undergraduate degrees has been sidelined in recent years by the significant shift towards the PGCE. Today, for over three-quarters of new entrants, their personal education is taken for granted by the state; it is assumed to have happened during their first degree. As a result, government policy has come to see initial teacher education as overwhelmingly concerned with the professional rather than the personal. And as we noted in Chapter 2, from the 1990s onwards, what professional education came to mean in England and Wales was almost entirely constructed in terms of the practical. Teacher education in England and, to a lesser extent, in Wales, has therefore become initial teacher *training*, not initial teacher *education*.

This training model is expressed in the government regulations known as professional standards that are used to frame and assess these sorts of courses in England and Wales (DfE, 2011c; Welsh Government, 2011). In both countries the professional standards focus exclusively on what newly qualified teachers should be able *to do* once they have completed their training. For example, the current English standards state a teacher must:

> Set high expectations which inspire, motivate and challenge pupils …
> Demonstrate good subject and curriculum knowledge …
> Plan and teach well-structured lessons …
>
> (DfE, 2011c: 5).

The English document contains virtually no reference at all to knowledge and understanding; as a result, there is little space in these regulations for a distinctive contribution from universities. By contrast, the Welsh standards do require new teachers to know and understand certain things, but these are virtually all concerned with knowledge and understanding of current Welsh government regulations such as the National Curriculum, the Foundation Phase, etc.

In Northern Ireland, regulations which are issued by the General Teaching Council rather than by the government itself, are characterised as competences rather than standards. However, in addition to a similar list of things those newly qualified teachers must be able to *do*, in Northern Ireland there is also a substantial emphasis on knowing and understanding. For example:

> Teachers will have developed a knowledge and understanding of contemporary debates about the nature and purposes of education and the social and policy contexts in which the aims of education are defined and implemented.
>
> Teachers will have developed a knowledge and understanding of the factors that promote and hinder effective learning and be aware of the need to provide for the holistic development of the child.
>
> (GTCNI, 2007: 13)

Important opportunities here for the contribution of universities to professional learning. A similar model is adopted for all students across the UK studying for a PGCE in postcompulsory education and training (Sector Skills Council for Life Long Learning, 2007); their courses, too, combine strong practical training with a strong programme of knowledge and understanding.

But the most significant difference is in Scotland. Here, standards – again defined by a General Teaching Council rather than government – not only mean standards for trainees, but there are also standards for courses of initial teacher education and these explicitly include reference to the contribution of universities. For example:

> Programmes of initial teacher education will be expected to: draw on a wide range of intellectual resources, theoretical perspectives and academic disciplines to illuminate understanding of education and the contexts within which it takes place … encourage student teachers to engage with fundamental questions concerning the aims and values of education and its relationship to society; provide opportunities for student teachers to engage with and draw on educational theory, research, policy and practice; encourage professional reflection on educational processes in a wide variety of contexts; develop in student teachers the ability to construct and sustain a reasoned argument about educational issues in a clear, lucid and coherent manner; and promote a range of qualities in student teachers, including intellectual independence and critical engagement with evidence.
>
> (General Teaching Council for Scotland, 2006: 4)

These different national regulations therefore have very considerable implications for the courses that universities are now able to offer. For example, the PGCE in England and Wales is now dominated by its practical and professional focus. Secondary students are required to spend 24 of their 36 weeks in school; primary trainees spent half of their time in school – 18 out of 36 weeks. And with so many standards to be covered, university-based work inevitably becomes narrowly professionally focused; there is a strong emphasis towards what Bernstein (1971) would have called an integrated code with all parts of the programme designed to support one end: students' practical work in classrooms.

But despite this heavy prescription, even in England, university-based elements do often include work on knowledge and understanding that goes well beyond government-defined standards and competencies. For example, one PGCE course leader from an English university described how in her course:

> Well, we had a day on assessment for learning and we looked at a range of theories of learning and how they did or did not fit in with that. When we do work on literacy, led by (X), he gives them twenty readings on different theories of literacy … and they read them because they do a project on literacy, looking at one pupil and they have to do the reading and develop a plan of how to respond. I do something similar on grammar.

Another PGCE course leader put it this way:

> The standards and Ofsted criteria obviously drive the way we assess; they have to but if you were to look at the secondary course, you would see different subjects have quite different philosophies underpinning their approach. English have a very particular philosophy, very particular, which is quite different to geography and history and so on.

Similar points about how, in reality, university teaching went well beyond what is formally required were made by most other PGCE course leaders interviewed in

England and Wales. By contrast, in Scotland and Northern Ireland, access to research-based professional knowledge is a requirement.

Broad policy differences within the four countries have also had major implications for the undergraduate degree. To begin with, they affect the length of courses. In England and Wales undergraduate courses can be either three or four years long. All of the courses in Wales are now three years of duration, while in England both exist, though there is a strong trend towards a shorter degree. In Scotland and Northern Ireland, the BEd or BA/BSc(Ed) in Education remains four years.

Despite the fact that they are first degrees, undergraduate three-year degrees in England and Wales have been swept up in government policy assumptions about training; the result has been the development of a strongly, some would say narrowly, professionally oriented degree with a strong emphasis on practical rather than theoretical forms of knowledge. For 66 per cent of the course, students are based in university rather than in school; the emphasis in these sorts of degrees is almost entirely professional. There is little room either for liberal, personal education or for theoretically based professional education at any depth. The dilemma for course leaders is how to do this at degree level. As this course leader explained:

> We are somewhat schizophrenic. We are standards-driven in that they have to cover classroom behaviour and being prepared for their first job, but at the same time, we want to make sure that they are working at degree level. We want them to develop the ability to stand back from government initiatives and critique them and see them against their own philosophy, making their own decisions in practice. We do not do that for Ofsted; they are not about that. We do it to make sure this is at degree level. If we can't do that, we are in trouble.

Of course, in England, four-year programmes do still exist and where they do, there is more opportunity for personal development and theoretical work. However, with the prospect of a significant rise in fees, there is strong market pressure towards the three-year model. Indeed, one case study institution was moving in this direction at the time of the fieldwork. In this particular course, the current fourth year, which was seen as qualitatively different from the other years, was devoted to advanced work in a subject specialism. The course leader was acutely aware of what was now in danger of being lost.

> What is driving the change from four to three years? It's driven by fees from the government; that has been the death knell. But we want to hang on to our specialisms. We are in the process of validating a three-year degree, but we are hanging on to our specialisms. We are a little island in the move towards generalism. Our BEd students are highly sought after because of their specialisms ... with four years, you can have subject teams, so I have a team of English people who are passionate about English. On a three-year

> course you can't afford them; gradually, staff become generalists working hard on a three-year model that will train emergent spe( hope that they will stay on and complete their master's in the. subject.

In sharp contrast, in both Scotland and Northern Ireland, the importance of the fourth year and, indeed, of a strong personal and theoretical dimension within such degrees has been consistently defended. In the Scottish case study institution, only 25 per cent of the four-year course was spent in school, giving significantly more time for university-based studies. The course also claimed 'on-campus delivery of the theoretical perspectives of teaching and learning throughout the four years of the course'. In addition, in their first year, students take an elective from anywhere in the university.

BEd degrees in Northern Ireland adopt a similar approach. For example, the website for one BEd degree describes the aim of education studies as assisting teachers in reaching a high level of professional understanding. 'Education studies consists of the study of the processes of schooling and the social context within which these take place. It employs the theoretical perspectives provided by the foundation disciplines in education, philosophy, psychology, sociology, history and comparative studies ...'. In England and Wales any references to 'the foundation disciplines' have long since disappeared from course outlines.

## *Managing initial teacher education*

Despite initiatives in England in recent years to move more and more initial teacher education into schools, initial teacher education is for the present at least, the core of the economy of most university departments and faculties of education. Without it, the system as a whole would be very much smaller.

But this involvement with initial teacher education is not without cost. From the point of view of departments and faculties themselves, offering courses in initial teacher education means working within parameters set by government or other professional bodies. It also means being subject to regular scrutiny by the different education and training inspectorates in each country. In England in particular, Ofsted inspections are extremely challenging and the consequences of not achieving a high grade are significant. As the head of professional programmes in one university put it:

> And I have to say the Ofsted 'Outstanding' label is phenomenally important to us. We were really disappointed with the primary; we were outstanding in everything else. It is very important.

Universities are perfectly used to working with external bodies in the validation of the professional courses they offer (in health, engineering, law, youth work, etc.). But in England and Wales in particular, where the regulations do not formally recognise the distinctive contribution that universities can make and where external scrutiny by inspectors can be invasive and at times confrontational, the price of offering initial teacher education is high. This is not to say that universities do not make a distinctive and principled contribution to the courses that they offer; they do. Nor is it to say that informally, government bodies such as Ofsted and the TDA don't value the distinctive contribution universities make to professional education; they do. But it is to recognise that the formal policy context in which initial teacher education operates in England and Wales in particular is a challenging one.

It is also important to recognise that engagement with initial teacher education is challenging from the perspective of universities themselves. While some vice chancellors may take little notice of the external control and scrutiny of teacher education programmes (unless they go seriously wrong), they do take notice of substantial shifts in provision that occur as student numbers rise and fall. We have already noted that in Scotland recently, primary numbers were cut by 57 per cent; this cut reversed substantial and rapid rises between 2003 and 2006, when primary numbers doubled. Reductions have been experienced in Wales recently, where there has been a 17 per cent cut in primary numbers and, to a lesser extent, in England. These sorts of fluctuations, over which individual universities have no control, make institutional planning extremely difficult. No wonder that some vice chancellors are, from time to time, sceptical about their continued involvement with education.

Within the ten case study institutions, it would appear that there have been two responses to these challenges; both involve diversification as part of the management of risk. In universities, particularly new universities, where education faculties can represent a significant proportion of university activity, there have been moves to reduce this dependence. As a respondent in one such university explained:

> there are consequences of the recent cuts in how the university looks at us. You have less staff and less students. They will be looking at us and saying, 'Education is forty per cent of our work and that is a problem'.

And a head of department said:

> Education was the largest part (of the university) and the dean was very powerful and the footprint of education was significantly larger than the rest. So, the restructuring we had last year was in part to change the balance; the aim was to hold education constant and to grow the other parts of the institution. They are not trying to shrink education but to grow the other areas.

The other response to these challenges has been that at departmental level. Virtually all departments and faculties of education have, in recent years, seen a substantial move towards the development of other sorts of courses, at both undergraduate and postgraduate levels.

As one Dean explained:

> I have been aware for a long time of the dangers of having all your eggs in one basket – the TDA-funded provision – the risks to that over the years are known to us all, so I would want a school of education that had different funding streams. We need diversification. From a financial point of view, I would like to see a third of our income being initial teacher education, a third being other teaching and a third from other things – research, international teaching.

## Other undergraduate provision

One recent example of this diversification has been the development of Foundation Degrees; as we saw in the last chapter, seven of the case study institutions offered such degrees. Sometimes these new degrees are offered in collaboration with other types of institution. For example, one of the case study institutions offered its Foundation Degrees at its home base and in partnership with 18 further education colleges across its region.

First launched in 2001–2002, Foundation Degrees are focused on access; their aim is to offer a route into higher education for people of all ages and backgrounds. Normally of two years in duration (longer for part-time study), they are designed to equip students for a particular area of work; they are also intended to provide pathways for successful candidates to progress to other qualifications. Many of the Foundation Degrees offered in education are specifically designed to provide qualifications for those already in the wider educational workforce, such as classroom assistants. For example, one case study institution described its Foundation Degree as 'A work-based degree for the children's workforce'. This particular degree was aimed at staff working in children's centres, social services, health care and the third sector (charity, voluntary and nonprofit organizations), as well as for childminders, foster carers and parent support workers. In another university there were a series of specialist routes for staff working in learning support, early years and youth and community work.

Another significant development, particularly in England and Wales, has been the growth in new undergraduate degrees that are primarily academic rather than vocational. Undergraduate degrees in educational studies or early childhood studies, most of which do not lead to a professional qualification, have flourished in recent years. These sorts of degrees not only have the advantage of sidestepping the intensive government prescription and scrutiny involved in initial teacher education, but they are also much more secure in terms of student numbers. For example, one case study institution, where undergraduate initial teacher education numbers have been reduced, had withdrawn entirely from those programmes. Instead, the same staff was now involved in offering a degree in educational studies. Most other institutions offered such courses in parallel with their conventional teacher education degrees, giving their staff the opportunity to work on a different type of programme, one under their own control.

What is interesting about these new degrees is how dramatically different the curricula are compared with initial teacher education programmes. For example, the first aim of one childhood studies programme was to:

- provide an academic programme of study that develops a deep understanding of young children and early childhood through the integration of theoretical and practical modes of study.

It involved the development of knowledge and understanding of:

- national and international conceptions of young children and early childhood;
- major philosophies, theories, research and ethical issues underpinning the academic study of early childhood;
- the historical, cultural and legal frameworks that underpin the disciplines and practices of professionals working with young children and their understandings of quality.

An educational studies degree at a different university included modules on: education and policy; education and diversity; education, democracy and caring; education and globalisation; education and ethics.

Though broadly 'applied' in orientation, what *applied* means in these degrees is very different from what it means in most courses of initial teacher education. For the most part, the professional orientation is approached indirectly by studying propositional knowledge of different kinds.

For anyone familiar with BEd degrees in the 1980s, before the 'turn to the practical' in teacher education, these courses will seem strangely familiar. Although clearly highly relevant for prospective teachers, none of these course elements would now appear in courses of initial teacher education in England and Wales. In terms of aims, content and student numbers, today they have more in common with degrees offered in other social science faculties than with initial teacher education degrees. Deans and vice chancellors can therefore perhaps be forgiven for encouraging them, for thinking that these sorts of degrees are more familiar and more straightforward for universities to manage than programmes of initial teacher education.

## Postgraduate provision

The other dimension of teaching – and one that has again seen substantial development in recent years – is postgraduate work, master's and doctoral degrees of different sorts. In 2009–2010 UK departments and faculties of education awarded 725 doctorates – roughly the same number as business and administration (a much larger discipline) – and 5,695 other higher degrees, including master's degrees of different sorts. Overall, it awarded twice as many higher degrees as economics and twice as many as sociology and social policy combined. There is also evidence (HEFCE, 2009) that all of these numbers have risen substantially since the late 1990s.

Although the qualifications offered at postgraduate level are fairly standard – MEd, MA, MSc, EdD, PhD – there is a range of very different types of provision on offer, particularly at master's level. Just as in undergraduate provision, the majority of these courses are broadly applied in orientation; programmes of study attempt to relate propositional knowledge, of many different sorts, to issues arising from educational policy and practice. But how they try to do that varies substantially. At times those links are close and direct; very often they are indirect.

### *Master's degrees*

Master's degrees in education can be characterised as falling into three major types, each demonstrating a different interpretation of the word *applied*. At one extreme are those masters' courses that are academically led, such as disciplinary-based courses in the sociology of education, the economics of education, the philosophy of education. Although popular in the 1980s and 1990s, today such courses are only available in any number at the London Institute of Education. It currently offers nearly 60 specialist master's degrees, some of which are disciplinarily-based. One example might be the MA in the philosophy of education. As the course website states, the course aims to give:

> comprehensive grounding in philosophy of education; to explore the relevance to education today of ethics, political philosophy, philosophy of mind and epistemology to enable students to think philosophically about their own educational concerns and to help students argue a case and to evaluate the arguments of others on controversial issues.

Core modules include: Philosophy of Education: Values, Aims and Society; Theory and Policy in Education: An Introduction; and Understanding Education Research.

Although applied in the very broadest sense, it is clear that in these sorts of courses, the world of policy and practice is to be understood *through* the lens of the discipline itself. There is a strong demarcation between ways of interpreting educational phenomena within the discipline and those used by practitioners in the everyday world of practice. There are established bodies of knowledge into which students are inducted so that whatever the teaching method adopted, the underlying theory of learning is didactic. There are bodies of knowledge, principles, procedures and dispositions that students are expected to learn or otherwise acquire.

Although the disciplinary-based master's degrees are probably the most 'pure' versions of this type of course currently available in the UK, there are many others that have some features of this approach. Another course at the IOE is the MA in the sociology of childhood and children's rights. This course draws on a more diverse body of theory and research, but it is still very much academically led. Its core modules are: Children's Rights in Practice; Researching Childhood; and Theories of Childhood and Children's Rights. Candidates are expected to draw on this diverse body of knowledge in order to 'develop their theoretical and analytical skills in learning to critique current professional practice with children' (IOE Website). Other case study institutions visited offered similar academically led programmes.

In their approach to knowledge, these sorts of courses are therefore very similar to master's courses offered in many other disciplines that are professionally oriented – social policy, management and administration, etc. Although broadly applied in orientation, their relationship with the world of practice is indirect; they are primarily academically led. In this sense they are very different from a growing number of courses offered by departments and faculties of education where students themselves have much more say in the selection and pacing of knowledge and where there is a much closer integration of different sorts of propositional knowledge derived from theory and research, with practice. This is the world of 'action research' (Stenhouse, 1970, 1981; Carr and Kemmis, 1986) or 'practitioner enquiry' (Cochran-Smith and Lytle, 2009; Campbell and Groundwater-Smith, 2007, 2010; Groundwater-Smith and Mockler, 2008), a movement that had its origins in the UK and is now an established approach to research and development across the developed world.

Several of the case study institutions offered courses based on these principles. One, for example, offered an MA entitled 'Practitioner Research: Improving Professional Practice'. As the website explained:

> Study on this course allows you the opportunity to research aspects of your professional practice and to gain accreditation at Masters Level. Through close scrutiny of your work, practitioner research is a powerful form of continuing professional development, which develops knowledge about and insights into practice.'

Over the past few years, Scottish institutions have been involved developing a similar approach with the Chartered Teacher Scheme, a school-based master's programme for experienced teachers (Christie, 2006). In England, a national Masters in Teaching and Learning based on these principles was launched in 2009 by the outgoing Labour government, though it was subsequently withdrawn by the current government (Burton and Goodman, 2011; Furlong, 2011a). Though there are important differences between these schemes, what they have in common is a distinctive approach to knowledge. Different knowledge contents (propositional knowledge, practical knowledge) are intentionally interrelated with one another. And, crucially, it is the individual student who is responsible for the selection of the knowledge made available by the university and it is the student who is required to use this knowledge to investigate their practice, to design interventions and to evaluate outcomes. Unlike more traditional master's programmes, these courses are therefore not academically led. Propositional knowledge of many different sorts is certainly a key ingredient, but it is the practitioners themselves who define the questions to be addressed; it is practitioners themselves who judge the relevance of different sorts of knowledge for their own professional concerns.

Though based on very different epistemological assumptions, academically led and practitioner-led master's courses are frequently offered within the same department or faculty of education. They are seen as having different purposes for different audiences. However, more common than either of these two sorts of degrees are those based on a different set of principles, where the students are given some control over the selection, pacing and organisation of knowledge (through choice of particular modules), but they do so within traditionally defined and separated subject areas. Here is the traditional MEd degree offered by virtually all departments and faculties of education; it is the largest form of master's provision currently available.

In the MEd degree large numbers of academically led modules are typically made available; in most cases but not all, the modules available are designed to reflect the interests and expertise of the academic staff. It is then up to the students themselves to select those modules that are most appropriate to their particular professional interest; sometimes there are suggested pathways to be followed and sometimes there are not.

As the website for one of the case study institutions explained:

> The MEd/Postgraduate Diploma programme offers a flexible course of study open to both full-time and part-time students. Students may pace their study as best suits them ... The MEd is organised into a number of programmes (made up of core and optional modules) and you will normally register with one of these ... The programme system offers students both choice and coherence and is suitable for most people. Students whose interests do not fit into these programmes may be able to register for an Individually Constructed Programme.

These are then academically led courses. However, where such courses differ from more traditional master's degrees is that in the element of choice in terms of modules available, the student has some degree of control over the programme. In most cases this is done at an individual level, with the student selecting modules that seem relevant to his or her professional world. In other cases, however, those choices are made at an institutional level. For example, some case study universities visited had entered into strategic relationships with their local authorities or with particular schools; it was then up to those authorities to decide which of the available modules were most appropriate for the professional needs of their particular staff.

## *Doctoral degrees*

The final type of teaching to consider is doctoral work. We have already noted that UK departments and faculties of education are major providers of doctoral degrees; only psychology amongst the social sciences provides more. But there are two different types of education doctorates currently available in British universities: the PhD and the EdD. The first PhDs in education were awarded in the USA at the end of the nineteenth century. The first EdD degree was also introduced in the United States at Harvard University in 1920, but it was not until 70 years later that the first EdD was awarded in the UK at the University of Bristol in 1992. After that, numbers of EdD programmes spread rapidly, with 29 new programmes being started in the next six years. Of the sample of ten case study institutions, all offered PhDs and eight now offer EdDs, though, as we saw in the last chapter, the numbers on those programmes vary substantially.

Both degrees have much in common. According to the Quality Assurance Agency (QAA), they are both concerned with 'the creation and interpretation of new knowledge, through original research or other advanced scholarship, of a quality to satisfy peer review, extend the forefront of the discipline and merit publication'; and they are both intended to provide students with 'a detailed understanding of applicable techniques for research and advanced academic enquiry' (QAA, 2008: 4). But these fundamental aims are addressed in somewhat different ways, with the EdD being more professionally oriented and the PhD being more research-oriented.

As one director of graduate studies put it:

> The difference is between a research and professional doctorate? For the professional doctorate, it is something that has the hallmarks of a research degree but with the specific remit to feed back into the professional world itself.

A case study institution described the target audience for their EdD in this way on their website:

> It is aimed at busy professionals who wish to undertake a substantial investigation into an area of current professional practice in education or training. It aims to provide students with a thorough grounding in theory and practice of educational research; professional competence; and transferable employment skills.

By contrast, the PhD is much more focused on developing academic researchers of the future. As well as making a substantive and original contribution to knowledge, the PhD is concerned with research training. As another director of graduate studies put it:

> I also think it's really, really important that what we're doing is enabling people to be good researchers. Not just to do a PhD, but to be good researchers; even if they're not gonna be going on into academia, still, it's very, very important and useful. I don't like the word skill, but you know what I mean... So, I feel very strongly that they do need that grounding.

The professional focus of the EdD is reflected in the structure of the course: typically a substantially taught programme, sometimes with a choice of modules, followed by a dissertation of between 40,000 and 60,000 words. It is also reflected in the nature of the assignments students undertake and in their dissertation, where they are expected to examine issues arising within their own professional practice. As in the MEd degree, students are offered access to forms of knowledge that are academically led. At the same time, they are encouraged to draw on those academic frameworks in ways that are relevant to their own professional practices. By contrast, the classic PhD can be characterised as being more academically framed. Through their dissertation, students are inducted into formal ways of engaging with theory and methodology; in this way they enter into the world of academia as novitiates.

And what about the students? Unfortunately, comparatively, little national data is available on EdD students as a separate group; we do, however, know more about PhD students (HEFCE, 2009). For example, we know that since the late 1990s, numbers of PhD students in education have grown by some 14 per cent, though numbers in many other subjects have increased much more. We also know that a very large proportion of students studying for the degree are doing so on a part-time basis – some 70 per cent; that is the largest proportion in any discipline. We know that most students in education have no financial backing and that they are considerably older than those in other subjects. And we know that education has the highest number of female full-time PhD students of any discipline and is amongst the largest proportion of nonwhite students (HEFCE, 2009).

The fact that doctoral students in education are older, more frequently working without financial support and are overwhelmingly studying part-time presents particular challenges. Added to that is the fact that nearly 50 per cent register for the degree with no master's degree. These students will therefore be studying education for the first time at doctoral level (HEFCE, 2009). In this regard, education is quite distinctive when compared to many other social science disciplines where most students will at least have a first degree in the subject.

Another distinctive feature – and one revealed through the fieldwork – is the very different nature of doctoral training available in different institutions. Probably half of the institutions visited freely admitted that their capacity to supervise at doctoral level was a challenge. As one dean put it:

> We have quite a lot of PhD students, but we must be at our limits now, because we have not got that many staff with PhDs who have doctorates themselves and can therefore supervise.

The sorts of support available for students in these institutions was therefore very different from that available in research-intensive universities, where there was not only supervision capacity but also well-developed institutional procedures for the support of doctoral students. The London Institute of Education, for example, has a doctoral school. Strongly influenced by the expectations of the ESRC and, behind that, the European Bologna Process (Bologna Process, 2007–2010), students are bilocated, both in their department and in the doctoral school. In the doctoral school there is a strong emphasis on broadly based research training and on interdisciplinarity.

Although perhaps not institutionalised like this, some other institutions visited also had well-developed support procedures. A director of graduate studies in another research-intensive university spoke of developments in research training and supervision. In research training they had recently initiated a strategy of joint teaching, where lecturers would engage in public debate in front of their students about different methodological procedures and principles. The institution had also recently moved to the appointment of second supervisors for all of their doctoral students.

With the privilege of large numbers of students and the supervision capacity to support them, these departments and faculties of education are now in a position to experiment with and develop the principles of high quality doctoral training. Recent moves by the ESRC to establish interdisciplinary doctoral training centres across social science disciplines and, in many cases, across institutions will intensify this process in the future. It will also intensify the difference between the minority institutions able to participate in this sort of provision and the majority that are not.

## Conclusion and evaluation

So what of the quality of the teaching programmes offered in education? How good are they? If we first look at initial teacher education in England, there is strong evidence that in terms of what is formally required by government, standards are high. Ofsted (2011) reports that most teacher education programmes inspected over the past four years have been judged to be either 'outstanding' or 'good' and there is evidence that there is substantially more 'outstanding' provision in university-led programmes (47 per cent of primary and secondary courses) compared with employment-based programmes (19 per cent). Estyn's (the Welsh inspectorate) evaluation of the quality of teacher training in Wales is slightly less glowing but still very positive. In the period 2004–2010, 75 per cent of provision was rated as grade 2 (on a 5-point scale); none was rated as grade 1, though none was lower than grade 3 (Estyn, 2011).

Inspection procedures in Scotland and Northern Ireland are somewhat different from those of England and Wales; they are less summative and less comparative. Instead, they focus on selected aspects of provision that have high policy relevance. For example, the most recent four reports from Northern Ireland Inspectorate (e.g., DENI, 2011) focus on the preparation of teachers in literacy and numeracy; overall standards on these key issues were judged to be 'very good'. In Scotland the most recent reports examine teacher education courses in relation to the Curriculum for Excellence, a new, integrated approach to curriculum provision for all 3- to 18-year-olds. The inspectorate reports 'significant progress' (HMIE, 2010).

But that is to evaluate teacher education programmes only in official terms. Many would argue that however good they are, programmes in England and

Wales, in particular, are overly technical and narrow in their scope. With nearly half of all courses in England being judged as 'outstanding' and 90 per cent at least 'good', it is clear that universities are now adept at providing the forms of training that government demands. But so, too, are growing numbers of schools running their own courses with very little university involvement. Just because Ofsted gives the universities glowing reports does not necessarily mean that they are currently allowed or encouraged to provide the best forms of initial teacher education possible.

There are particular problems, it would seem, in relation to the three-year undergraduate route into teaching. Of course, high quality personal education *can* be provided through well constructed vocationally oriented programmes. Vocationally oriented degrees of all different sorts have been the cornerstone of the expansion of higher education ever since the 1960s. At their best, vocational degrees can achieve all that is offered in terms of liberal, critical education by more traditionally academic programmes. I would disagree with Nussbaum (2010), who insists that the humanities are the preserve of liberal education. As Schwab (1978) demonstrated many years ago, well constructed science degrees can provide high quality liberal education; so, too, can vocational degrees. And it is evident that many of the courses offered in Scotland and Northern Ireland do achieve very high standards of both personal and professional education for their students; so, too, do many of the remaining four-year programmes in England.

It is perhaps not unrelated that these programmes often attract students with much higher entry qualifications than those for three-year degrees. But in England and Wales, not only are there continuing questions about entry qualifications for the three-year degree (Smithers and Robinson, 2011), but we must also face up to challenging questions about what can effectively be achieved in three years, whatever the entry requirements. Can necessary levels of personal and professional education be reached when the equivalent of one year must be spent in school and when the government prescribes, in such detail, an extensive list of practical competences that must be mastered? If Donaldson's insistence that the four-year undergraduate course in Scotland is too narrow as a preparation for new teachers has any validity, then how much more telling is it as a critique of three-year courses in England and Wales?

If we look beyond initial teacher education to graduate programmes, then, unsurprisingly, there is less objective evidence on the quality of provision. What we do know, however, is graduate teaching in the discipline faces a number of particular challenges, challenges that some courses are successful in overcoming and others less so.

Some of these challenges are programme specific. For example, as has already been noted, the lack of capacity for supervising doctoral work at many newer universities means that their numbers of students will always be limited. Small numbers combined with the fact that so many doctoral students are part-time means that the doctoral experience available to students studying in this very large group of universities will inevitably be very different from that available in research-intensive universities, where there are large numbers of doctoral students, many working full-time.

There are also challenges in relation to those master's courses based on the principles of practitioner enquiry. While the aspiration directly to harness the skills and knowledge available in universities to the development of practice is laudable, in reality, the approach does present some problems. One of the dangers of some, but certainly not all, practitioner enquiry is that it does not always build on what is known as effectively as it might; as a result, students simply reinvent the wheel. Nor in every case are the findings from this form of research made publically available; practitioners are not always required rigorously to present and justify their methods or the implications of their findings beyond their own very particular practice. As Groundwater-Smith and Mockler (2008) have argued, sometimes there is too much emphasis on the celebration of the results of practitioner enquiry rather than its careful scrutiny. Practitioner enquiry that simply celebrates might well be a useful professional development for those teachers who engage in it but, by definition, cannot count as research. As a result, it has a somewhat problematic role in the development of the discipline.

And there are more generic challenges as well. One of the biggest is that most students studying for a higher degree in education are studying it for the first time; they have no background in the subject. This places them in a very different position from students studying in most other social sciences, where an undergraduate degree is taken for granted. As one director of graduate studies put it:

> Because I come from sociology and I know that from day one of my undergraduate degree, it was theory method, theory method, theory method, then it was like that all the way through until I finished my PhD. As you know, in education you've got students coming from all sorts of disciplines that might be very, very unfamiliar with the social sciences.

This is a challenge that is met effectively, it would seem, in those master's degrees such as disciplinary-based degrees where there is a strong emphasis on inducting students into established bodies of knowledge. In the example of the MA in the philosophy of education described above, students are exposed to a range of aspects of the subject at some depth, giving them substantial opportunity to develop their expertise in what, for most, will be an entirely new area of study. At the other end of the spectrum are professionally led master's degrees, based on the principles of practitioner enquiry. Here there is no pretention of developing students as academic experts in their field. They are first and foremost practitioners; this is their area of expertise and they draw on skills and knowledge made available through the university in order to develop that expertise.

Where there may be more of a challenge is in relation to some MEd programmes. As was argued earlier, despite their professional focus, the fundamental rationale of most modules offered is academic. Nothing wrong with that. But if that is their rationale, to what extent does the programme of modules students select provide sufficient coherence, rigour and depth for study at master especially when students are studying the discipline of education for th time? Similar questions might be asked of EdD as well. How both sorts programmes address this challenge varies a great deal.

So, overall teaching in education presents a rich, diverse and very large field. It is still dominated by initial teacher education – two-thirds of its provision – but in recent years it has diversified substantially with the development of new sorts of degrees from Foundation Degrees to new doctoral degrees.

Initial teacher education still lives with many of the dilemmas it always has, dilemmas about its contribution to personal as well as professional education; dilemmas about how best to provide professional education that is both practical and critical at the same time. It also continues to suffer from excessive government intervention. Only for a very short period of time – in the 1960s and 1970s – did governments consider that mass teacher education should be left entirely to the providers themselves. In every other period from the mid-nineteenth century onwards, teacher education has been seen as too important to leave alone; that has been true of governments of every political persuasion.

As to the rest, within the discipline today, one can find examples of the sort of university courses that are as rigorous and/or as professionally relevant as any in the social sciences today. But as an applied discipline, education does face a number of specific challenges; in some cases it deals with those challenges successfully in other cases less well. But in that regard it is probably no better or worse than many other applied disciplines. Perhaps its greatest challenge is that, because of the discipline's involvement with the teaching profession, all of education's provision is subject to more public scrutiny than many other disciplines. So, too, is its research and that is the subject of the next chapter.

# 6 Educational research today

> No field of modern human endeavour, whether within or beyond the academy, can flourish without a strong research base. The enlargement of our understanding, the enhancement of the quality of public services, the nation's economic productivity, the well-being of the community, the wisdom and effectiveness of public policy all depend on the maintenance of a vigorous research culture.
>
> (BERA/UCET, 2012: para. 98)

Fine words. They were written as part of the recent review of educational research in the UK by two lead bodies in the field: the British Educational Research Association and the Universities Council for the Education of Teachers (BERA/UCET, 2012). Their sentiment is certainly clear, but is that the reality of educational research today in the UK? At the end of Chapter 3, we noted that in the closing years of the twentieth century, educational research was subject to vigorous criticism, both in the UK and internationally. It was accused of being inaccessible, irrelevant and of low quality. But where is it today, 15 years on? Is it flourishing? Has it finally got its act together in terms of accessibility, relevance and quality?

The aim of this chapter is to explore these questions. My view is that things have certainly improved substantially in the intervening years; significantly increased funding (it doubled during the last RAE period) and the cumulative impact of research assessment exercises have, I believe, driven up quality. There has also been a fundamental transformation in the seriousness with which governments have taken educational research. For example, in the early 2000s the Labour government funded a number of important initiatives to support the development of educational research in England. These included the establishment of a National Educational Research Forum (1999–2006) to advise on the strategic direction for educational research and the setting up of the EPPI-Centre to undertake and encourage systemic reviews of educational research to parallel those undertaken within medicine by the Cochrane Collaboration. They also funded a number of new research centres, such as the Centre for Research on the Wider Benefits of Learning and the Millennium Cohort Study at the London Institute of Education. At the same time, the ESRC funded the National Centre for Research Methods, the first of its kind internationally. Other government agencies in England – the TDA, General Teaching Council for England and the British Educational Communications Technology Authority, to name but three – also developed strong research profiles. And in Scotland, the Higher Education Funding Council and the then Scottish Executive Education Department jointly funded the Applied Educational Research Scheme specifically to develop research capacity (Taylor *et al.*, 2007). But perhaps most significant of all was the funding of the UK-wide Teaching and Learning Research Programme (TLRP). At £43 million, TLRP (2000–2012) was the largest ever single social-research programme funded in any discipline.

All of these initiatives have helped to increase the quality and relevance of educational research. But that is not to say that everything in the garden is rosy; it is not. As we will see, educational research capacity is not uniformly distributed between and within institutions; there remain significant numbers of education academics who, for a whole variety of reasons, are not research-active 20 years after most of the system joined the university sector. There are also some very serious challenges to be faced in the future funding of the field and there remain some thorny epistemological questions to be faced by the discipline as a whole. Despite these challenges, the underlying story is, I believe, a positive one for educational research over the past 15 years. Whether it will continue to be so remains to be seen.

## Defining the field: what is educational research today?

Perhaps the first place to begin is with definitions. In Chapters 2 and 3, we noted that during the twentieth century, what educational research was changed substantially. Initially defined as the study of what 'great men' had said about education – Plato, Aristotle, Rousseau and more – in the early years of the past century, it was progressively transformed into a branch of psychology, with a particular emphasis on assessment and the study of intelligence. After the war – and especially after the Robbins Report (Robbins, 1963) – educational research diversified into 'the disciplines' of education: sociology, psychology, history and philosophy. The latter part of the century saw further diversification; firstly, through the influence of bodies such as the Schools Council, with their focus on subject-based pedagogy and then with the explosion of social theory more generally and the postmodern turn. Also influential in recent years has been the practitioner-researcher movement premised on the argument that professionalism necessarily demands a process of reflection on action and, therefore, all are potential researchers in relation to their own practice.

And where does this leave us today? If we hold a mirror up to educational research now, what we see is something that is rich, complex and diverse ... hard to pin down. Some look in the mirror and see a discipline, some see a field and some see no coherence at all, just muddle. Defining educational research today, then, is difficult.

In 2004 Lyn Yates, the Australian educationalist, published a popular book called *What Does Good Educational Research Look Like?* (Yates, 2004). In it she emphasised how much educational research is differentiated. It is differentiated in terms of methodology, from randomised control trials (RCTs) to action research; in terms of theory, from atheoretical positivism to postmodernism; and in terms of purposes, policy research, applied and practice-based research and blue skies research. On all of these counts, she argues, there is substantial variation across the field. As a result, educational research becomes highly vulnerable to critique, to fashion and, particularly important in the UK, to government intervention. One is perhaps left wondering if, in other social science disciplines, it would be necessary, after 100 years of the development of the field, to write a book with such a title. In most disciplines things are much clearer; there is more consensus as to what good research is than there currently is in education.

More recently, this diversity has been made official by the 2014 REF panel for education. Their attempt at a definition of educational research is equally multifaceted, equally complex; even so, it is worth quoting at length because it provides such a valuable overview. The Panel says: 'Research in education is multidisciplinary and is closely related to a range of other disciplines with which it shares common interests, methods and approaches ...' It includes research:

- that addresses education systems, issues, processes, provision and outcomes in relation to *different sectors*, such as: 'early years, primary, secondary, further, higher, medical, workplace, adult and continuing education. It also includes teacher, health care and other forms of professional education, vocational training; and informal, community and lifelong learning';
- that addresses a range of *substantive areas*, such as: 'curriculum, pedagogy, assessment, language, teaching and learning; children, young people, student and adult learners; parents, families and communities; culture, economy and society; teacher training, professionalism and continuing professional development (CPD); special and inclusive education; participation, rights and equity issues; technology-enhanced learning; education policy; the organisation, governance, management, effectiveness and improvement of educational institutions; education, training, workplaces, industry and the labour market; comparative, international and development education';
- that employs a range of *theoretical frameworks and methodologies* drawn from a range of different disciplinary traditions, including but not limited to: 'anthropology, applied linguistics, economics, geography, history, humanities, mathematics, statistics, philosophy, political science, psychology, science and sociology';
- and that deploys a range of *different qualitative and quantitative methodologies*, including: 'surveys, experiments and controlled trials; ethnography, interview and narrative enquiry; action research and case study; evaluation research; critical theory and documentary analysis; analytic synthesis and systematic review' (HEFCE, 2012: paras. 26–28).

This diversity, whether we call it richness or muddle, is of fundamental importance in assessing where educational research is today, particularly because of the epistemological challenges it raises. These challenges will be considered in more detail later in this chapter. Before doing that, however, it is necessary to ask some more basic questions about the size and shape and funding of the system.

## The size and shape of the educational research system

In Chapter 4 evidence was presented concerning the numbers of educational academics in the UK entered for successive Research Assessment Exercises (from 2010, the RAE was rebranded the Research Excellence Framework, REF). Of course, university-based research is much broader and more inclusive than that which is measured by any research assessment exercise. This is particularly true in a strongly professional field such as education, where there is a presumption that academic staff will engage with the world of policy and practice through their teaching, their writing and other forms of public engagement. Nevertheless, the RAE does provide us with an important insight into the world of educational research at its most formal level. After all, research that conforms to the norms set down by the RAE/REF is that sort of research that is valued by universities, by the funding agencies that support them and, behind that, by the government. It is also the type of research that is most visible nationally and internationally; that is why it is so valued by universities in the increasingly competitive international market in which they now operate (Brown, 2010). In much of what follows, the analysis is informed by this formal conception of research. In other words, it is research – whatever its approach – that explicitly aims to build on what is known in a particular field, that aims to contribute to the public stock of knowledge (thereby allowing critical engagement) and that is conducted in accordance with the methodological protocols associated with its chosen tradition.

In 2008, 1,696 academic staff members from UK departments and faculties of education were entered for the RAE (2008a). In absolute terms, the number of academics formally designated as research-active is high within the social sciences, roughly equivalent to psychology and twice the size of either economics or sociology. However, as was noted in Chapter 4, those entered represented only 31 per cent of education academics employed at the time, a proportion that is significantly lower than in all other social science disciplines. It is also important to note that in absolute terms, the number of active researchers is dramatically lower than in other major areas of social policy, such as medicine and health. If one includes nursing and other allied professions, over 8,000 researchers were entered, even though those combined fields are probably only about one and a half times the size of education. It is also much smaller than business and management, where there were 3,300 entries. In short, when viewed as a social science, education has a reasonable number of active researchers. When viewed as an applied discipline closely linked to a major area of activity within civil society, the number of active researchers is comparatively quite small.

Perhaps part of the explanation for the low percentage of entries to the RAE lies in the fact that over successive RAEs, universities have been becoming more and more selective in who is entered. As the last RAE Education Panel noted in its subject overview (RAE, 2008b) overall, there was a drop of roughly 15 per cent, comparing the 2008 entry with that of the 2001 RAE. Numbers were particularly down in submissions from the research-intensive universities – the Russell Group. There were, however, some important variations with significant increases in Scotland (by 63 per cent), presumably encouraged by the more inclusive funding formulas adopted by the Scottish Funding Council. In contrast, numbers in Wales fell significantly, with Northern Ireland remaining much the same.

Another explanation for the relatively low entry rate is the high percentage of teaching-only and hourly paid staff employed in education. Although the move to teaching-only contracts is something that is happening across all of higher education (Brown, 2010), as we saw in Chapter 4, percentages in education are considerably higher than in comparable disciplines.

RAE results cannot only tell us about numbers of academic staff designated as research-active, but they can also give an insight into their distribution. Again in Chapter 4, we saw evidence of how the ten case study institutions described there had a variety of different profiles in terms of RAE entry. Some institutions appeared to have entered virtually all of their academic staff, indicating the existence of a strong research culture; at the other extreme, some quite large faculties only entered a handful of their staff.

This considerable variation is also revealed by the RAE results overall. For the 2008 RAE and the forthcoming 2014 REF, publications are rated on a four-point scale, from one star to four stars. One star is work that is of national significance; four stars is work that is considered world-leading.

Table 6.1 shows that of the 82 institutions that were entered to the RAE in education in 2008, there were four institutions with 30 per cent or more of their publications ranked as world-leading and a further 16 institutions where 15, 20 or 25 per cent of their publications were ranked in this way. Fifteen institutions had 10 per cent of their outputs rated as world-leading and a further 23 had 5 per cent. The remaining 24 institutions had no work rated at this quality.

However as Table 6.2 shows, the numbers of staff returned in all institutions varied considerably. At one extreme there was the London Institute of Education with its 218 members of staff entered; at the other, there were 28 institutions that entered only between 1 and 9 members of staff.

*Table 6.1* Numbers of education entries in 2008 RAE by percentage of 4* work

| Percentage of 'World Leading' publications – 4* | +30% | 25% | 20% | 15% | 10% | 5% | 0% |
|---|---|---|---|---|---|---|---|
| Numbers of institutions | 4 | 1 | 8 | 7 | 15 | 23 | 24 |

Source: RAE (2008a)

*Table 6.2* Size of 2008 RAE entries by institutions

| Numbers of staff entered | 60+ | 40–59 | 20–39 | 10–19 | 1–9 |
|---|---|---|---|---|---|
| Numbers of institutions | 3 | 8 | 13 | 30 | 28 |

Source: RAE (2008a)

One way of looking at this is to suggest that these figures reveal a strongly segmented field. At one end there were 20 highly successful institutions with a research culture that was both high quality and broadly distributed, with at least 20 active researchers working at the highest levels of international excellence. At the other end there were those 28 institutions that returned under ten members of staff; all but one of those institutions had low levels of work graded at 4* (0 per cent or 5 per cent).

However, at the same time we need to recognise that over half of all institutions did have at least 10 per cent of their work judged to be world-leading and 70 per cent of all institutions had at least 5 per cent of their work judged in this way. So, although there are a relatively small number of institutions with high densities of research excellence amongst a significant percentage of their staff, the RAE 2008 also demonstrated very clearly that there are small pockets of research excellence distributed across the system as a whole.

## Research funding: a golden past, a worrying future?

Funding for educational research in the UK comes from two explicit sources. Firstly, there is external funding that comes from a range of different bodies – research councils, government, industry, charities, etc. Most of this funding is awarded on the basis of competitive tendering. Then there is core funding for research provided to universities on an annual basis by the government through its various funding agencies. It is this funding (know as QR, quantum research) that is distributed to university departments differentially, depending on their performance in the most recent research assessment exercise. In addition, of course, there is funding for research that is not explicit, that arises from the voluntary time that academics put into their research work over and above that which is paid for through QR. Inevitably, this indirect funding is almost impossible to quantify.

At a national level, funding for educational research is very substantial, though, for a number of reasons, it is now in a worrying decline. During the last RAE period (2001–2007), the average annual funding from research grants of various sorts was £48 million (RAE, 2008b). Each of the 1,696 individuals entered raised, on average, over £100,000 in research funding. By 2009–2010 the annual figure had risen to over £60 million. Add to that QR funding for education, which, in 2009–2010, was £22.5 million and we have a total budget of over £80 million a year. As BERA/UCET (2012) show, there was a very substantial rise in funding over the period when New Labour were in office (1997–2010), though, as they also show, there were even larger rises in other social science subjects.

Where do the research grants come from? Looking again at data from the last RAE period (2001–2007), Figure 6.1 shows that the overwhelming majority of that funding (57 per cent) came from various government agencies; 17 per cent came from research councils; 11 per cent from charities; 5 per cent from EU governments; and 2.6 per cent from industry.

Education to date has therefore not been particularly successful in winning research grants from the European Union (other social sciences have been significantly more successful) and, given the size of the discipline, its success in winning Research Council grants is only modest. For example, BERA/UCET (2012) report that between 2001 and 2011, education accounted for 9 per cent of the ESRC applications and 6 per cent of the awards. Psychology, a discipline of roughly equal size in terms of numbers of staff entered for the last RAE, made 24 per cent of the applications and received 27 per cent of the awards. Other disciplines such as sociology, economics and politics – all significantly smaller than education – were also more successful.

And the dependence on funding from government bodies of different sorts is a cause for concern in two different ways. Firstly, there is the current economic crisis. BERA/UCET (2012), in their report on the current state of educational research, give evidence of significant numbers of government research and evaluation contracts being cancelled since the current Coalition government has come to power (education projects to the value of £7.5 million were cancelled during the government's first six months in office). In addition, a number of key government agencies such as the General Teaching Council for England and the British Educational Communications Technology Authority, both of which were significantly involved in funding research, were also summarily closed by the new government. A concern of a different type is that government funding in particular is far more likely to be strongly applied in nature, a point that will be discussed

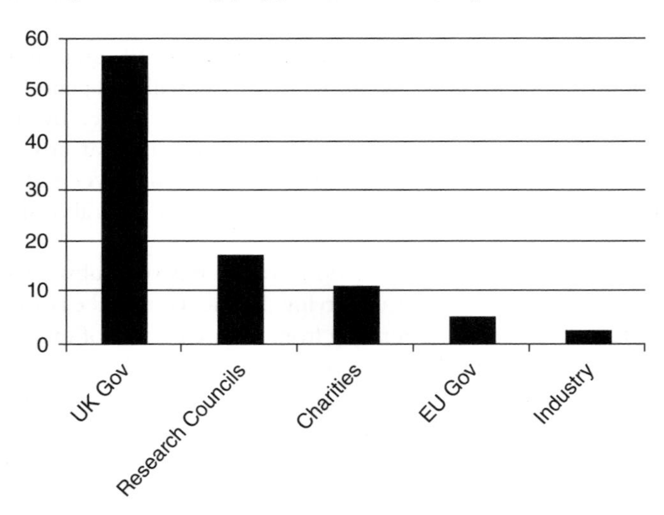


*Figure 6.1* Sources of educational research grants reported for 2008 RAE

Source: RAE (2008a)

in more detail below. Moreover, both government agencies and charities (also a very significant source of funding) often have less stringent peer-review procedures compared with Research Councils and the European Union. In turn, this may have important consequences both for the quality of work undertaken and the capacity development of applicants.

And what of the core funding for research, QR? Unfortunately, there are concerns here too. As we noted above, over the past decade education departments and faculties have returned progressively smaller numbers of staff to successive research assessment exercise. As volume combined with quality (the definition of which is regularly changed by funding councils) are the primary drivers of the overall QR budget and its distribution in each field, this has had important consequences for education as a whole. BERA/UCET (2012) present evidence to suggest that QR has fallen by some 45 per cent since 1996. At that time, as I noted in 1998, education, because of its size, attracted the largest amount of QR for any discipline (Furlong, 1998). Now a further significant reduction has been announced for 2012–2013. No other social science has seen a reduction anywhere near as large as this; indeed, subjects like psychology and particularly business and management have seen significant rises in their QR income over this period.

There is, however, variability of QR funding levels in different countries within the UK. The Funding Council in Scotland continues to have the most generous formula, while in Wales more stringent procedures mean that from 2011, no university is receiving any core funding for educational research. In England only research graded at three or four stars is to be funded from 2012–2013. All of these changes result from a policy, pursued by successive governments, of a progressive movement away from the dual-funding model. In the future it is intended that QR funding overall will become progressively less and less significant for the support of all forms of university-based research – except, that is, in science, technology, engineering and mathematics (the STEM subjects). Because of its reducing size and comparatively weak profile when compared with many other social sciences, education has experienced a more rapid decline in this source of funding than some other subjects.

## Research staffing

Of course, all of this is only to focus on the marginal funding for research, funds raised through competitive research bids and competitively won core funding. In reality, the most important resource for educational research is neither of these; it is in the core staff whose funding comes primarily from teaching. In the early 2000s there were significant rises in staff associated with initial teacher education in order to respond to increasing demand, but today education currently faces some very serious challenges. The current demographic downturn in the school system is having a significant effect on the demand for new teachers; this, in turn, has been causing a considerable contraction in numbers of teachers in training and, hence, of the academic staff who teach them. A second challenge in England, if not elsewhere in the UK, is the current move to a School Direct model of teacher education instituted by the Coalition government. As is discussed in more detail in Chapter 8, under this model, schools will progressively find themselves in the driver's seat in the provision of teacher education, purchasing what services they need in an open, competitive market from universities and other providers, including commercial providers. And, finally, there are the consequences of the marketisation of higher education more generally, with the charging of full fees for undergraduate and (presumably before long) postgraduate courses. All of these different forces between them mean that the future size and shape of education faculties in UK universities is currently in question. As was noted in the last chapter, most teaching programmes in education are likely to look very different in five years' time; this, in turn, will have a major impact on the future size and shape of the country's capacity for the production of educational research.

## Academic networks: learned societies, journals and conferences

So far we have only considered the institutional bases of educational research. In reality, that is only part of the story. One of the things that Martin Lawn and I learned from our recent review of one small part of the field of education – the so-called 'Disciplines of Education' (Furlong and Lawn, 2010) – was that most institutions today only give very indirect institutional support to them, to the sociology, psychology, philosophy, etc. of education. Unlike the past, today there are very few dedicated lectureships and professorships or even taught courses in these or, indeed, in many other specialist areas (the Institute of Education is one of the few exceptions here). And yet at another level, we found that these disciplinary perspectives do survive and are relatively strong. This is because instead of finding support in institutional structures, individuals now do so through a whole range of networked activities – learned societies, specialist conference, specialist journals – and that phenomenon is not merely confined to the traditional disciplines of education; it is true of very large numbers of specialist subfields within education.

Mapping learned societies in the UK that have an interest in education is not something that, to my knowledge, has been done. In the US the Department of Education hosts the Education Resource Organizations Directory, which lists almost 1,000 educational organisations involved in educational research. The nearest British equivalent would be the British Academy's Directory of Subject Associations and Learned Societies in the Humanities and Social Sciences. That covers 280 such societies, 25 of which would appear to have an interest in education. But, in reality, the directory really only presents a very partial picture.

A relatively cursory Google search confirms that there are many, many UK organisations supporting educational research through conferences, publications, networks, advocacy and sometimes funding. These fall into a number of different categories. Firstly, there are national broadly based learned societies such as the Royal Society or the Royal Society of Arts, which support educational networks and sometimes programmes of educational research that are relevant to their core objectives. Then there are more specialist learned societies such as the Institute of

Physics, the Royal Geographical Society and the Historical Association. These bodies have a broad remit in their subject areas, including the funding and support of specialist educational research.

There are also bodies specifically focused on research that include but are not limited to education. The British Psychological Society and British Sociological Association, for example, both have strong educational branches within them. A particularly important group of learned societies are those that specialise in educational research itself. The British Educational Research Association (BERA), the Scottish Educational Research Association (SERA), the British Educational Studies Association and the Society of Educational Studies are broadly based bodies that support conferences and have significant roles in journal and book publishing. BERA is particularly important here, with its annual international conference, its 30 special interest groups and its suite of four journals, including the UK's leading generalist research journal, the *British Educational Research Journal*. BERA sees itself a lead body in educational research in the UK. As such, it is also involved in advocacy and capacity building for the research community as a whole. BERA and organisations like it are generalist research bodies. Another group of research-based societies provide more specialised research support; bodies such as the Philosophy of Education Society of Great Britain, the Gender and Education Association, the Association for Science Education and the Society for Research in Higher Education. Again, these sorts of bodies support journals, conferences and other networks.

And all of this rich activity is closely paralleled by other national bodies in which British academics frequently participate: the American Educational Research Association (AERA), the Australian Association for Research in Education (AARE). And, finally, there is a growing number of transnational bodies as well: the European Educational Research Association (EERA), the World Council of Comparative Education Societies and even the World Education Research Association. Of these, EERA is particularly worthy of note, with its 28 networks (inclusive education, history of education, etc.), its journal and its increasingly important annual conference.

When we come to look at journals, the picture is even richer or perhaps even more bewildering. In 2010, in preparation for their 2012 Research Excellence Assessment, the Australian Research Council published a list of research journals, mainly in the English language, that it had classified and ranked in terms of quality. Of the 20,713 journals listed, 629 were classified as 'education' and a further 300 as 'pedagogy and curriculum', though this latter category mainly focused on pedagogy and curriculum in higher education teaching. After undertaking this mammoth exercise, the Australian government announced in 2011 that it would not be using this ranking system in their 2012 Research Excellence Assessment; nevertheless, the list does provide a useful insight into the huge number of education journals now available.

Academic journal publishing is now a major global business, with companies such as Taylor & Francis, Elsevier and Wiley dominating the market. Taylor & Francis, for example, currently publish 220 educational journals, 136 of which are based in the UK (70 in the USA; 2 in Singapore; 2 in South Africa; 10 in Australia). Taylor & Francis is part of Informa plc, a global group which describes itself as 'an international business in the media sector', academic publishing is only one part of their activity. Academic publishing is only one part of their activity. By contrast, Wiley is primarily an academic publishing house, characterising itself as a 'global information and education company'. It currently publishes 105 educational journals. Elsevier is also a global company, publishing a total of 2,000 academic journals, 16 of which are in the field of education.

And, finally, what of conferences? All of the learned societies and associations mentioned above will hold one or more conference each year. These vary massively in size from the largest – AERA often with 15,000 participants – to very small colloquia-based in single institutions, with 30 or so participants. But the actual number of such events is almost impossible to quantify. One website – Conference Alerts, which covers academic conferences worldwide (http://www.conferencealerts.com/) – for 2012, lists 30 conferences a month in the subfield of higher education alone. It lists similar numbers in ICT and teaching and learning. Such lists are certainly not systematic, but they do demonstrate the sheer volume of the networking and presentational opportunities that are now available worldwide for the footloose academic.

As Martin Lawn and I observed (Furlong and Lawn, 2010), these are the collective spaces where much of academic life in the field of education is now lived. It is an immensely rich and diverse field. Support for educational research, rather than being provided by universities alone, is increasingly provided by complex networks, increasingly undertaken within a transinstitutional, often transnational framework. And these spaces for academic life are made possible by rapid transport, by digital communication and by a somewhat surprising (some would say exploitative) collaboration between academic voluntary work (running societies, editing and reviewing for journals) and some of the world's largest global corporations. One of the consequences, as we will discuss in Chapter 9, is that these movements have also helped spawn a global employment market for the research elite.

## Quality and diversity

Institutionally, therefore, educational research in the UK today is in a relatively strong position, even if there are important segregations within it. In absolute terms, it has a large number of research-active staff, a significant proportion of whom publish at the national level and beyond. Over the past 15 years or so, it has also been relatively well funded and it is supported by a rich and diverse range of journals, conferences and thriving learned societies. All very positive. Whether, though, it will be able to maintain this strong institutional position is now very much open to question given the economic crisis and policy changes currently being pursued, particularly by the English government.

But what of its quality? Has all this activity and investment meant that it has got better? Inevitably, this is much more difficult to judge. However, we can gain some insight from two important reports in recent years. The first is a review commissioned by the ESRC in 2008 (Torrance, 2008) to examine the quality of the educational research it had funded in recent years. Torrance reviewed 71 final research reports and concluded that:

> Many of the research projects reviewed are at the forefront of current debates and advances in the field, particularly with respect to 'evidence-based policy and practice'; the use of mixed method designs; and the development of new sociocultural understandings of learning' (broadly, sociocultural theory). User involvement also features strongly in ESRC funded work, especially in the Teaching and Learning Research Programme (TLRP). Empirical research on learning draws extensively on sociocultural theory, across a range of educational phases and topics. The use and interrogation of theory in naturally occurring educational settings is a significant strength of ESRC-funded education research. Related work on the role of social and cultural capital in learning, community cohesion and social reproduction also features in current ESRC research.
>
> (Torrance, 2008: 1)

Other strengths included excellent work on assessment and its relationship to teaching and learning, computer-assisted learning and multimodal analysis. Although not without criticism – particularly because of its overwhelming emphasis on the school system – Torrance argues that educational research in the UK has recovered from the criticisms of the late 1990s. 'If they ever were justified, they certainly are no longer' (2008: 20). At the highest levels of peer-reviewed, nationally funded research, therefore, this is a strong endorsement of quality.

The other major report on quality in recent years is the 'Subject Overview', provided by the last RAE panel (RAE, 2008b). Their review is inevitably more broadly based than that of Torrance in that it covers all forms of research, not merely that funded by the ESRC. Overall, they, too, give a very positive report.

> It is the view of the subpanel that the quality of outputs has improved substantially since 2001 and that this should be widely celebrated. About 80 per cent of the outputs were assessed to be at international standard (two stars and above), with over 40 per cent being judged as internationally excellent or better (three stars and above) and 11 per cent as world-leading (four stars). At most, 3 per cent of outputs submitted were judged to be below national level.
>
> (RAE 2008b, p. 3)

As a result, they suggest that our best departments and faculties of education 'can compete on equal terms with the strongest departments anywhere in the world' (p. 3).

The reason for the significant improvement, the panel suggests, is institutional investment: in new chair appointments, in staff development and capacity building, in funded studentships and postdoctoral fellowships. Nevertheless, within this general trend, the panel noted that there was still a wide range of quality. While there was world-leading research in almost every subfield, at the lower end they noted insufficient building upon other work, including testing hypotheses/research questions in new contexts. The contrast between the innovative and the pedestrian was especially acute in research in higher education, assessment, early years, adult education and in subject-discipline focused work, including ICT.

The panel made some particularly important comments on disciplinary-based work: philosophy, history and sociology. Most of this work they judged to be excellent. It was also seen as vitally important because of its potential to interrelate with other educational-research traditions. Government funded research, though, presented a more mixed picture. The quality of the best government sponsored and targeted research was excellent, both rigorous and effective in informing policy, with enough funding to sustain large multidisciplinary teams over many years. However, other areas suffered in quality through being too closely tied to shifting government and government agency priorities, tight timescales, a focus on description rather than analysis and limited theorisation. This loosened the links with social science and sometimes involved over-simplistic assumptions about teaching and learning.

Overall, then, a generally positive picture from both of these major reviews. Nevertheless, before we get too excited, we need to remind ourselves that only one-third of education academics were entered for the last RAE; two-thirds were not entered at all. And many institutions offering large teaching programmes entered only a very small proportion of their staff. If we add to this the fact that, as we saw in Chapter 4, only 23 per cent of education academics currently have a doctorate as their highest degree, we perhaps get a more balanced picture. At the higher levels, the quality of educational research is now good, but there is still a long way to go for the discipline as a whole to become genuinely research-led, to become genuinely part of what higher education would expect it to be.

## What have we learned?

Asking questions about the size, shape and quality of the system is one way to assess the current state of educational research in the UK. A rather different and perhaps more challenging way of posing that question is to ask what we now know as a result of educational research that we did not know ten years ago. Of course, in the social sciences and humanities, unlike the natural sciences, there are few sudden breakthroughs, few eureka moments. The best we can aspire to is the slow accumulation of insights and even then we know that such insights seldom last forever; they necessarily atrophy as educational contexts, policies and, indeed, learners themselves change over time. As Berliner (2002) famously argued, education is the hardest science of all. Nevertheless, the question of what we have learned recently is an important one, though I suspect that every educational researcher would have his or her own list. What is clear is that we have learned a range of different sorts of things.

Firstly, we have a great deal substantively. The sheer range of what we have learned can perhaps be most effectively illustrated by giving some recent examples from my own department. We have, for example, learned a great deal in the past ten years about the importance of early-years education and the long-term difference to children's life chances that high quality provision can make (Sylva *et al.*, 2011). We are also starting to learn much more about what high quality parenting looks like for very young children as well (Scott *et al.*, 2012). At the other end of the educational system, we know a great deal more about the relationship between further and higher education and the economy. Policies based on human capital theory that think only about the supply of skills rather than also looking at demand for skills in the economy are increasingly recognised as inadequate (Keep *et al.*, 2006; Pring *et al.*, 2009).

In relation to the teaching profession, we know more about how teachers learn during their initial teacher education (Hagger and McIntyre, 2006) and we know more about teacher learning during their early years in the profession (Mutton *et al.*, 2011). We also know more about the informal ways in which subject departments in secondary schools contribute to that process (Burn *et al.*, 2007). We know more about the consequences for learning that have come about through the saturation of young people's lives by new technologies, the blurring of formal and informal boundaries and the new literacies that such boundary crossing demands (Davies and Eynon, 2013; Furlong and Davies, 2012). And we know more about other forms of boundary crossing too; those that come about through the demands of different forms of interprofessional collaboration necessary for the effective support of vulnerable children. Here we know more about the institutional strategies and personal skills needed for such collaboration to happen effectively (Edwards, 2010).

At the pedagogical level, we know more about second-language acquisition and the critical significance code switching – by both student and teacher – in the learning process (Lo and Macaro, 2012). We also continue to learn more about effective teaching of mathematics (Nunes *et al.*, 2012; Watson, 2009) and the teaching of reading (Nunes and Bryant, 2006).

I could go on.

All of these examples are very different in terms of topic, educational sector, theory and methodology, but what they have in common is that they are all based on high quality social scientific research and they are also strongly applied. Most of the researchers referred to here have been centrally concerned to utilise their work to engage in conversations directly with the world of policy and practice and the same is true of the majority of educational researchers; it remains a very strongly applied discipline. And in recent years, in addition to learning more substantively, we have learned a great deal about how to engage with our different publics more effectively than in the past. In this regard, the TLRP (The Teaching and Learning Research Programme) was particularly important in that it insisted on the centrality of user engagement throughout the life of all of its constituent projects with a range of different sorts of users involved in the design and management of research from its very inception. TLRP also emphasised the importance of knowledge synthesis (linking findings from different projects so that insights could become more cumulative) and knowledge transformation (writing in ways that allowed knowledge to be accessed by different audiences for different purposes). As such, it taught the research community a great deal about how to improve the relevance and impact of its work (TLRP, 2009).

However, a rather different thing we have learned (or perhaps been reminded of) in the recent past is that not all research in the field of education needs to be motivated in this way. In his BERA presidential address, Whitty (2006) drew the important distinction between ***educational*** research – research that is explicitly focused on 'making a difference' in the world's policy and or practice – and ***education*** research, which is academically driven, focusing first and foremost on understanding. As one of the major social institutions of contemporary society, Whitty persuasively argued that academic enquiry in the field of education is just as legitimate as in any other field.

Another point, equally important, is to acknowledge that not all research in education sees itself as part of social science; other research is based on different intellectual traditions, draws inspiration from the humanities, history, philosophy, English and from the arts.

A final thing that we have learned more forcefully in recent years concerns the boundaries between researchers and research. All of the examples presented above see researchers as external to the fields of practice that they investigate; the findings they report are the result of research undertaken by professional or at least quasi professional researchers. But while that approach to educational research remains the dominant one in many of our universities, a very different tradition based on the principles of action research has become progressively more influential. That tradition, drawn from the work of Stenhouse (Stenhouse, 1970;1981; Carr and Kemmis, 1986) and developed further by Schön's notions of 'the epistemology of practice' (Schön, 1983), fundamentally challenges the distinctions between researcher and research. As was noted in the previous chapter, many (though not all) in departments and faculties of education now recognise the power and importance of different forms of practitioner enquiry in facilitating practitioners' own engagement with research. In some universities, particularly those that are strongly professionally oriented, supporting practitioner enquiry of different sorts has become a major strand in their research agenda (Campbell and Groundwater-Smith, 2007; Cochran-Smith and Lytle, 2009; Groundwater-Smith and Mockler, 2008).

## The challenge of diversity: where do we go from here?

Educational research then has taught us a great deal in recent years, both substantively and about the research process, about different types of research and about different forms of public and academic engagement. But one cannot ask questions about what we have learned without confronting the challenge that it brings. That is the challenge of coming to terms with diversity. For what these few examples – mostly drawn from just one department of education in the UK – have demonstrated very clearly is the diversity of educational research. That diversity is not just in terms of topic or educational sector, but in terms of method (I deliberately selected examples to include research based on design experiments, randomised control trials, longitudinal cohort studies, large-scale surveys, interview studies and detailed qualitative case studies); in terms of theoretical framing (from atheoretical empiricism, to labour economics, to child development); and in terms of fundamental purpose (academic and applied research and practitioner enquiry). What can we make of that diversity? On a larger scale, as anyone who has tried to come to grips with the conference programme for the American Educational Research Association annual meeting knows only too well, when one is confronted with the full range of educational research as a whole (in the case of an AERA conference, 15,000 participants, 8,500 individual papers), it quickly become a bewildering experience! Indeed, perhaps the AERA conference programme, with all its theoretical, epistemological, methodological and substantive diversity, might serve as a symbol for the field as a whole.

So, the final challenge for educational research today is to ask if that matters. Does it matter that the field today embraces such diversity? One reading of the story that this chapter has told is that educational research today – even where it is strong – is a world of subcommunities, each with its own specialist conferences, specialist journals and networks supported by status-hungry universities and an equally hungry global-publishing industry. Communities that perhaps come together for the latest research assessment exercise, for BERA, for AERA, but otherwise swim in parallel streams.

In short, is educational research really no more than what Clark Kerr, back in 1963, described as a 'series of individual faculty entrepreneurs held together by a common grievance over parking' (p. 15)? This was the challenge that Martin Lawn and I posed in our recent book on the current position of the disciplines of education, which, we suggested, were today no more than ghosts of their former selves.

> Journals arrive without a past, reflecting (often creatively) new areas of work and old journals linger on, supplied by the necessity of research audit publication. The internationalization of fields of study and the growth of cross-border study creates hybrids of different disciplinary histories and their production or microstudies, which avoid the problems of the past while looking to the future and action.
>
> (Furlong and Lawn, 2010: 10)

We were writing only about the current position of the educational sub-disciplines of sociology, psychology etc., though the same might be said of education as a whole. But, again, does this matter or is it simply the condition of the modern university? At present, one can discern three different responses to that question, each very different.

The first response is primarily methodologically focused, arguing that the majority of educational research is not fit for purpose since it is not based on a rigourous science of what works. What is needed, instead, is what Gorard (2002) characterises as design science in education, an approach to research that came to ascendency in the US with the No Child Left Behind initiative of Bush years (Feuer *et al.*, 2002). Probably the clearest demonstration of this approach to research in the UK is the Institute for Effective Education at York University, led by Robert Slavin. Back in 2002 Slavin argued that education was on the brink of a scientific revolution that had the potential to profoundly transform policy, practice and research.

> At the dawn of the 21st century, education is finally being dragged kicking and screaming into the 20th century. The scientific revolution that utterly transformed medicine, agriculture, transportation, technology and other fields in the 20th century almost completely bypassed the field of education.
>
> (Slavin, 2002: 16)

The most important reason for the extraordinary advances in medicine, agriculture and other fields, he argued, was the acceptance by practitioners of evidence as the basis for practice. In particular, it was the randomised clinical trial – more than any single medical breakthrough – that had transformed medicine.

> Imagine that there were programs underway all the time to develop, evaluate and disseminate new programs in every subject and every grade level ... over time each area would experience the step-by-step irreversible progress characteristic of medicine and agriculture because innovations would be held to strict standards of evaluation before being recommended for wide scale use.
>
> (Slavin, 2002: 17)

It is these ideas that have become central to the Institute for Effective Education, established by the Bowland Trust at York University in 2007. Its long-term aim is to use rigorous research methods, particularly experiments and randomised control trials, combined with systematic reviews in order to establish what works in every subject area at every stage of the school system. As they say in their 2009 Annual Report:

> our vision for the future is that the gap between research, policy and practice will close. Educators and policymakers will have easy access to research and confidence in its reliability and purpose. Using evidence will be as important in teaching as it is in medicine or science.
>
> (Institute for Effective Education, 2009/10: 6)

In short, one response to the bewildering diversity of educational research described above is to argue implicitly that most of it is not worthy of the name. This line of reasoning then plays the science card, arguing that there is a way out of the impasse: the development of more rigourous scientifically based research.

A radically alternative view is presented by Carr (2006, 2007), who argues that although educational researchers 'often behave as if they belong to a single intellectual community' and indeed argue for recognition as such – for purposes of funding, political influence and a mission of social amelioration through education – the sad truth is that educational research now embraces so many traditions, paradigms, theoretical perspectives, methodological frameworks and academic disciplines that it cannot claim to meet even the most minimal criteria of homogeneity that any notion of a research community presupposes and requires. Carr therefore argues that it is unsurprising that any identity educational research may have stems more from its institutional embodiment in conferences, research journals and learned societies than from any internal intellectual coherence.

Carr begins his critique by arguing that what he calls theory – the various products of research and scholarship – has, as we have already observed, changed over the twentieth century, from philosophy to science, to the disciplines of education and then to forms of theories in use exemplified in the work of Stenhouse and Schön. (Actually, I would disagree with him here. It is not that one form of theorising in education has succeeded another; all of these different theoretical discourses are very much still with us, hence the dismaying Tower of Babel that we have.)

But, he argues, all of these different approaches have been based on foundationalist principles. Foundationalism, argues Carr, does not refer to any particular argument or theory, but to the general belief that the only way that we can adequately justify our beliefs – the only way we can show that they are rational and true – is to show how they rest on some basic beliefs or foundations, that do not themselves need justification. They are self-evident or otherwise necessarily true. This, Carr argues, is no more than the continued working out of the Enlightenment project. As he says elsewhere these Enlightenment commitments and beliefs are familiar enough, the most important of which is 'the conviction that the practices and institutions of society can be rationally reformed by making them less dependent on dogma and tradition' (Carr, 2007: 1, quoted in Lee, 2010).

Carr then makes the case that from a whole variety of different perspectives, foundationalism – the pursuit of truth that stands outside of history – can no longer be sustained. We are now, he argues, firmly in a world of postfoundationalism. The way in which postfoundationalist thinking is articulated within different philosophical traditions and academic disciplines, Carr argues, varies. But what they all have in common is the shared conviction that the time has now come to abandon the search for epistemological foundations that can guarantee the truth of theoretical knowledge. Hence, he suggests, the familiar postfoundationalist slogans: there are 'no unmediated facts'; 'no neutral observation language'; 'no telling it as it is'; 'no view from nowhere'; 'no escaping politics'.

> These postfoundationalist slogans are underwritten by a range of philosophical arguments that collectively show how any idea that we can occupy a position outside of history and culture is a myth.
>
> (Carr, 2006: 146)

In a rather dramatic flourish, Carr therefore comes to the conclusion that 'the educational theory project has run its course and that the time has now come for us to bring it to a dignified end'.

For the busy and committed educational researcher, Carr's arguments are seriously disturbing because, at one level, they seem self-evidently true. How could one seriously engage with the vastly different approaches to truth claims that are made on the basis of educational research today without recognising that such claims are always historically situated, that research does not nor ever could stand outside of the world of practice, that it is a form of practice in and of itself? Should we then give up the whole enterprise and put educational research to a 'dignified end'?

Actually, that is not quite the end of the story for Carr. He goes on to argue that although theory (for our purposes here, the products of research and scholarship) does not stand up as an independent source of truth, it does, on occasion, still work. However, instead of working through truth claims, it works rhetorically.

> The practical influence of educational theory thus has nothing to do with its meeting criteria of objectivity, rationality and truth and everything to do with the rhetorical role that this mode of discourse is able to play in a particular educational context at a particular historical moment.
>
> (Carr, 2006: 152)

In short, it can sometimes work rhetorically, politically; at a particular time in history and with particular communities, it can be persuasive. Perhaps, then, it is still worth doing. And this brings us to the third and much more pragmatic pluralist response to the current diversity of educational research.

This pluralist approach has been embedded in organisations such as BERA in the recent past, in the TLRP and, indeed, in the current REF panel's definition of research. Perhaps sidestepping the more fundamental questions that Carr has raised, it takes the view that in the world in which we live and work, many different forms of educational research can be persuasive. If it is undertaken well, within its own terms, educational research can work rhetorically amongst academic, policy and practitioner communities.

This was the line of argument I put forward in my BERA presidential address in 2004 (Furlong, 2004). I recognised the diversity of educational research and the very different methodological and theoretical commitments of BERA members. However, I argued that on BERA's 30th birthday, it needed to do two sorts of growing up. It needed to grow up enough to see the diversity of the educational research community as a strength, not a weakness, tolerating differences and contradictions and promoting dialogue amongst those who hold different perspectives. Secondly, I argued that educational researchers should be grown-up enough to insist that each different sub-community engages in its own robust review of what quality is and how it can be promoted. And from my observation, BERA has now adopted these principles wholeheartedly, though I would not claim that it was I who made that happen. (As Carr would irritatingly observe, I was merely going with the historical tide!)

Successive research assessment exercises and the forthcoming REF have taken a similar approach. We have already noted that in the hugely inclusive definition of educational research quoted at the beginning. The same is true for the TLRP and most particularly for the Strategic Forum for Educational Research that TLRP finally sponsored (SFRE, 2010). That forum, which ran from 2008 to 2010, was designed to bring together the full community of educational researchers and research users from across the UK. Its task as educational research's single most significant ever investment, the TLRP, came to an end, was to take stock. Its aim was to look at quality and capacity across the four nations of the UK, to look at the contributions of different research and theoretical traditions, to look at the current forms of engagement with research by different users and to make recommendations on the processes and infrastructure needed to address the further development of quality and sustainability in UK educational research. And the SFRE did all of these things most effectively, though whether anyone was listening as the New Labour government came to an end is a moot point!

In this pluralist response to research diversity, it is not that Carr's arguments have gone away. Most of us know too much about the partiality of knowledge production not to recognise the difficult truths he raises. Critically, these are truths not just of education, but for the academy as a whole. But as critical realists such as Young (2008) would remind us, while we collectively angst about the relativity of knowledge, powerful knowledge continues to exist in our society. Rationally produced knowledge of many different sorts may be partial; educational research may no longer have the aura of fundamental truth with which to speak to power. But partial though it is, it is all we have. To be rhetorically persuasive, it therefore needs to be as good as it can be in its own terms.

These are issues that go to the heart of the purposes of education as a university-based discipline; they are issues to which we return in the final section of this book. But before we do that, we need to ask *why* it is that the discipline of education, its institutions, its research and its teaching is currently shaped in the way that it is. That is the purpose of the next three chapters, Section III.

# Section III

# Why are we where we are?

# 7 Globalisation, neo-liberalism and the emergence of the enterprise university

> To a significant extent, universities have been self-organising institutions ... To emphasise their independence from temporal imperatives, they have retained the monastic and cathedral symbolism of rectors, deans and readers. They have sought to count rank and ritual as equal to cash reward ... Entwined into this formal pageantry, like Ariadne's thread, has been an individualism which asserts itself as a total right to academic freedom, expressed with equal plausibility as a responsibility to both defend and criticise the dominant culture of the day. Without evident discomfort, this same energy has driven genetic engineers and physicists to extend the borders of the known universe and, as they say, go where no enterprise has gone before, dragging commerce and politics with one hand and holding the *Book of Common Prayer* in the other.
>
> (Marginson and Considine, 2000: 1)

## Introduction

The aim of the previous three chapters has been to describe university departments and faculties of education in the UK as they are today. What we have seen is that, as a discipline, education does have some important strengths. Much of its teaching is rated as high quality by students, by employers and by government agencies; there is also evidence of some very high quality research, at best, certainly equal in quality to the very best that is produced anywhere in the social sciences today. In addition, it is a very lively intellectual field, with large numbers of refereed academic journals, learned societies and specialist academic conferences. But we have also seen that despite these strengths, the discipline is flawed in a number of key ways: its institutions are highly differentiated and, internally, its institutional position is often insecure; it is too dependent on technical rationalist teaching, which, in turn, has implications for staffing and for opportunities for their professional development; as a research field, it is epistemologically divided and often theoretically weak, dominated by small-scale applied research; as a result, its research is not always cumulative.

But why is education as a discipline like this? Once it finally arrived at the medieval high table in the latter decades of the twentieth century, why did it not take on the character of other university-based professional disciplines such as medicine or law? Why did it not achieve the academic freedoms of the traditional university as characterised by Marginson and Considine above? The answer is that by the time education finally arrived, universities were changing in fundamental ways. So, too, was the management of research, the school system and, beyond that, teaching profession. All were being subject to a range of different pressures that have come to shape education in new and different ways. The aim of this and the next two chapters is to explore the different forces that currently help to make education as a discipline what it is in the UK today.

This first chapter begins by looking at the background to those pressures; that is, globalisation. But following the work of Rizvi and Lingard (2009), it is argued that globalisation does not work directly and independently as a force in shaping educational policy and practice. Rather, globalisation works by being 'imagined' by governments around the world as necessitating neo-liberalism. As we will see, the philosophy that there is no alternative to the market in all aspects of public and personal life has had a profound impact on both schools and on universities. Departments of faculties of education, which are based in universities but largely focus on the work of the school system, are therefore doubly influenced by neo-liberal policies.

After introducing the concepts of globalisation and neo-liberalism, this chapter particularly focuses on the impact of neo-liberal policies on universities themselves. In recent years neo-liberal policies have helped to change universities in fundamental ways; those policies include the massive expansion of the system and the development of new public management in all aspects of university life. The result has been the birth of the 'enterprise university' (Marginson and Considine, 2000; Marginson, 2009). It is argued that because of their historically weak institutional position and because of the dominance of the government as a purchaser of education courses, education departments and faculties in the modern enterprise university have been particularly susceptible to external government pressures, especially in relation to the professional education of teachers – still the core of their business. Those pressures have had a major impact on courses that are taught, the students and staff that are recruited and the research that gets undertaken.

But beyond university entrepreneurialism, how has neo-liberalism come to shape the discipline of education? Chapter 8 explores this question by looking at the background to recent policies on the professional education of teachers and the changing contribution of universities to it. Although policies have changed over time and are different in different parts of the UK, it is clear that it is neo-liberal ideas that have driven the policy agenda. Chapter 9 then focuses on the impact of neo-liberal policies on research but takes a rather different approach. Rather than staying at the national policy level, it examines the ways in which research management in the enterprise university has come to influence day-to-day realities of life in UK's departments and faculties of education.

Chapters 8 and 9 are, therefore, quite different in focus. They both explore the impact of neo-liberal ideas on the shaping of the discipline, but they do that in different ways; one looks at national policy, the other at institutional practice.

Therefore, they do not aspire to provide a complete overview of the impact of neo-liberalism on the discipline of education in the modern enterprise university; rather they are intended to explore two different moments in that formation process.

## Globalisation: imagining the necessity of neo-liberalism

If we are trying to understand contemporary policy and practice in education – whether that is at the university level or that of schools – then one of the most important influences to come to terms with is globalisation or, more accurately, a particular form of globalisation based on the ideas of neo-liberalism. We can gain some insight into how these two themes work together in education by looking at the work of Rizvi and Lingard (2009). Globalisation, as Rizvi and Lingard admit, is a highly contested notion. Drawing on the work of Held and McGrew (2005), they suggest that there are at least three different interpretations of globalisation identifiable within public discourse. There are *globalists* such as Giddens (1990) who argue that globalisation has emerged as the result of changed material realities. New technologies and new patterns of communication have helped to reconfigure time and space; as a result, new patterns of social interaction have emerged, producing a significant reconfiguration of the organising principles of social life and the world order.

At the other extreme, there are the *sceptics*: those who argue that the term globalisation is largely ideological and, as such, has limited explanatory value. Hirst and Thompson (1996), for example, suggest that the impact of globalisation has been largely exaggerated and that, anyway, there is nothing new about global changes that have been occurring at least since the end of the nineteenth century

The position adopted by Rivzi and Lingard is between these two extremes. As transformationalists, they argue that globalisation does indeed have a material reality; it has a hundred-year history, but the process of change has sped up dramatically recently. Drawing on the seminal work of Harvey (1989), they suggest that in the age of globalisation, time and space have become compressed through better communication, virtual contact, cheaper travel and digitisation. They also describe how capitalism has taken advantage of these possibilities, stretching the reach of markets and bringing the whole globe into its sphere of influence. However, Rizvi and Lingard also argue that there is nothing inevitable about the ways in which the material changes underpinning globalisation impact on the economy, on politics and on culture. Their impact, they suggest, varies considerably as a result of history, of ideology and a range of other political and structural processes.

In trying to understand the impact of globalisation, Rizvi and Lingard make the important point that public discourse about globalisation is often both descriptive and normative at the same time. As well as describing the material changes that underpin globalisation processes, public discourse frequently invokes the necessity of neo-liberalism. In this way, globalisation and neo-liberalism have become intimately entwined. Initially associated with Reagan and Thatcher, over the past 30 years, neo-liberalism has been adopted by political parties of the centre, the traditional left as well as the right; as Noam Chomsky (1999) has argued, it has become the defining political and economic paradigm of our time.

Neo-liberalism, as Robertson (2007) points out, is itself a development of liberalism: a utopian project promoted by philosophers such as Locke and Hobbes committed to the ideals of personal freedom and individualism. However,

> Neo-liberalism differs from liberalism in one important way: its commitment to neoclassical economics; that is, recognition that some state intervention is necessary to ensure that Adam Smith's hidden hand of the market can function. This means that freedom of the market, the right to free trade, the right to choose and protection of private property is assured by the state.
>
> (Robertson 2007:4)

In its first formulation in the Thatcher and Reagan eras, known as the Washington Consensus (Dale, 1999), neo-liberalism had a number of key themes: the rule of the market; the need to cut state expenditure on services such as education, except where it could be justified in economic terms; consumer choice in public services; deregulation; and privatisation, with the role of the state reduced to managing the awarding of relevant contracts and to ensuring that no single monopoly provider gains too much power in the market. Later interpretations, exemplified by New Labour's Third Way policies (and also echoed under Clinton in the USA) involved a variation on these principles where there was a continuing and even growing role for the central state in supporting markets, particularly in key social policy areas such as education and health. And, as we will discuss in the next chapter, these principles are, today, being refashioned yet further by the UK's current Coalition government. But despite these developments, throughout the past 30 years, the broad thrust of the necessity of neo-liberal augments has held sway.

Rizvi and Lingard argue that it is these ideas that have become common sense when thinking about globalisation. Drawing on the work of the Canadian philosopher Charles Taylor, they argue that neo-liberalism has become the 'social imaginary' of globalisation.

> A social imaginary is a way of thinking shared in a society by ordinary people, the common understandings that make everyday practices possible, giving them sense and legitimacy. It is largely implicit, embedded in ideas and practices, carrying within it deeper normative notions and images constitutive of a society.
>
> (Rizvi and Lingar, 2009: 34).

It is Rivzi and Lingard's distinctive position that globalisation is, for governments, for international agencies, as well as for ordinary people, 'imagined' as entailing neo-liberalism; as such, it becomes part of the general population's common sense: it becomes a necessity. Promoted by governments and international agencies such as the World Bank and the OECD that insist there is no alternative, promoted by the global media, promoted by the flow of people and ideas from business schools and think tanks, Rizvi and Lingard argue that these accounts are presented in a language that demands the implicit consent of national governments and ordinary people alike. In these ways, 'the neo-liberal social imaginary of globalisation is designed to forge a shared implicit understanding of the problems to which policies are presented as solutions' (p. 36). As we will see in the remainder of this chapter and those that follow, neo-liberalism as the social imaginary of globalisation has had profound implications for universities, for the teaching profession and for management of research.

This is not to argue that it has had the same effect in different countries and in different historical periods. As we will see most particularly in Chapter 8, when we look in more detail at contemporary policy in teacher education across the UK, there is ample evidence that different countries within the UK, let alone internationally, have interpreted neo-liberalism in different ways. And, as I have already indicated, the idea of neo-liberalism has also changed over time. Nevertheless, it is true that at a general level, neo-liberalism has been profoundly influential on all of our educational institutions. As a consequence, it has been highly significant in the current shaping of the university-based discipline of education.

## Neo-liberalism and mass higher education

As Becher and Trowler (2000) have documented so clearly, universities have changed fundamentally in recent years. One of the most significant changes has been the exponential growth of the system: its 'massification'. Over the course of the past three decades, higher education in the UK and, indeed, around the world has moved from an elite to a mass system of education. In the 1980s, when departments and faculties of education were becoming fully integrated into higher education proper, only 12 per cent of 18-year-olds were in higher education; by 2002 that figure had risen to 43 per cent. The rises slowed after that, mainly keeping pace with demographic changes. However, even today, further expansion is pursued. For example, the 2010 Browne Report on the future funding of higher education anticipated a further expansion of the system by 10 per cent over the next four years so that 'everyone who has the potential to benefit from HE gets the opportunity to do so' (Browne Report, 2010). And similar expansions have happened internationally as well. While some developing countries still educate fewer than 10 per cent of the 18–21 age group, almost all developed countries have dramatically increased their participation rates. Across the world, the percentage of the age cohort enrolled in tertiary education grew from 19 per cent in 2000 to 26 per cent in 2007, meaning that there are now about 150.6 million tertiary students in the world today (Altbach, 2010).

This worldwide move to massification has links both to globalisation and neo-liberalism. Marginson (1993), for example, traces the rapid expansion of higher education in the last decades of the twentieth century to the rediscovery of human capital theory, which, in line with neo-liberal principles, sees education primarily as a form of economic investment. As the OECD noted back in 1986:

> the development of contemporary economies depends critically on the knowledge, skills and attitudes of their workforce, in short, on human capital ... a basic policy goal permeating education in all countries is to increase the productivity of human resources, so as to enable more valuable output of work and thus allow higher wages and/or profits in the economy as a whole.
>
> (OECD, 1986, quoted in Marginson, 1993: 48)

Human capital theory had been significant in the 1960s, where *public* investment in education was seen as a vital key to economic growth. What has been different about the contemporary interpretation of human capital theory in an age of neo-liberalism is that it has emphasised private rather than public investment. Expansion of higher education is seen as essential for the modern economy but with the cost falling increasingly on families and individual students. Whoever pays for higher education, its expansion is seen a key contributor to economic performance where 'the key appears to be the ability of people to cope with changes and to turn them to advantage in the future' (OECD, 1986, quoted in Marginson, 1993: 48).

The impact of massification on universities has been profound but not merely in terms of the size of the system. The massive rise in student numbers led to the need for greater funding from the government. What that rise did not do, though, was to keep pace with the rises in numbers. Even before the changes in funding advocated by the Browne Report (2010), the UK government was anticipating a 40 per cent reduction in the higher education budget by 2014–15. As a result and in line with the principles of neo-liberalism, the costs of higher education have been progressively moved from the state to the consumer. And successive governments have also chosen not to increase core funding for the research element of academics' time in line with their expanding numbers; instead, they developed the Research Assessment Exercise (RAE, now rebranded the Research Excellence Framework, REF) to distribute that funding element on a competitive basis. As we will see, it is this significant reduction in state funding for universities that has been the stimulus for many of the changes that have overtaken them in recent years.

## Enter the 'enterprise university'

Much has been written in recent years about the changing nature of the modern university and its 'discontents' (Rothblatt, 1997) and although there are many different interpretations, one common thread concerns changes in their resourcing. Once generously publicly funded, the past 30 years have seen the unit of resource for both teaching and research in UK universities progressively reduced. As a result, the modern university in the UK and internationally has been forced to become much more entrepreneurial in its pursuit of funding. Slaughter and Leslie (1999), for example, document what they see as the rise of 'academic capitalism' across universities in five different countries. At an institutional level, as resources shrink, academic capitalism involves universities increasingly orienting themselves to the most secure government funding streams (for example, science and technology) and to external bodies (such as industry) that can provide research funding, even if that means moving from pure to applied or strategic research (Henkel, 2000; Lucas, 2006; Brew and Lucas, 2009).

At a personal level, academic capitalism describes a situation in which the academic staff of publicly funded universities deploy their 'academic capital' – their teaching, research, consultancy skills – in order to survive in an increasingly competitive environment. Clark (1998), in his study of five different European universities that he considered to be particularly entrepreneurial, describes a broadly similar process. However, for Clark, the point of university entrepreneurialism is not merely to make money; it is also to provide much needed independence from increasingly interventionist governments.

Closely aligned to the establishment of this more entrepreneurial culture within universities has been the development of new public management (Hood, 1995; Deem *et al.*, 2007) – an approach to running organisations that has become widely influential throughout the public-sector institutions in recent years. As Deem *et al.* (2007) note, higher education institutions in the UK are not constitutionally part of the public sector and, historically, have had considerable autonomy. But in the past 20 years, as institutions, they have been re-imagined and reshaped in the UK, largely as a result of the development of new public management. New public management involves a range of different strategies that now set the tone of day-to-day life in the modern university. Mainly borrowed from the private sector, these strategies include: the management of organisations through different competitive units, each identified as its own cost centre; an increasing discipline and parsimony in the use of resources; a move towards more hierarchical, hands-on management; and a much greater emphasis on explicit and measurable standards of performance.

As Henkel explains, it is the marketisation of higher education with the growing emphasis on income generation that has led to strong pressures on academic communities and institutions to change their cultures and structures to enable them to manage the new policy environment. As a consequence, universities have moved away from high-trust flat structures, the community of scholars. Instead, 'academic policymaking moved from the department to the centre. Institutional leaders, rather than protecting academics from external assessments, tended to promote compliance and use them as instruments of change' (Henkel, 2005: 162).

In their characterisation of what they call 'the enterprise university', Marginson and Considine (2000) integrate both of these types of changes: increasing entrepreneurialism and increasing managerialism. They argue that the term 'enterprise university' is more appropriate than academic capitalism because that suggests a one-dimensional institution solely dominated by profit seeking and an organisational culture that is totally reduced to the business form. As they argue, while parts of the new university are pure corporation, universities as a whole are more complex than that. '*Enterprise* captures both economic and academic dimensions and the manner in which research and scholarship survive but are now subjected to new systems of competition and demonstrable performance' (Marginson and Considine, 2000: 5). And enterprise, they suggest, is as much about generating institutional prestige as about income. This approach is neatly, if rather more enthusiastically, captured in this more recent comment from Shattock (2009: 4):

> Entrepreneurialism in a university setting is not simply about generating resources – although it is an important element – it is also about generating activities which may have to be funded in innovative ways in response to anticipated and/or particular market needs or driven by the energy and imagination of individuals, which cumulatively establish a distinctive institutional profile.

For Marginson and Considine, the modern university therefore now has a number of new and distinctive features: it is subject to strong executive control; university missions and governing bodies have taken on a distinctly corporate character; senates, councils, academic boards, departments, etc. have been supplemented (and sometimes supplanted) by vice chancellors' advisory committees and a private shadow university structure. Driving these changes, they suggest, is a redefined internal economy in which underfunding drives a pseudo market in fee incomes, soft budget allocations for special purposes and contested earnings for new enrolments and research grants. As they say, some elements of this market – particularly the education of international students – are, frankly, driven by a commercial and entrepreneurial spirit, now a key (though, by no means, always dominant) element of the enterprise culture.

Overall, a very different world from the financially secure self-governing community of scholars dedicated to the pursuit of 'truth'.

## The consequences for universities: specialisation, difference and relativity

> A university whose borders are so penetrable will have Romans and barbarians mixing freely on campus streets.
>
> (Rothblatt, 1997: 49)

So, what have been the consequences for universities of this more marketised reality? When Cardinal Newman originally proposed the idea of a university, it was explicitly designed to be an elite institution; as we have already noted, following Matthew Arnold's edict, its aim was to expose its students 'to the best that has been thought and known in the world'. Today it is a mass institution and far from following a single idea, massification and marketisation mean that it is increasingly characterised by *difference* rather than by any single idea. As Smith and Webster say:

> Different academics pursuing different knowledges, different teams of researchers combining and recombining to investigate shifting topics, different sorts of students following different courses, with different modes of study and different concerns among themselves, different employment arrangements for different types of staff – difference everywhere in this the postmodern, flexible, accommodating university.
>
> (Smith and Webster, 1997: 104)

In these circumstances they argue that it is absurd to try and express any grand organising principle.

Such changes are not completely new. As Barnett (2000) observes, ever since Clark Kerr (1963) introduced the idea of the multiversity in the 1960s, we have had to recognise the growing multiplicity of roles that the university is taking on itself. Nevertheless, recent developments have sped up that process of change in a dramatic way. And now 'the modern university stretches out here and there, amoeba like wherever it can find a response and sometimes still, even where it cannot' (Barnett, 2000: 14).

But the modern university is not only characterised by difference; it is also characterised by an increasing loss of epistemological confidence. Significantly, in the closing decades of the twentieth century, as was indicated in the last chapter, the development of a more marketised form of higher education (and the arrival of education) coincided with fundamental challenges to the epistemological bases of much of higher education.

For example, in 1990 writers such as Barnett were writing about the end of certainty throughout the whole of higher education:

> The idea of objective knowledge is central to higher education. But from various theoretical quarters – philosophy of science, sociology of knowledge, epistemology, critical theory and poststructuralism – the idea of objective knowledge and truth has come under a massive assault. What, if anything, is to replace objective knowledge is unclear. Pragmatism, relativism, meta-criticism and even 'anything goes' are all proposed. The very diversity of the alternative options is testimony to the collapse of some of our basic epistemological tenets.
>
> (Barnett, 1990: 11)

Twenty years later Barnett (2007) is now using this 'collapse' as his starting point. In a world of uncertainty, he asks, how do we understand students' continuing 'will to learn'?

In the last chapter the significance of this epistemological crisis of confidence for research was described by alluding to the work of Carr (2006, 2007), but the implications run much deeper. The end of what Carr calls foundationalism – certainty of knowledge that stands outside the social processes of knowledge production – means that in increasingly marketised institutions, there is no longer any basis on which to prioritise one teaching programme, one research contract, one consultancy over another. It all depends and probably depends on who shouts loudest.

And, as Smith and Webster (1997) suggest, in the face of this lack of confidence, there is a kind of passivity on behalf of universities, a marked reluctance by anyone to stand up and say what higher education is actually for. As Readings (1996) depressingly noted, there is no shortage of spokespeople claiming that what universities do for government and industry is excellent; what they don't do is articulate a common purpose of anything beyond the utilitarian. Not surprising, then, that Rothblatt (1997) argues that in order to solve the discontents of the modern university, we once again urgently need to think of its common purpose, its rationale; in short, its idea.

The issue of what, if anything, universities have to contribute to the study of education – their rationale in an age of uncertainty – is an issue to which we return in the final section of this book.

## The consequences for education

The changes that have overcome the modern university in the past 30 years have therefore been momentous. It has massively increased in size, lost its privileged and secure funding, been forced into developing an entrepreneurial approach to securing students, to securing research and to developing new third-stream forms of funding. It has had to diversify itself, moving into more and increasingly different markets and it has had to develop new and very different forms for managing itself internally; and all of this when, intellectually, it has lost its confidence about the value of objective knowledge.

And the result of all of this turmoil and transformation? The university has lost its central purpose, its core idea. Newman is dead ... or at least his voice is lost in a world of difference. After waiting outside the door for over 100 years, this was the university world that education as a discipline finally and fully entered in the closing decades of the twentieth century.

So what have the consequences been for education? The final section of this chapter will again draw on case study data to show that those consequences have been profound, both for the majority of departments and faculties that entered the university system in recent years and for the smaller number of university departments that had a much older history. The established university departments, whether they were Reading or Leeds or, indeed, Oxford or Cambridge, have, in the end, been just as caught up in the changing politics of the modern university as their cousins in the new universities and university colleges.

In looking at the implications for education of this brave new university world, there are two stories to be told: a larger story, concerned with increasing government penetration and control of the discipline; and a smaller story of entrepreneurialism and growing institutional differentiation. Both stories have had a profound effect in the shaping of the discipline – its staffing, its students, its intellectual aspirations and achievements.

## *Story 1: 'Fordism' and government control*

Marginson and Considine (2000) point out that one of the paradoxes of the new openness to outside funding that has been forced on the university system is that, in many cases, it has actually resulted in less not more choice within the system; it has resulted in 'a process of "isomorphic closure" through which universities with diverse histories choose from an increasingly restricted menu of commercial options and strategies' (Marginson and Considine, 2000: 4). This is particularly true in the field of education.

As we noted in earlier chapters, it is government funded initial teacher education and, to a lesser extent, government funded CPD courses for teachers that always have been and remain the core business of university departments and faculties of education. Even in our most well-established institutions – including the London Institute of Education – government funded courses remain a key part of the institutional budget. In some of the case study institutions visited, especially the newer universities, initial teacher education and government-mandated CPD constituted over 70 per cent of their budget. The significance of this dependence is this: as in any market relationship, where there is only one dominant or monopsonistic 'customer', then that customer, if it so wishes, can have a profound effect in influencing the product that is sold.

Because universities are now such market-sensitive institutions and because they no longer have any particular essential purposes (no core principles on which to insist), it has been extremely easy for successive ministers of education, particularly in England and Wales, to take more and more control of the teacher education system: to define the nature of the curriculum; to define the structure of courses and relationships with schools; to define the professional qualifications of those allowed to teach on those courses. In Northern Ireland – and particularly in Scotland, where the GTCS has significant power – things have been different; change has been slower but in England and Wales, since the early 1980s, different ministers of all political persuasions have made different demands on the system. As I and colleagues demonstrated in the MOTE studies (Furlong *et al.*, 2000), looking at changes to teacher education in England and Wales throughout the 1990s, by the close of that decade what had been put in place was a system that was highly sensitive and highly receptive to changing government demands. Simply by issuing a revised government circular and by issuing a new Ofsted inspection framework, between them, ministers in England and Wales were able fundamentally to change courses up and down the land if not overnight, then in the course of one year. It was a command-and-control system that many less democratic governments than our own would have been envious of.

In other words, in the course of one generation, government control in England and Wales was successfully reasserted to a degree that had not been seen since the nineteenth century. And the irony is that in a world of increasing relativity in terms of knowledge, in a world where, intellectually, as Barnett (1990) put it, 'anything goes', what successive governments put in place was ever narrower and more practically oriented forms of knowledge. As we saw in Chapter 5, courses based on technical rationalist principles now dominate much of the teacher education curriculum, particularly in England and Wales but even to some degree in Scotland and Northern Ireland. Despite the postmodern university, education courses have become increasingly 'Fordist' in design: any colour as long as it is black. And it is perhaps a testament to how much universities themselves have changed in recent years that even our most ancient of universities – even Oxford and Cambridge – have found it possible to accept and embrace these new forms of professional education. As long as the books are balanced and as long as their departments deliver on other things – especially success in the RAE/REF – then Oxford and Cambridge have found it possible to live with courses that are government-controlled, government-inspected and (supposedly) based purely on technical rationalist forms of knowledge.

Other changes have also taken place. In recent years English government policy has progressively increased the numbers of new teachers entering the profession who do not attend universities at all. As we will discuss in more detail in Chapter 8, employment-based routes into teaching, the Graduate Teacher Programme and TeachFirst (for high-flying graduates) now account for some 20 per cent of new entrants to the profession and the number is set to expand further in future years. At the same time, there has also been pressure on (entrepreneurial, market-sensitive) universities to accredit these training programmes, to find ways of awarding trainees a PGCE and even master's-level credit for work that is undertaken almost entirely in schools.

Fifteen years ago Smith and Webster (1997) warned that the modern university is in danger of becoming 'reduced to a servant of the professions, employers and industry and succumb to the penetration of the university by sponsors, by professional bodies, seeking accreditation on their own terms' (p. 10). In England, in the field of initial teacher education, this story has already become a reality.

And in the face of these challenges, departments and faculties, like their parent institutions, have remained passive. Paralysed (or, indeed, compromised) by their own entrepreneurialism, they have not managed to articulate any clear vision of what it is they are actually for. From the perspective of the government in England, universities are now just one form of provider of teacher education … one amongst a growing number.

### *Story 2: Entrepreneurialism, differentiation and degrees of freedom*

At the same time as successive governments have found it ever easier to define and manage the detail of teacher education in our universities, the new spirit of entrepreneurialism has helped many of those same departments and faculties of education develop themselves in different ways. As we will see in Chapter 9, the research assessment exercise (RAE/REF) has encouraged the majority of institutions to develop and strengthen their research profiles. Even in our newest universities, the institutional imperative for differentiation, for finding a place in the higher education market, has encouraged vice chancellors and deans to look for opportunities for developing a research profile in education for the first time.

But the enterprise university has also affected teaching as well as research. As we saw in Chapter 4, several case study institutions had, in recent years, developed new undergraduate courses in educational studies as a way of responding to increasing uncertainties about the BEd. As one dean explained very clearly:

> The educational-studies programme was started because of the BA (Ed) disappearing. We needed work for the BA (Ed) staff to do, so this programme was created to create jobs for the BA (Ed) staff, but it has gone very well and recruits about one hundred students a year.

In addition, all of the case study institutions visited now had growing numbers of international students. Those numbers were particularly strong in the older universities with more to sell in terms of positional advantage for their graduates, but even the most recently created universities recognised the importance of attracting international students. One recent university put huge amounts of effort into recruiting just four or five PGCE students from Canada each year; though small in number, these students were seen as very important for the income and status that they generated within the institution. At the other extreme, the London Institute of Education reported 163 full-time and 163 part-time students registered in its various master's degree programmes.

Growing numbers of departments and faculties have also begun exploring different markets for their teaching. Seven of the ten institutions visited offered teaching programmes overseas. While some of this activity was focused on capacity building in developing countries, the majority was more directly entrepreneurial. One Russell Group university, for example, had a well-established EdD programme that it had taught overseas for many years. Another university, an ex-polytechnic, offered its master's programmes in three different European locations. As the course leader explained:

> Well, it's very interesting. Practice-based research is a strong element of the programme, which is linked, really, to public-service professions. So, we've basically got lots of teachers, but we've also got nurses, social workers, police officers, people involved in prison service, a whole range of different people … But it's also got an international dimension, so UK work is all internationally focused in the sense that there's a lot of reference to different welfare systems, different comparative work, different research … But we also have cohorts in Germany, in Sweden and Holland. And they submit – one of our strengths but also one of our difficulties is that they can either submit in German or English and we're thinking of allowing Swedish and Dutch as well.

International teaching of this sort was seen to have many advantages in the current climate. As one particularly entrepreneurial dean explained:

> We therefore need more international activity of the sort we already are in China – we have a decent base out there, with a strong programme – that is good for research-income generation and good experience for colleagues and is stimulating new forms of research. We are close to having three or four programmes like that – one in Kazakhstan, one in China. If we get that balance right, even if things are rocked heavily here at home by the government, that will stabilise things. And if we can keep that drive forward, we can continue appointing people who are already research-active and successful.

The evidence from these ten universities is that many education departments and faculties are now experiencing new entrepreneurial freedoms, freedoms to run different sorts of courses (giving staff opportunities to teach courses other than those defined by government) and freedoms to recruit different types of staff (those with academic rather than primarily professional 'capital' and, therefore, potentially greater success in the forthcoming REF). As Clark (1998) noted in his study of five European universities, one of the greatest attractions of this sort of entrepreneurialism is that it provides universities with opportunities for greater freedom from outside control.

But at the same time, it is clear that that entrepreneurialism does come at a price; that price is that it has contributed to increased differentiation both within and between universities. Inside institutions, there has been a growing move to marginalise and even casualise those whose primary work is in teacher education. Increasingly, *core* staff are expected to contribute to both teacher education and one of the many other functions – research, other forms of teaching – that are part of the mixed economy of modern-day departments and faculties of education. Again, as we saw in Chapter 4, many of the institutions visited employed large numbers of part-time and casual staff; in most cases the casualised staff was employed to make key contributions to initial teacher education programmes. Some universities, it would seem, have found it easier to lower their expectations for research and scholarship from those whose main task is initial teacher education. Rather than seeing research and scholarship as something that must be fostered amongst *all* academic staff, too often, it seems, tenured posts are now reserved for those who already have a research track record or who are willing and able to teach higher-degree programmes, both in the UK and overseas. Therefore, entrepreneurialism may be one way for contemporary deans of education the keep the ship afloat; but too often, I would suggest, it has had the negative consequence of devaluing and deprofessionalszing those involved in what is still core business in education: initial teacher education.

And, finally, it is also important to note that the marketisation of higher education also serves to make ever more real differences between institutions. As is clear from the numbers of international students registered at the ten case study universities (See Appendix, Tables 3, 4 and 5), it is established institutions – and particularly those in the elite Russell Group – that are best able to offer international students positional advantage by taking their courses; it is they who are best placed to exploit this new market openness. That, in turn, means that they are more likely to have opportunities to recruit a broader range of staff and, in turn, they are better placed to compete for research funding. Those institutions that are primarily oriented to local or regional markets and that are primarily concerned with access for less advantaged British students have far less to sell in the international market. In the enterprise university, the Matthew Principle reigns supreme.

To return to the opening of this chapter, the driving force for change in many aspects of society over the past 30 years has been the rise of globalisation, a globalisation that has been imagined as demanding the pursuit of neo-liberal policies in virtually all aspects of public life. In higher education it is these policies that have given birth to the enterprise university, a new kind of cash-strapped university that fully understands the need to respond to and to exploit changing markets in teaching, in research and in other forms of trading. This is the university world that education as a discipline finally and fully entered from 1992 onwards. This is the university that has become highly responsive to government demands in relation to its core teaching programmes. This is the university that has exploited new opportunities for teaching and research both in the UK and increasingly internationally. If they are to survive and thrive, then departments and faculties of education, like their parent institutions, need to be entrepreneurial, fleet of foot, responding to the demands and opportunities they face.

But as we will see in the next two chapters, globalisation has also had a direct impact on the discipline of education in other ways too – both in relation to national policy on teacher education, which we examine in Chapter 8 and in relation to the management of research, which we consider in Chapter 9. It is the combination of these different forces on universities, on teaching and on research that helps to make the discipline of education what it is today.

# 8 Neo-liberalism and its impact on teacher education[1]

## Introduction

As we saw in the previous chapter, today's universities are very different institutions from those of a generation ago. Globalisation, interpreted as necessitating neo-liberal policies, has had a major impact on them. Universities in the UK, as in many parts of the world, now come in many different shapes and sizes; they have different histories, different missions, different types of student intake, different expectations of and opportunities for their staff. They are also highly differentiated within themselves; so much so that finding a common purpose, a common voice (beyond that provided by the ubiquitous graphic designer), saying what they are actually *for* is an increasingly difficult task.

What the previous chapter also showed was that what our contemporary universities *do* all have in common is that they are now nearly all highly entrepreneurial institutions. The fact that there has been less and less money to pay for their massive expansion has forced them to become entrepreneurial in seeking out new opportunities for teaching and for research. It has also forced them – and this is particularly important for an understanding of contemporary departments of faculties of education – to become much more market-sensitive. Successful university managers today must be fleet of foot, rapidly able to adapt their work to the demands of their funders. As we will see in this and the next chapter, this market sensitivity means that universities in general – and their departments and faculties of education in particular – are increasingly shaped by outside forces. Through their entrepreneurial market sensitivity, universities have lost much of their autonomy. Those not able to adapt quickly to the changing demands of their funders – especially where that is the government – are unlikely to thrive.

But beyond mere entrepreneurialism, what are the externally driven policies that now shape the discipline of education? Clearly, there are many, but in this and the next chapter, we examine two that have been particularly powerful. In Chapter 9 we examine the way in which research funding and especially research assessment (RAE/REF) has come to influence the day-to-day realities of life in UK's departments and faculties of education. This chapter takes a more macro perceptive. It focuses on policy in professional education – initial teacher education and continuing professional development (CPD). This is because professional education has been and remains one of the key elements in the economy of most departments and faculties of education and because, particularly in England, successive governments have taken a highly interventionist approach in this arena. These two chapters are therefore quite different in focus; one looks at national policy, the other at institutional practice. Therefore, they do not aspire to provide a complete overview of the forces that currently shape the discipline of education in the modern enterprise university. And, as we will see, sometimes those forces work in complementary ways; sometimes they are in tension. And, of course, it also has to be acknowledged that there are many other forces that shape the discipline as well: the economy and institutional histories to name but two.

Probably to the irritation of some readers, the largest part of this chapter focuses on England. This is because over the past 15 years, despite changes in the size of each system, the aims, aspirations and structures of teacher education in Scotland, Wales and Northern Ireland have been relatively stable. But in England teacher education has been at the epicentre of national educational policy, going through reform after reform; each one of those reforms has had major implications for the discipline of education in modern universities. In the second part of the chapter, I do turn to the rest of the UK – and particularly to Scotland – to document the very different ways in which neo-liberal policies have affected those countries. What these contrasts remind us is that there is nothing inevitable in the way in which globalisation in general or neo-liberal policies in particular impact on national contexts. While there may be a general direction of travel across the UK as a whole, different histories, different institutional structures and different political and educational cultures mean that those policies mean different things in different parts of the UK.

## Neo-liberalism, New Labour and the reform of teacher education in England

What is interesting in the English reforms that are the focus of this section is that on the surface, the three consecutive New Labour administrations and the current Coalition have pursued policies that have much in common. They have all deliberately challenged university autonomy in pursuing what Hoyle, with considerable prescience, described back in 1982 as 'the turn to the practical' (Hoyle, 1982). They have also justified the need for reform in relation to a common problem: how to raise achievement for all in order to meet challenges of globalisation. But, as we will see, the ways in which New Labour and the current Coalition have gone about that task have been very different. Both administrations can be seen to have imagined a necessary response to globalisation in neo-liberal terms. That, too, is something they have in common. But, as I will try and show, their interpretation of neo-liberalism has been somewhat different. They have therefore imagined very different things for the teaching profession; this, in turn, has had major consequences for the policies they have imposed on universities in relation to professional education.

### *New Labour and the 'modernization' of education*

In its early years in office, there was considerable debate as to whether or not New Labour 's Third Way policies represented a continuation or even an extension of what the previous Conservative administrations had begun (Power and Whitty, 1999; Mahony and Hextall, 2000). The reason that there was such debate, I would suggest, is because there was both continuity and change. There was a new vision or at the very least a new rhetoric, but to a significant degree, that was assembled by building on much that the Conservatives achieved. As Newman (2001: 46) stated at the time:

> The Third Way attempted to forge a new political settlement by drawing selectively on fragments and components of the old and reconfiguring these through the prisms of a modernized economy, a modern public service and modern people.

Modernisation, as Newman stressed, became *the* core concept for New Labour; it was seen as essential because of the massive changes overtaking society.

> Modernization is situated in a number of structural forces – globalization, competition and meritocracy – that are collapsed into a single unifying theme. Globalization occupies a special place at the core of these series of narratives that construct an imperative to change.
>
> (Newman, 2001: 48)

The sociologist Anthony Giddens, who was profoundly influential in the thinking behind the New Labour project, made a similar point when he stated that the primary purpose of Third Way politics was to restructure social democratic doctrines 'to respond to the twin revolutions of globalization and the knowledge economy' (2000: 162).

And in that modernisation project, education was being seen as crucial significance and remained so throughout the whole New Labour period (1997–2010). It was a national campaign, spoken about on many occasions with passion and commitment.

But why was educational reform so important for New Labour? The reasons are not hard to find. As Tony Blair himself said in his introduction to the Green Paper *The Learning Age*, 'Education is the best economic policy we have' (DfEE, 1998a). In other words, education under New Labour moved from being simply a *social* policy to being a *social* and an *economic* policy at the same time. In a world of intense competition between nations, as Lauder *et al.* (2007) have argued, education increasingly plays a key role. National prosperity, social justice and social cohesion are all seen to rest on the shoulders of education, on the creation of a highly skilled workforce with the knowledge, enterprise and insights required to attract the global supply of high-skilled, high-waged employment.

Because education was so important for New Labour, like the rest of the public sector, it had to be modernised – harnessed to the needs of the modern state. But how was that modernisation to be achieved? New Labour's approach to public-service reform had many points of continuity with the previous Conservative regimes. In particular, there was a continued focus on market mechanisms and the forms of new managerialism associated with them. The neo-liberal critique of the public sector was accepted as largely correct and there was a new realism about the necessity of markets. In the words of Giddens (2000: 164), 'There is no known alternative to the market economy any longer'. Labour therefore retained an emphasis on competition as a lever both for ensuring greater efficiency and quality in the delivery of services and as a means of securing innovation. It also continued with the forms of new managerialism developed under the Conservatives that were seen as necessary for the maintenance of such markets, though new managerialism was now presented as an entirely natural, rational and common-sense response to inevitable forces beyond the control of any individual state (Newman, 2001; Hughes, 2003). As a consequence, New Labour reinforced many of the core principles of previous Conservative government's neo-liberal reforms in education. Where it differed, however, was its view that, taken alone, markets would not achieve all that was needed. Again, as Giddens stated, 'Modernizing social democrats are not believers in laissez-faire. There has to be a newly defined role for an *active state*, which must continue to pursue social programmes' (Giddens, 2000: 7; emphasis added).

It is this notion of a market-based approach to the management of the public sector, combined with strong government intervention that characterised much of the New Labour project. As Robertson (2007) notes, the new direction in policy was not a rejection of the broad trajectory of neo-liberal economic policy, but rather its deepening and widening. Robertson quotes Joseph Stiglitz (Stiglitz, 2002), chief economist at the World Bank at the time who emphasised that society has broader objectives than merely the economic – they include better living standards, better health, sustainable development and more equitable development – and, most particularly, better education. In this new post-Washington Consensus, all of these different areas of social policy were important; all of them needed to be brought into the sphere of neo-liberal policy reform.

## *Modernising the teaching profession*

If Labour's plans for the modernisation of education were to be achieved, then the teaching profession – and behind that, teacher education – were going to be of key importance. Teachers themselves had to sign up to the government's national objectives; they, too, had to be modernised. As Tony Blair himself said:

> I have always said that education is this government's top priority. The teaching profession is critical to our mission … this Green Paper sets out the governments' proposals to improve the teaching profession … (It represents)

> the most fundamental reform of the teaching profession since state education began.
>
> (Tony Blair in DfEE, 1998b: 5)

Throughout the New Labour period, the aspiration to reform the teaching profession was a remarkably consistent one. The aim, set out originally in its Green Paper (DfEE, 1998a) just one year after New Labour came to office, was to change the ground rules of what teacher professionalism actually meant in order to harness that professionalism closely to the government's own educational reform agenda.

For a government bent on fundamental, centrally driven educational reforms, there were a number of problems with the teaching profession, the most pressing of which was teachers' perceived lack of accountability. Even before he came into government, Tony Blair was explicitly invoking an earlier Labour prime minister, Jim Callaghan (Blair, 1996), to argue the need for teachers to be far more accountable to their schools, their parents and communities and, above all, to the government. And if that meant challenging traditional notions of individual professional autonomy, then so be it.

From the very start, therefore, New Labour was confident that what was needed was a new professionalism relevant to the twenty-first century. That was the bold vision announced in the original Green Paper of 1998 and that vision remained remarkably consistent throughout the New Labour administration. Significantly, this new professionalism set its face against the notion of individual autonomy amongst teachers. As it stated clearly: 'The time has long gone when isolated, unaccountable professionals made curriculum and pedagogical decisions alone without reference to the outside world' (DfEE, 1998a: para. 13). Instead, it argued that modern teachers needed to accept accountability; take personal and collective responsibility for improving their skills and subject knowledge; seek to base decisions on evidence of what works in schools in this country and internationally; work in partnership with other staff in schools; and to welcome the contribution that parents, business and others outside schools can make to its success.

Being professional, from this point of view, was not something that could be achieved by the individual teacher; it was not based on the traditional vision of a professional, someone with *individual* knowledge, *individual* autonomy and *individual* moral responsibility (Hoyle and John, 1995). Instead, teachers needed to sign up to accepting a more collectivised, a more accountable and, in short, a more externally managed vision of their own professional expertise.

In reality, the aims of the Green Paper took over a dozen years to achieve and the policy went through a number of different phases, each of which had different implications for the role of universities in professional education.

### *Seeking the 'new professionalism': phase one*

As I have already indicated in Chapter 3, by the end of their period in office, previous Conservative administrations had developed a system of initial teacher education that was highly centralised and highly responsive to policy change. Market-sensitive, financially dependent universities showed themselves as only too keen to respond to the changing demands of the TTA/TDA and Ofsted. What the government and particularly the TTA/TDA had wanted in initial teacher education was a common system with common standards and procedures no matter where or by whom the training was provided. By the end of the 1990s, they had largely achieved it.

It is important to recognise that in terms of governance, the instincts of the previous Conservative government and New Labour were similar. Throughout their period of office, New Labour insisted on the maintenance of a competitive market in teacher education; as a result, they continued to encourage competition with universities, the main 'providers'. Schemes run by schools themselves (School Centred Initial Teacher Training – SCITT schemes) were encouraged despite their consistently low ratings by Ofsted and new routes into teaching were developed with the Graduate Teacher Programme (GTP) (an employment-based route, theoretically for older entrants), Teach First (another employment-based route for high-flying new graduates wishing to experience teaching for a year or two) and the flexible PGCE (a teacher education programme that could be taken on a flexible part-time basis). Inspection and the publication of results also remained core parts of the management strategy. Following Giddens' first line of argument that 'there is no alternative to markets', a highly competitive market was maintained as the first and unchallengeable principle of management of the sector. However, by the end of the 1990s, when a command economy had been achieved, Giddens' second principle – direct intervention by an active state – became possible. In this context, that meant defining the content of teacher education itself.

Until 1996 the content of teacher education had been only broadly prescribed. During the middle 1990s in particular, the most important influence was the market to which students were increasingly exposed, i.e. practice in schools. In sharp contrast, policies in the late 1990s sought to exploit the new control of the system to begin specifying the content of professional education in much more detail.

Two strategies evolved. The first was the issuing of a new circular, *Circular 10/97* (DfEE, 1997), which transformed the previously specified competencies into more elaborate standards. The second was the development of an 85-page national curriculum for initial teacher education, specifying in very great detail the content that had to be covered by trainee teachers in English, mathematics, science and information and communication technology (ICT). The English curriculum, in particular, was controversial with its insistence on whole-class teaching and the detailed coverage of the teaching of reading through phonics. But because courses were subject to high-stakes inspection by Ofsted, universities had little choice but to follow this new, externally defined curriculum. In the core areas that the national curriculum covered, it was now the government that had a key say in what new teachers learned in their courses; what they learned about *how* to teach as well as *what* to teach.

### *Seeking the new professionalism: phase two*

In reality, the national curriculum for initial teacher education, with its controversial specification of how to teach core subjects, was short-lived. After five years in office, the Labour government issued new documentation (DfES/TTA, 2002) that abandoned the national curriculum, perhaps recognising that if the new professionalism was to be achieved, then more direct strategies of intervention across the teaching force as a whole were needed. This, I would suggest, was an important turning point and marked the beginning of a move away from seeing initial teacher education on its own as the main strategy for challenging teacher autonomy (Furlong, 2005). This, in turn, had major implications for universities and their approach to teaching on professional education courses.

Instead of focusing on initial teacher education and in an attempt to ensure that *all* schools improved year on year, the government developed what they called their 'high-challenge, high-support' strategy (DfEE, 2001). First, they set ambitious targets.

> Our education system will never be world-class unless virtually all children learn to read, write and calculate to high standards before they leave primary school. We have therefore given top priority to a national strategy to achieve this goal, setting ambitious national targets for 2002: that in English, 80 per cent and in mathematics, 75 per cent of 11-year-olds should meet the standards set for their age. These targets are staging posts on the way to even higher levels of performance.
>
> (DfEE, 2001: 1.15–16)

Then they devised a series of prescriptive strategies that involved intervening in the detailed processes of how to teach, not just for teachers in training but for all teachers. In a move that also saw a major reassessment of the importance of educational research (Blunkett, 2000), these new prescriptive strategies were to be based on research evidence of what works.

In New Labour's first term of office, these interventions focused on the development of the national Literacy and Numeracy Strategies, later developed into the National Primary Strategy (DfES, 2006). In what was an unprecedented and highly controversial move, through these strategies, for the first time, a government took it upon itself to define what effective pedagogy should be in relation to these two key aspects of primary teaching. Although not formally statutory, the fact that the Literacy and Numeracy Strategies became key components within Ofsted inspections meant that in the vast majority of schools, they were, in effect, compulsory. It was a brave headteacher who chose not to follow the detailed government 'advice' set out in these strategy documents.

In New Labour's second term of office, this approach was extended to secondary schools with the Key Stage 3 strategy. Later children's welfare came to the fore through the *Every Child Matters* agenda (DfES, 2003) and, finally, the focus was on the personalisation of learning. Over time, therefore, the New Labour government's substantive agenda changed as its policies evolved; what did not change was its aspiration to use targets and research-based prescriptive strategies in the development of more direct control of teachers' classroom practice.

And what were the implications for initial teacher education of this rather different approach to reforming teacher professionalism? Instead of a National Curriculum for initial teacher education, in 2002 (DfES/TTA, 2002) the government returned to a more general and much shorter list of standards accompanied by guidance that linked these standards to the national strategies. At the same time, it encouraged more and more providers – schools, local authorities – to enter the training field. The Graduate Teacher Programme was substantially expanded during this period, eventually reaching 18 per cent of provision by 2007. School-led initial teacher training schemes (SCITTS) continued to be encouraged despite continued questions about their quality. Training now could be provided in any number of ways. It could be provided by: schools working with a university as the accredited provider on undergraduate and postgraduate programmes; or several schools working together, with or without the involvement of a university as part of a SCITT scheme; or a school or schools working together, sometimes in partnership with a university, local authority or commercial organisation to provide an employment-based route to qualified teacher status. (TDA, 2007: 1).

As a result, the idea that universities and schools might have different perspectives and different forms of knowledge to contribute to teacher education was increasingly squeezed out. New Labour policies insisted that all providers were identical. Now that practice in schools was increasingly centrally defined, all were capable of delivering an effective training on the technical list of standards that trainee teachers needed to meet. With this move, the TTA/TDA and a growing number of providers came to see teacher education as largely unproblematic, that getting it right was a technical matter, ensuring that there were the right number of school places for training, ensuring that teachers, in whatever scheme they worked, had the time and skills they needed for mentoring (Campbell *et al.*, 2005).

This was the policy context that was still in force in England during the fieldwork carried out for this book in 2010–2011. However, as we saw in Chapter 5, the reality of practice in many universities is much richer, much more complex than this. Many university-led courses still aspire to do more than offer student teachers a narrow, technicist, professional education. They take an expansive view, encouraging their student teachers to think, to reflect, to explore relevant theory and to question dominant practices in schools. Nevertheless, as we also learned in Chapter 5, Ofsted inspections and restricted resources mean that the pressure is always there to adopt a much narrower approach, just ticking the boxes. And the fact that now a few school-led SCITT programmes, with little or no university involvement, can be rated by Ofsted just as good quality as those provided by universities demonstrates that however valuable universities may think their contribution to professional learning actually is, they are swimming against the tide; it is not formally acknowledged.

### *Seeking the new professionalism: phase three*

But that is not the end of the story. Towards the end of New Labour's period in office, it was increasingly clear that taken alone, this target-based strategy was not sufficient (Hargreaves, 2006). Despite some improvements, the hoped-for year-on-year rises in measured achievement were not fully realised. Fuelled by the post-PISA analysis and by international reports such as the OECD's *Teachers Matter* (OECD, 2005) and then by the McKinsey Report (2007), the focus to increase school achievement shifted from targets to teacher quality, a focus that gave some new opportunities for universities. As the OECD report (2005: 1) put it: 'All countries are seeking to improve their schools and to respond better to higher social and economic expectations. As the most significant and costly resource in schools, teachers are central to school-improvement efforts.

As a first response, the government began to experiment with increasing quality by the recruitment of high flyers into the profession with the establishment of the Teach First initiative (a development of Teach for America). Then, following a visit to Finland by Lord Adonis, the then schools minister, government became convinced that the answer to further raising achievement was to make teaching a master's-level profession; all teachers should have the opportunity to study for a master's degree at some stage during their careers. If teachers in Finland, which was so successful in competitive international assessments such as PISA, had this opportunity, was this not the key to success in raising teacher quality? The English Masters in Teaching and Learning (MTL) was conceived.

In headline terms at least, the MTL was to be a very different approach to raising achievement from that which went before. As a government publication said at the time:

> World-class teaching is characterised by a sophisticated understanding of effective classroom practice, highly skilled professional expertise and high quality engagement with children, young people and their parents and carers. The MTL will develop and build on these characteristics.
>
> (DCSF, 2008).

Once again, it would seem that the ordinary classroom teacher was emerging as *the* key figure in the raising of achievement; someone who was highly skilled, who had access to research-based forms of professional knowledge and who was able to deploy that knowledge in complex and uniquely different classrooms settings.

In line with this changing vision, the MTL was developed with a number of key principles in mind, principles that drew on research about the conditions for effective professional learning for teachers. The focus was to be on early professional development; it was to be largely school-based, though with strong university support. School-based work was to be supported by a coach and the whole programme was to be personalised.

The MTL therefore signalled a very different approach to professional learning form the recent past; it also reimagined a new role for universities in professional education. Did that mean, therefore, that after 12 years in office, the Labour government intended to abandon its commitment to the new professionalism? Was there to be a return to a more individualised conception of teacher professionalism? The truth is that behind the very positive headlines of the new master's degree, there were a number of very important tensions; tensions that, had it survived, would have made it hard to deliver some of its aspirations. This is because the new degree, which was intended to have a common framework across the whole of England (TDA, 2009), was written with two different voices.

On the one hand, there was a progressive commitment to make sure that the MTL was indeed tailored to individual learning needs; it was to be 'a personalized, professional-learning journey' (TDA, 2009: 12). At the same time, however, the programme had to: 'align with induction and performance-management requirements' (p. 6). Programmes, for example, *had* to include work on the national strategies for literacy and numeracy and on personalisation. Everyone also *had* to consider the role of assessment data in evaluating effective learning. Despite the avowed commitment to a 'personalized learning journey', government insisted that students on the MTL addressed nationally defined priorities.

Therefore, the aim of the MTL was not to abandon the new professionalism. Instead, the ambitious hope was that by giving teachers opportunities to research, to evaluate, to critique these national priorities for themselves, in their own classrooms, they would, over time, develop the personal commitment needed to make them effective. They needed to learn for themselves how personalisation could work in their classrooms; they needed to know for themselves how to use performance data to increase measured student achievement. Rather than abandoning the new professionalism, I would therefore suggest, the English MTL implied an ambitious new strategy for achieving it through a more personalised learning experience.

The aspiration to establish a single degree with common content and assessment procedures across the whole of England was an enormously ambitious one. It was also enormously difficult; the negotiations between regional groups of universities and the TDA were complex and protracted. My guess is that only New Labour, with its uncompromising commitment to central prescription, would have dreamt of taking on such a task. But why it was important, why universities supported the scheme despite its difficulties was that for the first time in a generation, the MTL offered a new vision for the role of universities in professional education. It recognised that, at master's level at least, they did have something important, something essentially distinctive to contribute. Whether this reformation of the teaching as a centrally defined master's-level profession could have been achieved we will never know. The Labour Party lost the election in 2010 and within a few months of coming to office, the incoming Coalition government abandoned the MTL and, indeed, the vision of the new professionalism.

### *A conclusion for New Labour*

Before moving on to the current Coalition government, it is important to reflect on New Labour's period in office in terms of the key policy drivers it put in place in relation to teacher education. Certainly, there is evidence of the government seeing teacher education as a key element in its response to the pressures of globalisation. The unrelenting focus on developing a new professionalism for teachers with greater accountability to nationally set targets was rhetorically driven by concerns to ensure the international competitiveness of the English school system. The surface story, particularly towards the end of their period in office, might have been the need to increase England's position on international league tables such as PISA. But behind that concern lay a much more powerful competitiveness that saw achievement in education as centrally implicated in global economic competition. Back to Tony Blair's mantra: education is the best economic policy we have. The search for the new professionalism and the implications this had for universities in their contribution to teacher education were centrally part of this story.

But it is also important to reflect on how that was to be achieved and the role of neo-liberal polices in that process. As we have seen, neo-liberal policies – the maintenance of a competitive market in the provision of teacher education – were of central importance to New Labour. Globalisation was consistently imagined by New Labour in neo-liberal terms. But neo-liberalism – and this marks a key difference from the current government – was not seen by New Labour as an end in itself. Markets were not expected, independently of government, to deliver the right sort of teacher education. The competitive market amongst providers of teacher education was seen under New Labour as a tool of governance. Intense competition between resource-hungry entrepreneurial providers was encouraged because it gave government the opportunity to intervene on an unprecedented scale in defining what teacher education and, indeed, what professional practice should be. It was this emphasis on centralised provision, made possible by a competitive market amongst a widening group of financially dependent providers – where universities were only one amongst many – that was the hallmark of New Labour's policies. And it is the challenge to this approach that has become the hallmark of the Coalition government that replaced them.

## The 2010 Coalition: neo-liberalism re-formed?

> This White Paper signals a radical reform of our schools. We have no choice but to be this radical if our ambition is to be world-class. The most successful countries already combine a high-status teaching profession; high levels of autonomy for schools; a comprehensive and effective accountability system; and a strong sense of aspiration for all children, whatever their background. Tweaking things at the margins is not an option.
>
> (Cameron, 2010: 4)

The UK's first Coalition government since the Second World War came to power in 2010. It is a coalition dominated by the Conservative Party, supported by the much smaller Liberal Democrat Party. Significantly, the Liberal Democrat Leader, Nick Clegg, was appointed as Deputy Prime Minister, though, in many public spheres, including education, it is Conservative policies that have held sway. Just six months after coming to power, a new White Paper – *The Importance of Teaching* (DfE, 2010) – was published, signalling a radical new agenda for schools and for teacher education. Once again, the role of universities in teacher education was set to change.

One of the distinctive features of New Labour education policy was that in relation to teacher education, it was so straightforward, so linear. The biggest challenge to our economy was globalisation and education was central to responding to that challenge. In order to do that, education had to be re-modelled on neo-liberal lines. The teaching profession therefore had to be reformed; a new professionalism had to be developed to ensure that teachers would take on government-defined strategies and targets. Universities and other providers of teacher education were required to deliver teachers willing and able to embrace this centrally defined, target-driven culture.

What is very different about the Coalition government is that its analysis of what is wrong with the English educational system, the challenges it faces, is more complex, more multifaceted. As Bochel notes, social policy under the Coalition is complex and dynamic (Bochel, 2011). However, as we will see, the government's answers to these problems are largely one-dimensional; they primarily put their faith in what the market can deliver.

Coalition discourse about education is built on at least four core concerns. The first, like New Labour before them, focuses on global competitiveness. Again, as the prime minister and deputy prime minister put it:

> So much of the education debate in this country is backward-looking. Have standards fallen? Have exams got easier? These debates will continue but what really matters is how we're doing compared with our international competitors. That is what will define our economic growth and our country's future. The truth is, at the moment we are standing still while others race past.
>
> (DfE, 2010).

However, despite regular comparisons to our global competitors, few, if any, policies seem directly focused specifically in this direction. As we will see below, for the Coalition, the primary purpose of education is profoundly *not* utilitarian; in marked contrast to New Labour, education is not directly part of economic policy. Rather, education is about the preservation of our cultural heritage; it returns to the Arnoldian tradition of exposing young people to the best that has been thought and said. So, beyond the general urging to be 'amongst the best in the world', there is very little appetite to adapt the educational system to the needs of a twenty-first-century global economy or, indeed, any economy.

The second concern, often spoken about with force and passion, is inequality. Again and again since coming to office, ministers and senior officials have spoken of the failures of our current system to deliver equality of outcomes. As Michael Gove, Secretary of State for Education, put it:

> no country that wishes to be considered world-class can afford to allow children from poorer families to fail as a matter of course. For far too long we have tolerated the *moral outrage* of an accepted correlation between wealth and achievement at school; the *soft bigotry* of low expectations…
>
> (DfE, 2010, emphasis added)

However, despite the passion, to date there has only been one policy directly focused on addressing inequality and that is the so-called pupil premium: additional school funding for students from poorer backgrounds. But because of overall cuts in school budgets as a result of the recession, the vast majority of schools – even those with large numbers of disadvantaged students – are facing substantial cuts in their budgets rather than rises (BBC, 2010). Therefore, if a reduction in inequality is to be achieved, it will be so done as an outcome of other strategies aimed at more general educational improvement.

In sharp contrast, there has been a great deal of activity in relation to a third dimension of their policy discourse, one that has strong links with Margaret Thatcher's administration in the 1980s. This has been the need to return to more traditional neo-conservative notions of knowledge, where schooling is fundamentally concerned with the maintenance and transmission of an agreed cultural heritage.

As Nick Gibb, the Minister for Schools put it: 'I believe strongly that the teaching of knowledge – the passing on from one generation to the next – is the fundamental purpose of education' (Gibb, 2010a).

Or as the secretary of state for education, Michael Gove, put more colourfully in a recent speech to Cambridge University:

> We may not all be able to inherit good looks or great houses, but all of us are heir to the amazing intellectual achievements of our ancestors. We can all marvel at the genius of Pythagoras or Wagner, share in the brilliance of Shakespeare or Newton, delve deeper into the mysteries of human nature through Balzac or Pinker *by taking the trouble to be educated.*
>
> (Gove, 2011, emphasis added)

Policies designed to achieve these ends include the development of the new English Baccalaureate – not a qualification in itself but a performance measure of how many 16-year-olds achieve five higher-level GCSE passes in traditional school subjects: English, mathematics, science, modern foreign languages and either geography or history. And in an extension of such thinking, in 2012 it was firstly announced that some 3,000 'pseudo academic vocational qualifications' would be downgraded, no longer eligible for inclusion in school league tables

(Guardian, 2012) and then that GCSEs themselves might be scrapped with a return to more traditionally academic 'O' levels (Telegraph, 2012a).

At the same time, the National Curriculum is being reformed in order to focus on 'the essential knowledge and understanding that all children should acquire' (DfE, 2011a: para. 12). All of these measures are intended fundamentally to reshape the content of schooling on narrower, more traditional lines. Indeed, many secondary schools, aware of the implications of the English Baccalaureate, have already started to reduce the numbers of teachers they want to employ in other subjects; for example, religious education, citizenship education and a whole range of vocational subjects that are no longer part of the cannon. This, in turn, is having major consequences for universities that prepare such teachers.

A final concern and one that is linked to their most radical proposals, is the over bureaucratisation of day-to-day life in schools. Instead of trying to prescribe the detail of teaching and school management from the centre, the Coalition government has talked about the importance of devolving as much power as possible to the front line, though retaining high levels of accountability at the same time. Their stated aim is to 'cut away unnecessary duties, processes, guidance and requirements so that schools are free to focus on doing what is right for the children and young people in their care' (DfE, 2010).

Interestingly, the principles of reform in the structure and governance of education are common across much of the public sector, including health and social welfare. In 2011 the Coalition published a White Paper (*Open Public Services*, Cabinet Office, 2011) that set out its view on how to achieve better public services. At the heart of the White Paper are five principles:

- Greater choice wherever possible
- Decentralisation to the 'lowest appropriate level'
- Diversity of provision by opening up public services to for-profit and not-for-profit providers
- Fairness and, in particular, fair access
- Accountability, with an emphasis on local democratic accountability (Centre for Market and Public Organisation, 2011).

In short, the answer to improving the quality of education – for greater equality, for global competitiveness – is the same answer as it is in health or social welfare. It involves a rolling back of the state and establishing a diversified market of provision underpinned by rigorous but simple accountability structures. Like New Labour, neo-liberalism, the pursuit of markets, is central to government thinking. But now, rather than being linked *directly* to the challenges of globalisation, rather than being the means whereby government can impose its will in a centralised way, neo-liberalism is understood in more traditional terms. It is being presented as the key to a new localism: the aim is to abolish centralised bureaucracies and allow a wide variety of different agencies to deliver state services.

This is the 'Big Society'; this is David Cameron's big idea (Cameron, 2010) and it is an idea that is central to educational reform – the reform of schools and, linked to that, the reform of teacher education.

Unlike under Margaret Thatcher then, public services, especially health and education, are important. In this there is continuity with New Labour. But it is a revitalised public sector based on the principles of Open Public Service that will deliver what is needed. In education it is these principles that will deliver the raised levels of achievement needed to ensure global competitiveness; they will also ensure greater equality of achievement, even for the most disadvantaged sectors of society.

And, of course, underlying these different political aspirations is the expressed need to deal with the consequences of the banking crisis of 2008. Shrinking the state, moving more services and reduced services away from government go hand in hand with saving money. In these circumstances rolling back the state is both financially and morally justifiable for the future health of the nation.

In higher education these ideas have already found expression in the end to public subsidy of undergraduate teaching except in subjects where there is a perceived direct link to the economy: science, technology, engineering and mathematics (the STEM subjects). From now on students will have to pay the full market rate for their university education through a complex programme of loans. And in order to increase competition, private universities are expected to grow in number. In the schools sector these same principles underpin a commitment to the establishment of publicly funded Free Schools, where, as in Sweden (Allen, 2010), parents and other not-for-profit groups can now apply to establish a state-funded independent school. And all existing schools can now apply to be established as an academy so that they are entirely independent of their local authority.

What are the implications of these different lines of argument for teacher education and particularly for the role of universities?

## *The Coalition and teacher education*

> For too long left-wing training colleges have imbued teachers with useless teaching theories that don't work and actively damage children's education.
>
> (Unattributed government source, Telegraph, 2012b)

Neo-conservative thinking on teacher education policy was evident from the start. Nick Gibb, Minister for Schools, for example, was reported as saying to his civil servants just a few days after coming into office: 'I would rather have a graduate from Oxbridge without a PGCE teaching in a school than a physics graduate from one of the rubbish universities with a PGCE' (Gibb, 2010b). Less confrontational but equally significant was Michael Gove's announcement that one of his flagship policies – the development of Free Schools, led by parents and others as independent state-funded schools – would not be required to employ qualified teachers. Such schools, he suggested, need to be free to employ inspirational teachers from wherever they can find them. For the secretary of state, teaching, it would seem, is a combination of inspiration and a craft.

> Teaching is a craft and it is best learnt as an apprentice observing a master craftsman or -woman. Watching others and being rigorously observed yourself as you develop is the best route to acquiring mastery in the classroom.
>
> (Gove, 2010)

And these ideas of personal inspiration and teaching as a craft have found expression in two complementary policies. The first has been the expansion of Teach First, the scheme initially devised by New Labour to attract high-flying new graduates into teaching. And a new and similar scheme has also been announced – Teach Next – a new entry route for career changers, including men and women returning from the Armed Services. Even with expansion, the numbers on these programmes are likely to be small, but the government's very public commitment to them is symbolically significant.

In order to attract the most academically able, the government is also using the national bursary scheme for teachers in training in a more focused way. Graduates with excellent degree results in shortage subjects (physics, mathematics, chemistry) can now receive a bursary of up to £20,000 during their training year; however, those with less than a 2.1 degree will have to cover the full cost of their training themselves. And in line with the government's neo-conservative principles, no bursaries will be provided for those training to teach in a whole variety of social sciences or vocational courses, however good their degrees. Primary courses that encourage specialist rather than generalist teaching will also be encouraged. Again, there are important implications for the shaping of university-based provision here.

But the government's most radical and far-reaching proposals take their inspiration from its neo-liberal commitments through the development of School Direct training. The 2010 White Paper recognises that over the past 20 years, teacher education in England has already become overwhelmingly practically oriented. But in sharp contrast to teacher education in some of the most successful school systems (Finland, Singapore, Korea, Shanghai), it argues that this move has not gone far enough.

> Too little teacher training takes place on the job and too much professional development involves compliance with bureaucratic initiatives rather than working with other teachers to develop effective practice.
>
> (DfE, 2010: 19)

Under the School Direct model, schools themselves will increasingly be in the driver's seat. Firstly, a school will apply to offer a training place; if approved, it can advertise the place, select the trainee and then choose an accredited teacher education provider to work with to help them in providing the training. Funding will flow from the provider to the school to cover the costs of the training they contribute. However, because schools will be able to choose which provider to work with (it will be a free market of public and private universities or newly designated Teaching Schools), they will, in effect, be able to dictate how much training they wish to purchase and how much they will provide themselves. Initially beginning with 900 places in 2012–2013, it is anticipated that the scheme will expand rapidly in the coming years (Gove, 2012).

There are two other dimensions to the policy. Firstly, in direct competition with universities, individual schools or chains of academies will themselves be encouraged to become accredited providers of initial and in-service training that other schools can purchase from them. And in a parallel move that will profoundly alter the role of universities in post-compulsory education and training, all FE colleges will be able to apply to be accredited trainers for their own staff. Secondly, these initiatives are accompanied by a new and slimmed-down list of teachers' standards, intended to provide a framework of clearly defined minimum standards against which both trainees and experienced teachers' performances can be judged. The 150 pages or so of guidance that accompanied the previous standards has been removed so that providers of teacher training have the flexibility to design the programmes that best meet the needs of their schools.

Here, then, is the very essence of the Coalition government's neo-liberal inspired new localism, a diversity of public and private competitive providers with minimum but flexible standards that can be adapted to local need. And the consequences for the university sector? They could well be dramatic. As the Secretary of State for Education, Michael Gove put it in June 2012:

> The cumulative impact of these changes on initial teacher training will be revolutionary. By the end of this parliament, well over half of all training places will be delivered by schools, whether through direct provision; Teach First; School Direct; or our new employment-based route. Most of the rest will be doing PGCE courses in existing providers rated outstanding. The weakest providers will no longer be in business. They will have been de-accredited following Ofsted inspections or unable to persuade schools to commission support from them.

In England the shape of teacher education and, therefore, of the university-based discipline of education could be fundamentally different in five years' time. As these market-based reforms take hold, it is now clear that size of the sector will certainly become much smaller.

## Teacher education reform in the rest of the UK?

Finally, one must ask: what of the other UK countries after devolution? Were they involved in a similar maelstrom of reform? How have they responded to the pressures of globalisation that appeared to be driving so much of the agenda in England? While it would seem that all four countries are concerned about their

PISA results and while all four countries have taken on board OECD (2005) and McKinsey (2007, 2010) messages about the importance of raising teacher quality as the key to raising achievement, the ways in which each country has gone about this task is somewhat different. Certainly, there has been change in Scotland, Northern Ireland and Wales in the post-devolutionary period, but until recently, most of that was change in the structure of provision rather than in the nature of the courses that were offered. So, for example, in Scotland, following the Sutherland Report (Sutherland, 1997), all of the former teachers colleges were amalgamated into just seven research-led universities. In addition, in recent years there have been major fluctuations in student numbers; first, a sudden increase in the early and mid-2000s, then a dramatic cutback of 40 per cent in 2010 (Scottish Funding Council, 2010). The result has been that some schools of education suffered losses of academic staff of up to 30 per cent.

Wales has experienced similar changes. Following the *Review of ITT Provision in Wales* (Furlong *et al.*, 2006), the Welsh Assembly Government authorised a reduction in overall primary numbers by up to 50 per cent and secondary by up to 25 percent. They also agreed to the rationalisation of provision into three collaborative 'university centres for initial teacher education', covering different parts of the country. Launched in 2011, each of the new centres involves two universities working together on a joint programme of courses. In Northern Ireland there has, to date, been less dramatic change in terms of numbers, though it is clear that reform is on the way. Indeed, the Minister for Education and Employment (Farry, 2011) recently stated that he believed that 'the current system of teacher training is neither affordable nor sustainable'. Amalgamations of the formerly independent and religiously based teachers colleges into Queens University have been proposed but are currently on hold, mired in sectarian division. Integration, though, is the preferred direction of travel advocated by the current government.

Institutional change is therefore a common experience across all three countries, but despite that, the basic model of teacher education has, until now, remained largely the same since devolution. Wales, although now granted autonomy, has done little in this field to assert its independence; indeed, the Furlong Review (Furlong *et al.*, 2006) was specifically disbarred from raising questions about the structure and content of courses. As a result, initial teacher education in Wales is still largely wedded to the legacy of policies devised in the 1990s by Margaret Thatcher's government. There are, though, signs of significant change for qualified teachers with the recent announcement of a master's degree that will be available for all newly qualified teachers (Welsh Government, 2012).

Scotland and Northern Ireland, in contrast to England and Wales, have managed to retain their commitment to a more traditional university-led model of initial teacher education. There has been little experimentation with alternative employment-based routes into teaching and the four-year undergraduate route into teaching remains strong, attracting very high quality entrants. And while standards or competencies have been introduced in both Scotland and Northern Ireland, they are very different from those of England in that they both stress the intellectual grasp and theoretical understandings that teachers are expected to demonstrate, rather than simply practical skills. Scotland has also introduced guaranteed placements for newly qualified teachers and a school-based master's-level qualification – the Chartered Teacher Scheme – for more senior staff.

The recent Donaldson Report (Donaldson, 2011) confirms Scotland's different approach. As Menter and Hulme (2012) note, it extols a need for extended professionalism (p. 10), enhanced professionalism (p. 14), redefined professionalism (p. 19), a reinvigoration of professionalism and a reconceptualisation of teacher education to support this (p. 15). In marked contrast to the approach adopted in England, Donaldson asserts, 'Scotland's universities are central to building the kind of twenty-first-century profession which this Report believes to be necessary' (2011: 104).

But as was noted in Chapter 4, Donaldson also argues that in order to make the best use of the university system, the undergraduate route into teaching needs fundamental reform. One of the key weaknesses of the current BEd degree, Donaldson argues, is that its narrow professional focus can lead to an overemphasis on technical and craft skills at the expense of broader and more academically challenging areas of study. He therefore recommends that these new degrees should involve staff and departments beyond those in schools of education. If carried through, this recommendation will have further major implications for the staffing structure and perhaps even the viability of some Scottish schools of education.

At one level, then, all very different from the policies pursued in England. But in the end, how different is it? Does the Scottish and Northern Irish experience amount to a fundamental rejection of neo-liberal policies in education? In their research comparing Scottish and English policies on teacher education, Menter *et al.* (2006) conclude that despite very important differences between two countries, the fundamental direction of travel is broadly similar. In Scotland, as in England, teacher education has been taken under the umbrella of national education policy; it is now centrally part of the drive to raise competitive standards in schools. To that end, what teachers should know and do has been defined, if more broadly than in England. Differences between Scotland and England, they suggest, would therefore 'seem only to reflect different gradations of neo-liberal influence' (p. 282) rather than fundamental differences.

Interestingly, what these differences highlight is the lack of determinacy of globalisation in relation to specific policies. Such diversity brings us back to Rizvi and Lingard (2009) and their observation that globalisation does not, of necessity, demand the pursuit of neo-liberal policies however strong such ideas are amongst our national policymakers. Neo-liberalism is simply part of the dominant social imaginary of globalisation. And we have learned that neo-liberalism itself does not involve a static group of set policies. As we have seen in relation to England, interpretations of neo-liberalism have changed over time. And as the case of Scotland demonstrates, neo-liberalism can work hand in hand with policies and traditions that perhaps on the surface seem to point in a different direction.

## Conclusion

So, what has been the impact of these neo-liberal teacher education policies on the discipline of education over the past 30 years? Obviously, government funded teacher education is not the only factor that shapes the discipline; there is research and many other forms of teaching as well, but for the most part, these have been less directly exposed to changing government ambitions. It is because professional education is so central to the economy of most departments and faculties that its influence on the field as a whole is so profound.

One thing that has changed in England and Wales, though much less so in Scotland and Northern Ireland, is the nature of knowledge in professional programmes. Far from the vision of personal, liberal education put forward in the Robbins Report (Robbins, 1963), most professional courses in England and Wales are now highly practical affairs, based around nationally defined professional standards. Those standards, together with the regular high stakes inspection of courses by Ofsted in England and Estyn in Wales, mean that all courses now need to be able to account for themselves in technical rationalist terms. In reality, of course, not all courses or individual lecturers confine themselves to technical rationalist objectives. There are many examples, most famously the Oxford Internship Scheme (Benton, 1990), but many others as well, where university lecturers continue to insist on what is expected in Scotland and Northern Ireland, on what Cochran-Smith (2008) calls an 'expansive rather than narrow notion of practice', where there is an insistence on the discussion of ends rather than simply means. But that does not mean that there is not still a relentless pressure in a different direction.

But there are two other important consequences in England and Wales as well, in many ways even more profound. The first has been the impact on the staff recruited into university departments and faculties of education in recent decades. With the constant pressure to deliver teacher education programmes that are highly practically oriented, there has been strong incentive for managers to recruit staff who themselves have primarily professional rather than academic capital. They are recruited mainly for their strong experience in schools or colleges rather than because they have research experience or higher degrees. Moreover, the demands of professional courses are such that there is then often little time or, indeed incentive for such staff themselves to develop a research profile or to register for a higher degree. From the individual academic's point of view, undertaking research or studying for a higher degree is difficult because it is based on a different form of knowledge from that which they are engaged in day to day in their teaching. From an institutional perspective, there is often little incentive to ensure that all staff develop academic profiles. If it is not demanded by a government directive or by and inspection framework, then what is the incentive to pay for such a costly distraction from the real task of delivering courses?

As a result, a significant divide has grown up in many departments and faculties of education; a divide between those whose main teaching is focused on professional courses and those who have more conventional university duties, teaching academic undergraduate or higher-degree courses and undertaking research. As we saw in Chapter 4, in some universities that division has been made even more extreme by the employment of large numbers of hourly paid and casual staff on professional courses. And as we will see in the next chapter, that division has, in some institutions, been encouraged by successive rounds of the UK's research assessment processes: the RAE/REF.

Another important consequence has been the further encouragement of entrepreneurialism in departments and faculties of education. As was noted in the previous chapter, seeking out new sources of income from research and from teaching is now common across many different university faculties because it helps to balance the books. But in education there is another incentive as well. It is not only financially important, it is also important because it can provide greater freedom from government intervention. Teaching a new course in China, developing an undergraduate degree in educational studies or early childhood studies, pursuing international students, setting up a new research centre, all of these activities and many more provide important opportunities to develop forms of activity that are less controlled by government. They also allow the recruitment of more conventionally qualified academic staff who can combine teaching with research. Of course, whether this secondary economy survives the substantial raise in student fees outlined by the Coalition government remains to be seen. Nevertheless, it is this bid for freedom from government control that has been significant in the shaping of education in many of our contemporary universities. In the next chapter we turn to consider the way in which research and particularly successive research assessment exercises have also come to shape the discipline of education.

## Note

1 An earlier, shorter version of this chapter was published in *The Educational Forum* (the official journal of Kappa Delta Pi) as Furlong (2013).

# 9 Educational research in the 'enterprise university'[1]

> The nature of university research has constantly evolved, from a chilly reluctance to accept that empirical and experimental research (as opposed to speculative scholarship) had a proper place in the university in the eighteenth and early nineteenth centuries through a stable coexistence (if not harmony) between teaching and research in the twentieth-century university to the current imbalance in favour of (overmanaged) research.
>
> (Brew and Lucas, 2009: xvii)

## Introduction

The focus of this chapter is on educational research and how it is increasingly shaped by the contemporary enterprise university that has emerged as the result of 30 years of neo-liberal higher education policy. At one level, even to ask the question 'How is research shaped by universities?' is counterintuitive. This is because one of the most powerful aspects of being an educational researcher is that we experience it as a highly personal affair; it is something that we want to shape ourselves; it demands significant personal engagement, as well as huge amounts of personal time. That it is very personal is reflected in how we train new researchers in education. In education, the humanities and most other social sciences, our procedures are different from many of the more traditional sciences. We encourage new researchers to find research questions that are 'theirs'. We encourage them to discover for themselves what sort of researchers they want to become. And what sort of researcher they do become – their theoretical, their methodological and their substantive commitments – is also highly personal. They become part of every researcher's identity, part of who they are in their professional lives as academics. In short, research is something that all of us live in profound and personal ways. But while this personal dimension of research is very important, in reality, it presents only one side of the truth about the shaping of educational research in the modern university. By looking at the experience of the last research assessment exercise – the RAE 2008 – this chapter explores the institutional side of the shaping of educational research.

As has been noted before, it is an interesting irony that the reason why successive generations of educationalists in the college sector aspired to join the university system was because they thought that it would give them academic autonomy: the right to determine the nature of their work (Neave, 1988). What we now know, however, is that the move into the university sector was, in the end, a pyrrhic victory. The end of the twentieth century not only saw the final arrival of education as a university-based discipline, but, as we have already noted, it also saw the fundamental restructuring of the university system. As higher education and science became increasingly important instruments of national economic policy, it was more and more difficult to think of academics as self-regulating communities. As Henkel argues, the relations between higher education and the state were redefined on neo-liberal lines and, as a result, 'Higher education institutions and their members were subject to unprecedented government steerage and scrutiny' (Henkel, 2005: 159). As was demonstrated in Chapter 7, the consequences have been contradictory. On the one hand, universities now acting as corporate bodies have become more powerful; at the same time, they have become less coherent by 'embracing conflicting values and multiple functions and loosening institutional boundaries' (Henkel, 2005: 172).

One of the key ways in which academics and their institutions have been steered has been through the competitive assessment of their research. The Research Assessment Exercise (RAE), now called the Research Excellence Framework (REF), is one of the key features of university life in the UK. Every five or six years, since 1986, research across the whole of the UK's higher education sector has been comparatively assessed, largely by peer review. And depending on the outcome of the quality judgments that have been made, core university research funding (known as QR) has been distributed differentially to all public universities in the UK. In 2011–2012 the Higher Education Funding Council distributed £1,558 million of QR funding, representing approximately 24 per cent of the total core government funding for higher education. Not surprisingly, since so much is at stake, research assessment is taken extremely seriously by every university in the UK.

Of course, research assessment is not the only external force that shapes educational research. Over the past 20 years, it has also come to be influenced by a range of other factors. For example, there has been an increasing recognition at both the international and the national levels of the legitimacy of the policy originated quest for answers to social and economic problems and the need for research to contribute to solutions (Nowotny *et al.*, 2003); as a result, the idea of evidence-informed policy and practice has rapidly gained support and has come to shape educational and other research agenda throughout this country and internationally. A 'new social contract for research' in education has been developed (Demeritt, 2000), involving substantially increased funding – doubling during the previous RAE period – in exchange for increased accountability for and direction of the content and methods employed.

And now, in the pursuit of research that can provide policy-relevant answers, there are other pressures too. For example, the European Union is currently leading a challenge to the traditional disciplinary structures of academic research.

As the Commission argues, 'New ways are needed to address the asymmetry between relevant scientific and societal problems and the disciplinary structures underpinning the University' (European Commission, 2005: 14). Interdisciplinarity (furthering expertise through common developments), transdisciplinarity (interaction leading to radical epistemological rethinking) and increased cross-border research mobility are therefore needed to overcome 'traditional disciplinary clustering' (European Commission, 2006: 31). The development of the Economic and Social Research Council's doctoral training centres, which will encourage greater interdisciplinary work, are a current manifestation of this policy drive in the UK.

At the same time as these attempts to harness academically led research to the world of policy and practice, there has been an increasing recognition on the part of governments internationally that higher education is only one source of knowledge. From the 1980s onwards, the UK's Foresight programme (Henkel, 2005) – strongly influenced by Gibbons *et al.*'s (1994) ideas about Mode 2 knowledge production – called for new ways of working between universities, industry and the public sector. And the 'pathway to innovation is now seen as often beginning in industry rather than the university and as entailing more variable, complex, uncertain and interactive patterns of communication and collaboration between the university and industry' (Henkel, 2005: 160). Education, along with other professional disciplines 'struggling to wriggle out from under the condescension of more established and more 'academic' disciplines' (Nowotny *et al.*, 2003: 179), has embraced this approach. There has been a rise in interest in action research, practitioner enquiry (Mockler and Sachs, 2010) and a whole range of other applied and practice-based approaches to research (Furlong and Oancea, 2006).

All educational academics, therefore, whether they are aware of it or not, are caught up in these and other policy movements, movements that help to shape the nature of educational research and the world in which researchers live. They help to directly influence academics' institutional lives and, indirectly, their personal commitments. Potentially, there is a large and complex story to be told about the current shaping of educational research. This chapter has more modest ambitions, focusing on only one of those factors: research assessment.

In exploring the impact of the RAE/REF in education, this chapter looks at three different but overlapping levels of analysis. The first is at the level of the university itself, exploring the ways in which universities increasingly see themselves as institutions functioning in competitive markets where research is a key part of their institutional positioning. The second level looks at the internal management of research at both university and departmental levels and its links to the rise of new public management. Finally, we need to consider the impact of both of these issues on the identity of individual researchers – what sort of researchers they aspire to become. As we will see, competitive research assessment is implicated in each of these different moments for all academics.

Evidence is again drawn from the ten case study institutions that have been discussed in earlier chapters, supplemented by national data from a parallel survey undertaken by Oancea on behalf of the British Educational Research Association (Oancea, 2010). Interviews in the case study universities covered reflections both on preparations for the last 2008 RAE and the consequences afterwards for institutions, departments and individuals. The 2008 RAE outcomes for education in these ten universities varied significantly: two departments achieved high scores; four achieved medium scores and four had lower scores, although all had had at least some of their research judged as internationally excellent.

In terms of financial outcomes, for seven of the case study departments, the 2008 RAE resulted in an increase in core funding for research (albeit only a marginal increase in three cases). For the remaining three, already highly successful departments, the 2008 RAE resulted in a decrease of core funding for research because a revised funding model distributed that funding more widely than in the past (Hazelhurst *et al.*, 2010).

## The institutional story: the RAE and the market positioning of universities

In relation to university-based research, Brew and Lucas (2009) suggest that globalisation and neo-liberalism have had at least three different impacts. First, with the support of the World Bank and some other international agencies, free-market modernisation has been promoted, which emphasises research production and skills formation as one of the primary purposes of the modern university. Second, governments now regard their universities as key agents for securing competitive advantage internationally, with research performance as a key component in that process. Finally, the universities themselves now compete for students (especially PhD students and also young researchers), as well as collaborating in major research projects in an international marketplace that is largely unregulated by public authorities.

At the institutional level, therefore, research is now a core part of universities functioning as neo-liberal institutions. Reduced government funding has encouraged them to become more entrepreneurial in their search for research funding and in order to compete, they have to position themselves within those markets. Some institutions – the research elite – find themselves located in highly competitive international markets; others are primarily oriented to the UK or even to a particular sub-region of it. Whatever market they find themselves in, a key strategy for all universities, Brew and Lucas argue, has been differentiation. And research has increasingly come to be privileged for its contribution to that differentiation process, building university brands that enable them to compete more effectively (Marginson and Considine, 2000).

While such trends are seen to affect all types of higher education institutions in the UK and in many other countries as well (Slaughter and Leslie, 1999), it is acknowledged that the ways in which such processes work in practice will also be strongly influenced at the local level. Institutions, as well as the different disciplines within them, are likely to be positioned differently. To what extent can we see these processes at work within the ten case study institutions?

Interviews with senior education colleagues in the case study universities confirms that the ways in which education's 2008 RAE result was interpreted varied considerably between institutions depending on a range of different factors, including institutional 'vision' (i.e., market position), history, culture and the distinctive position of education within the institution. In simple terms, it was possible to distinguish three different types of education faculties in different types of university. At one end of the continuum are the established elite, those based in the Russell Group and the 1994 Group of universities, where, institutionally, there was an expectation that all staff would be research-active. For this elite group, where national and international visibility in terms of research is core to the institution's mission and market position and where, from historical success, research funding has become part of core funding, success in the RAE was seen as essential for departmental survival. Senior colleagues in institutions of this type reported very strong, centrally driven pressure on them; for example, the aspiration to eliminate research graded at a level of 2*(on a four point scale) in the next assessment round, with tough decisions being made about who was entered for the 2008 RAE and who was not (as one director of research put it, 'There was blood on the carpet').

And for the successful, despite the overall reduction in funds available, there were rewards in the confirmation of their position as part of one of the UK's leading universities. For those that were not successful for whatever reason, there was continued insecurity with reduced funding and, in some cases, robust external reviews of their future. Although there was no evidence that as a result of the 2008 RAE, any university department of education I visited was threatened with closure, there was talk in some institutions of 'disinvestment' in terms of future research capacity. As one respondent explained: 'It's all focused on the mission and deciding and, with scarce resources, where are you going to put your money? Where are you gonna make your mark?'

At the other end of the continuum, there were those institutions (including many of the post-2000 universities) where there was probably not an institutional expectation that research was a part of core activity (Oancea, 2010). In the case study institutions of this sort, the research success of individuals and small groups was seen as a bonus. As the director of research in one such university department explained:

> We had a different view as to what we intended to achieve in the exercise. We were actually quite surprised to have had any funding at the end of the exercise. We were not actually expecting to achieve any financial gain out of this. [Rather] it was part of the strategy for increasing the status of research within the institution and to have as many people as possible in the School of Education feel that they had crossed the line into being research-active.

In this new university there was evidence that the relatively modest success of the education group had encouraged the institution as a whole to reconsider its strategic vision, to behave, in the words of one respondent, 'like a proper university'. As another respondent said:

> The VC wants to change the culture from mainly, if not entirely, teaching, which it was, to a culture where research is considered the norm and everybody's duty will be to carry out research. There will be a very strong encouragement for people to be involved in research or penalties will be imposed.

Then there is, in national terms, a much larger group of universities in the middle (many post-1992 universities, the ex-polytechnic sector and some pre-1992 universities), where the development of research is clearly part of the institutional vision, but where different faculties and individuals within those faculties are at different stages of development; where there is an established commitment to developing research but not, as yet, an expectation on the part of the university that everyone would be fully research-active. As one respondent in a post-1992 university explained:

> Like most universities of our type, we have areas of research excellence and then we have areas like education with an aspiration to excellence and some areas that are entirely teaching and not doing any research at all.

Typically, case study universities of this type were on a journey to become more fully research-active, but it was clear that the speed of that journey varied considerably.

What the evidence demonstrated, therefore, was that nearly every type of institution could and did see research as part of its bid for differentiation within its marketplace; for some, research excellence was about maintaining their position within the world market; for others, it was about beginning to present themselves as a 'real university'. However, it also became apparent that different institutions did that differently, depending on a number of factors.

For example, the ability of many new universities to utilise the outcome of the RAE in this way was significantly affected by the structure of the RAE rewards system itself. As market-oriented institutions, such universities showed themselves to be highly sensitive to the fact that the funding was much more widely distributed than in previous RAEs. As has already been noted, even small amounts of new money were significant in alerting VCs to the potential of looking at education as a player in the marketing of their institutions. On the other hand, for those already dependent on funding derived from previous RAE exercises, the 2008 funding formula brought significant uncertainty. There were also very important differences nationally, particularly with Scotland, given its different funding formula, being encouraged and rewarded for entering a large number of researchers (Hazelhurst *et al.*, 2010).

How the RAE was interpreted in relation to each university's market position also varied, depending on a range of other factors going on at the time: the outturn for the RAE in the institution overall; the internal impact of the preferential funding for STEM subjects; in Scotland, the significant downturn in student numbers and changes to student-funding arrangements; and, of course, the credit crunch. As a respondent from a department that was seen by its university as having a weak result explained: 'So, basically, there was this crunch point of the credit crunch, plus the results'. All of these factors were external to institutions, but how the RAE played out in positioning education within universities was significantly dependent on internal factors as well, including politics.

Given the complexities of the RAE 2008 assessment system – with profiles rather than grades – it was possible to play the system in a variety of different ways. Some education faculties had done that successfully. As one dean put it: 'Moving the stats around any way you wanted to, it's only natural'. Others had fared badly, having been outmanoeuvred by other dominant faculties insisting on formulations that were most favourable to them.

It was also apparent that some institutions were much more accepting of a mixed profile than other comparable institutions. For example, one large faculty in a post-1992 university that entered 15 researchers and achieved a midrange outcome was seen in a positive light; another faculty of similar size that entered far more people and achieved a better result was strongly criticised because of its low entry rate. A recent change of vice chancellor had meant that the previous inclusive philosophy and slow progress towards more research productivity was now being challenged. As one respondent explained: 'This is a university that clearly sees itself on its way in terms of being a serious research-driven university in a number of key disciplines'. Because of the relatively low entry rate compared to other faculties serious questions were being asked as to whether or not education was part of that new vision. 'When they put up this graphic and benchmarks, including non-submissions ... education just fell out of the mix basically ... People really decided they're disinvesting there; that's not where they're putting their money'.

What is clear from the evidence, therefore, is how much the RAE and its outcomes are now bound up with the marketisation of higher education. Although such processes were clearer in some institutions than others (one dean, for example, described his university as 'a money-driven organisation'), there were many examples of institutional positioning, institutional differentiation and internal jockeying for scarce resources throughout the evidence. But in that process of marketisation, it is also clear that the history of education's long journey to the university sector was also very much in evidence. As Hazelhurst *et al.* (2010) note, by 2001 only one ex-polytechnic had crossed the dividing line to get significant core research funding, although ten old universities had slipped out of the funding regime. In the 2008 RAE the rules had changed so that even small pockets of international excellence could be recognised, but, again, only one ex-polytechnic received any substantial funding (i.e., over £300k), while the numbers of old universities without substantial funding increased substantially. Even with the more distributed funding regime of the 2008 RAE, 85 per cent of the funding remained with the pre-1992 university sector.

## New public management

A second feature of the modern university that is relevant to understanding the impact of the RAE is new public management (Hood, 1995; Deem *et al.*, 2007), an approach to running public sector organisations such as universities that has come about as a consequence of neo-liberalism at the institutional level. As Deem *et al.* (2007) note, higher education institutions in the UK are not constitutionally part of the public sector and historically have had considerable autonomy, but in the past 20 years, as institutions, they have been re-imagined and reshaped in the UK, largely as a result of the development of new public management.

As Henkel (2005) explains, it is the marketisation of higher education with the growing emphasis on income generation that has led to strong pressures on academic communities and institutions to change their cultures and structures to enable them to manage the new policy environment. As a consequence, 'academic policymaking moved from the department to the centre. Institutional leaders, rather than protecting academics from external assessments, tended to promote compliance and use them as instruments of change' (Henkel, 2005: 163). A key question, therefore, concerns the extent to which the 2008 RAE was managed through and therefore served to further develop and embed the principles of new public management in faculties and departments of education. Again, the evidence shows a complex story, although, overall, the direction of travel seems clear.

In considering the evidence, it is perhaps helpful to return to Hood's (1995) original presentation of what he calls the seven doctrinal components of new public management. In one sense, the whole of the RAE is centrally bound up with the development of new public management in that, as Hood suggests, one of its core principles is the move towards more explicit and measurable standards of performance as against trust in professional standards and professional expertise. And after 20 years of the RAE, it is clear that it has indeed established its legitimacy as a form of accountability in research. What the fieldwork for this study and Oancea's (2010) national survey demonstrated was that whatever other reservations respondents had about the outcome of the 2008 RAE, they almost universally considered that the judgments of the panel were fair as far as their own institutions were concerned; the measurement of research performance via the RAE is now widely accepted as legitimate within the education community in the UK. But new public management has a number of other features as well, all of which were visible in different degrees in the ways in which the RAE 2008 was managed and in its consequences.

For example, Hood suggests that new public management involves a move towards the disaggregation of public organisations into separately managed and separately accountable units. Every one of the university departments visited demonstrated that they were, indeed, seen as separate units in relation to their success in the RAE. Universities varied substantially in terms of the financial autonomy they granted individual departments and the transparency of their resource allocation mechanisms. Some senior colleagues were fully aware and had control over the financial outturn of the RAE for their departments' budgets. Others had a much more vague notion; as one head of department commented: 'Yes, there is a line somewhere in the budget, but nothing has gone in it yet'. And, as we will see below, universities also varied in terms of central planning in relation to RAE submissions. Nevertheless, the structure of the RAE itself meant that, in most universities, education was now seen as an autonomous player in a competitive field.

That brings us to another of Hood's doctrinal assumptions in new public management: competition. There was lots of evidence that competition – personal, departmental or national – is now a key part of institutional life for education academics. Moreover, in virtually all universities, education has become a competitive unit in itself. This was despite the fact that, in some institutions, what constituted the subject of education was immensely diverse. In one university, for example, it covered sports studies, health sciences, counselling, refugee studies and autism, as well as conventional primary and secondary teacher education. Nevertheless, in research terms, personal, departmental and national accountability were largely seen in terms of RAE units of assessment.

Another feature of new public management that Hood notes concerns the move towards more private sector methods of management, with increased differentiation of staff, separation of functions and hierarchies of accountability. Such an approach is potentially very different from the flat management structures based on individual autonomy and collegiality that have characterised universities in the past. Here a complex picture emerged with some institutions having moved further down this route than others, although, again, there was a clear direction of travel. For example, many institutions showed evidence of the emergence of different sorts of academic, some of whom were designated as research-active, with lower teaching loads and others who were considered teaching only.

Increasingly, these differences were reflected in different contracts. Research-active academics (as opposed to research staff) were more likely to have full-time, permanent contracts and perhaps lighter teaching loads than those who were considered not to be research-active. As part of the staffing for initial teacher education programmes, there was also evidence of the increased use of nonresearching part-time staff. As one head of department explained:

> Certainly now, though, we have a much more differentiated workload model that has come in this year ... at the moment we still have an academic contract that covers all staff but that is changing.

As a consequence of these processes, divisions were increasingly visible between academic staff. As a colleague in a different institution put it:

> I think [the RAE] definitely exacerbated the teaching-research divide … which we particularly have here, because there has been such a strong culture of teaching here and people who are very committed to teaching.

Such divisions reflect the prioritising of a different type of 'academic capital' (Deem and Lucas, 2007) amongst education academics. Traditionally, schools of education were staffed by academics who were expected to have strong professional experience. However, the evidence suggested that in many institutions, staff who had *only* professional capital, acquired through their experience in schools, were being marginalised. Even those institutions that had only modest research profiles talked about teaching-only staff as a thing of the past for core posts. For the future, they were looking for new recruits who would have both research and professional capital.

Increased differentiation of academic staff on lines that were relevant for research assessment was increasingly common. A different form of differentiation was evidenced in the increasing professionalisation of research administration. Virtually all of the colleagues interviewed reported that their departments had now appointed professional research administrators. As one colleague put it:

> One of the good things now in the environment here, we've got somebody who's, basically all the invitations to tender and so forth come through her and she circulates things out, but she also coordinates stuff, so we know who is putting bids in, you know? So, there are processes developed, you know, which are better.

In some institutions research administrators held relatively senior positions, helping to oversee the RAE submission process.

Another feature of new public management mentioned by Hood concerns the move towards more hands-on management, with senior managers wielding substantial discretionary power. In many of the institutions visited, respondents talked of the centralised processes that had been developed in undertaking preparation for the RAE. In some institutions that control came from the very top:

> It was central because we had the deputy vice chancellor who was overseeing the research process. And the vice chancellor himself had a very clear view about what we could put in and what we couldn't. There were a series of meetings where, if there was any potential to submit, we looked at everything on the table and then the university's research committee … looked at each of the proposals and they made a judgement.

In other institutions the process was led by one or more senior colleagues in the department itself; nevertheless, it remained a hierarchical process, with colleagues required to offer up their work for scrutiny. The process of hierarchical management as well as differentiation were well brought out in this statement from one respondent:

> And of those people, we were in a process probably for two or three years before the RAE, where our output was being monitored, we were expected to draw up action plans ... and things would be happening. We were given a degree of structure in relation to that, whereas other people were not really included in that kind of structure. It was very much ... a particular group who were looked at as though they were going to be part of that submission.

The power of such scrutiny, as we will see below, became apparent in those cases where colleagues felt bruised by final decisions about whether or not to enter them for the RAE.

In all these ways, therefore, it is clear that the RAE was significantly involved in the further embedding of the principles of new public management in university departments and faculties of education: it increased and rendered visible forms of accountability, it legitimised divisions between different types of academic and it increased the hierarchical nature of some aspects of university management. Yet we also need to be aware that the impact of these processes was again uneven. For example, departments within our most established universities seemed to find themselves in a contradictory position. The RAE placed a great deal of pressure on all academic staff in terms of research performance; at the same time, internally, such departments struggled to protect a degree of professional autonomy for colleagues as well as some procedures of collective decision-making. Many of the newer universities were, perhaps for the first time, experiencing considerable pressures to change. As a respondent in a post-2000 university said:

> Clearly, you have an institution that, historically, has grown out of a local authority college and there are a number of members of staff who certainly were not appointed with any intention of doing research. Now the institution has gained university status and in the course of doing that, the entry to justify university status required close examination of CVs and justification of scholarly activity.

Another said:

> You know, from 1992 we were kind of left alone to carry on and nothing much changed, but because of the external drivers in the main within the university, then that could not continue for much longer.

Of course, the RAE was not the only factor that was driving change; financial pressures and changes in status were also very important. But the RAE was always part of the institutional mix, speeding up and legitimating change, demonstrating to senior university colleagues both the importance of research in their university's mission and the necessity of increased managerialism in order to achieve the changes that were needed.

## The RAE and academic identity

Finally, I want to consider the issue of the impact of all of these changes on academic identity; what it means to be an education academic today. As was indicated at the beginning of this chapter, the experience of being an educational researcher is an immensely personal one. Research is something that we put ourselves into; for many of us it is a key part of our professional identity. And yet we also have to recognise the potential impact of neo-liberalism and the increasing marketisation of universities together with their associated forms of new public management. These may well have consequences in redefining what it means to be a successful academic; pressurising us to achieve; differentiating us; encouraging us to define ourselves as particular sorts of academics; for some, sharpening the focus on research and, for others, marginalising it.

Certainly, these are predictions made by some commentators in their analysis of the university system at large. Henkel, for example, states,

> What was clearer [by the early 2000s] was that the research policies being pursued at national and institutional level[s] were raising fundamental questions for what it means to be an academic. While at one level, they were reinforcing the value of research, they were also making the right to research conditional on attracting income and delivering regular assessable output that met increasingly demanding evaluative criteria.
>
> (Henkel, 2005: 165).

Brew and Lucas (2009) make a similar point. They argue that one of the most significant features of recent policy changes has been the emergence of a distinct and separatist research culture. On the one hand, the relentless pressure for the division of academic labour has helped to spawn a new class of academic: a research elite. These are premier-league researchers who can move between universities with ease in this country and internationally, commanding enhanced (if not premier league) salaries. At the same time, they suggest that current policies have put pressure on the traditional all-round academic; those who want to teach students, undertake (some) research and contribute to the wider life of their university have now been placed on the defensive. Yet even those in the premier league, it is suggested, no longer have the autonomy they once did. While their research reputation is now highly valued as a form of currency in universities, it is no longer merely personal. Successful researchers are expected to exploit their work's strategic potential in order to enhance their university's income and influence as well as their own personal academic reputation.

Yet the picture painted in the literature is not all one way. There is also recognition on the part of some commentators that the external forces that have been shaping the university research system have been confronted by counterforces. Academic disciplines, strongly defended by elite members, it is suggested, have been important in the maintenance of an academic agenda. As Becher and Trowler, (2000) and Martin Lawn and I (Furlong and Lawn, 2010) recognise, discipline remains a strong source of academic identity in terms of what is important and what gives meaning and self-esteem. Henkel (2005) sums up the position by suggesting that the commitment to academic autonomy remains strong, even amongst university managers, but that its meaning has changed; it is something that has to be achieved.

> The right of academics to determine their own agenda now must be against competing rights. Academics no longer work in a bounded space. Rather, academic autonomy has become something that must be realised by managing multimodality and multiple relationships in a context where boundaries have either collapsed or become blurred ... It seems that all scientists must negotiate between social and institutional pressures and preservation of identity.
>
> (Henkel, 2005: 173)

But, of course, not all academics have the same resources with which to negotiate their autonomy, especially in the sort of stratified university system where education faculties are located.

So, to what extent are these views corroborated by evidence from the post-2008 RAE? To what extent did the RAE put pressure on academic identities? One of the most powerful messages to be learned from the data from the case study institutions was that the experience of undertaking research remains a highly personal affair, in part because of the personal demands it makes on people. As one respondent explained:

> I know from my experience here, it doesn't happen in your allotted hours. It happens in weekends, in the evenings and whatever, you know, 'cause you have a massive teaching commitment as well.

That personal commitment was revealed most clearly in those instances where individuals had, for whatever reason, not been included in the RAE and where that exclusion had not been well handled by management:

> So, it's really, for real knocked down my confidence as a researcher and also my motivation. And that kind of treatment is really bruising. And people don't realise ... You've still got the papers you still can be pleased with. But, actually, it's more than that, isn't it? It affects your whole identity and your whole sense of self, really, as a researcher, you know?

But we also need to be aware that not everyone displayed the same sense of disappointment as this respondent. For some, not being entered or expected to be entered was a huge relief. This is because education as a discipline employs many different types of academic. As was noted in Chapter 4, in 2008 only about 1,700 of the 5,000 academics employed in education departments and faculties across the UK were entered for the RAE; the overwhelming majority were not entered. Many of those are likely to be people whose primary teaching commitments were in initial teacher education.

The differences in professional identity for this group of staff are, in part, historical. As one head of department in a post-1992 university explained:

> We have a different mission and we have staff who were brought in for a different mission and you can't expect in a short time they will change from being really good teachers to really good researchers; it is not realistic.

From the interviews undertaken in the ten case study institutions, it became apparent that there were at least four different types of research identity. Firstly, there were the research elite, although the opportunities to recruit such staff varied significantly. Some institutions had invested heavily in attracting existing successful academics in the run up to the RAE. Some of these were from overseas, with staff attracted by the opportunities for research-led careers in academically prestigious British universities. Other institutions were more constrained in establishing new posts, although perhaps were in a position to exploit existing vacancies to increase their research capacity. Others had no such opportunities at all. As the head of department in one new university explained: 'No, we didn't do any of that. No research fellows or additional funding. It was all with existing staff'.

A second category was the career researcher, those who constructed their professional identities primarily through research even though they were frequently on a short-term contract. The expansion of research funding over the previous RAE period meant that there was a growing number of these types of academic in a wide range of institutions, often working on projects led by other, senior colleagues. There was also a growing number of postdoctoral fellows working on their own projects, particularly in institutions with substantial core research and external funding. Then there were those who were not entered for the RAE, those whose professional identity was primarily concerned with teaching. As we have already seen, in many institutions the RAE meant that the status of these staff, despite their importance in teaching and administration, had diminished; sometimes that lower status was reflected in their contracts. In one institution, for example, those not entered in the RAE even had a change in title from university lecturer to university teacher.

But the largest group of those entered into the RAE were those who had to maintain a profile as a teacher as well as a researcher; identities that, particularly in the field of education, were sometimes experienced as inimical. In many new universities with high teaching loads, the pressures were particularly intense. As one successful researcher explained:

> I'm going tomorrow to ... to supervise a student on placement. It is an hour and a half away by train ... That's very time-consuming. I also have the master's degree which I teach, [and] we've got thirty students on that. Okay, we teach that on Saturdays, you know, in our spare time. That's actually a

> very time-consuming degree to teach because the limited number of Saturday contacts means that an awful lot of it is done by e-mail, which is even more time-consuming.

A pressure of a different sort that affected all of those involved in initial teacher education concerned the nature of knowledge. As Murray and Male (2005) note, in teacher education, experiential knowledge is seen as a key element. This is not only true for student teachers; it is also true for their lecturers. Possessing experiential knowledge of school teaching is central to their professional credibility. Murray and Male suggest that this emphasis is created in part by the rhetoric of partnership between schools and HEIs as the dominant orthodoxy of teacher education in England and by the historical resonances of the 'recent and relevant' requirements of the 1980s. Teacher educators are therefore surrounded by what Maguire and Weiner (1994) describe as 'a discourse of relevance'. However, as a discourse, it is very different from that which underpins the majority of educational research. Unlike the conventional lecturer who teaches on an undergraduate course or someone who teaches mainly at a higher degree level, teacher educators experience two modes of being an academic. Maintaining an identity that can operate effectively in both a research-oriented and in an experiential discourse is potentially extremely challenging.

That is not to say that there are not some forms of education research that are themselves closely related to the world of practice and some respondents described struggles to have this sort of research legitimated as relevant for the RAE. As one director of research explained:

> We really had to fight tooth and nail ... because they were sort of applied developmental, curriculum development type work. We had to fight really hard ... for them to be included, because quite a number of colleagues here [say] that's not real research.

As Oancea has argued (2010), the RAE has increasingly come to define what being a successful researcher in education actually is. One lecturer in a pre-1992 institution agreed. 'It limited the breadth of projects in which I got involved; the need to publish according to RAE criteria shaped my research decisions.' For some academics in education, the research identity offered through the RAE was compatible with other aspects of their work; for many others, adopting such an approach was experienced as highly challenging.

## Lessons learned

So, what have we learned about the way in which the RAE has helped to shape the discipline of education? What is clear is that over the course of the past two decades, research, including educational research, has become part of the drive for the competitive marketisation of higher education. Marketisation is something that affects all institutions, not merely those that appear in *The Times* list of top-ranking universities. In all education departments in all types of institution, there are clear expectations that they should contribute to institutional differentiation and competitive success however it is understood by their parent university. What is also clear is that the 2008 RAE extended and developed this process. One of the perhaps unintended consequences of the more widely distributed funding model used in 2008 (Hazelhurst *et al.*, 2010) was that the RAE drew more and more universities into the research game. Even where overall RAE achievements were relatively modest, research was seen as something that could help in the institution achieving its mission.

It is also clear that the RAE served further to embed the principles of new public management. Increased levels of accountability, differentiation, hierarchal hands-on management processes, all of these were visible across the system as a whole despite important differences at the local level. Finally, it become apparent how, often in subtle ways, research assessment impacts on what it means to be an education academic today. For the successful, how it encourages the development of a research-focused identity; how it marginalises other, more rounded academic identities; how it fosters a certain approach to knowledge; and how that is often experienced as existing in tension with the forms of knowledge that are dominant in teacher education.

Although none of these processes were actually started by the 2008 RAE, it is clear that the exercise was profoundly influential in furthering them. In conclusion though, it is important to reflect on this comment from Nowotny *et al.* (2003: 184):

> It is a mistake to imagine that accountability is being forced upon universities and other research institutions by hostile external forces, even if mutual trust, once rooted in the collusion of political, administrative and academic elites, has been eroded. The processes of assessment and accountability have been deeply internalized.

Perhaps one of the most important findings from this study was that the RAE education panel was seen as having done its job properly; its judgements were seen as fair. What this observation demonstrates is how much research 'performativity' (Ball, 2003) is now an everyday aspect of academic life; it has become deeply internalised by the research community.

## Conclusion

The aim of the previous three chapters, Section III, has been to try and explain why education as a discipline is currently shaped as it is: why we are where we are. The answer put forward has been that by the time education finally arrived in the university sector, universities themselves were changing in fundamental ways. Swept up by the forces of globalisation (imagined as necessitating neo-liberalism) and by the universal collapse of certainty of knowledge, our universities have increasingly become primarily entrepreneurial institutions, driven more by the necessity of finding a place in the market than by any core principles of what their contribution to society might or should be. And it was these entrepreneurial universities that education finally and fully joined in the late twentieth century; these are the sorts of market-sensitive institutions that have helped to make education the discipline that it is today.

In Chapter 8 we saw how these market-sensitive institutions are now highly vulnerable to the changing policies of governments in relation to the education of teachers. Universities, particularly in England but also to a lesser degree in the rest of the UK, have provided very little resistance to government agenda for the teaching profession, which are themselves caught up with neo-liberal ideas. The same is true in relation to research. National competition for research achievement – again, driven by the market – fundamentally shapes the external and internal management of research, as well as the types of opportunities made available to some staff and not to others.

As has been argued before, most of these challenges are common to the university system as a whole. Education, as an applied discipline and as a discipline that was late arriving at the university high table, is perhaps no more than an extreme example of the difficulties that face universities as a whole. And, as we have also noted, in the face of those challenges, few have been willing to stand up and say what universities are actually for, to say what universities can uniquely contribute to the study of education. That is the challenge that, with a good deal of trepidation, is taken up in the final part of this book.

## Note

1 An earlier version of the chapter was published in *Power and Education* as Furlong (2011b).

# Section IV

# Rescuing the university project?

# 10 Re-imagining the university

> The university is an autonomous institution at the heart of societies differently organised because of geography and historical heritage; it produces, examines, appraises and hands down culture by research and teaching ... It is a trustee of the European humanist tradition; its constant care is to attain universal knowledge; to fulfill its vocation, it transcends geographical and political frontiers and affirms the vital need for different cultures to know and influence each other.
>
> (Magna Charta Universitatum, 1988: 1)

The university is one of Europe's most influential and enduring creations and this powerful reaffirmation of its core principles was drawn up in 1988 in celebration of the 900th anniversary of Europe's first university: Bologna. In order to achieve its noble ends, the Magna Charta goes on to argue that a university needs to uphold certain key principles: research and teaching must be inseparable; it must be 'morally and intellectually independent of all political authority and economic power'; and individual academics must be free to research and teach as they see fit. 'Freedom in research and teaching is the fundamental principle of university life and governments and universities must ensure respect for this fundamental requirement' (1988: 1).

Despite the fact that the Magna Charta Universitatum was written only 20 or so years ago, it is surprising how wide of the mark it now seems given the reality of the contemporary university. As we have seen in previous chapters, even our most ancient universities do not always live up to these principles and many of our newer universities were never set up to do so in the first place. For example, the principle of autonomy for institutions and for lecturers has been challenged and undermined in a whole variety of different ways, particularly by the drive to marketisation; the constant search for new sources of funding, with new student groups to teach and new research contracts to take on board, has challenged and undermined both sorts of autonomy. At an institutional level, the marketised university has to be highly sensitive and responsive to its funders, whether that is industry, the government or, increasingly, students themselves. At a personal level, lecturers may experience less and less autonomy in determining what it is they teach and what it is they research; they, too, must respond to the realities of their own market. Autonomy, as a universal principle, as envisaged by the Magna Charta, has gone. And the new soft economy that now dominates many universities has increasingly driven a wedge between teaching and research. As we saw in Chapter 4, large numbers of university academics in education, as in other disciplines, have become teaching-only staff, 'casualised' in different ways.

But perhaps the biggest challenge to the vision of university as laid out in the Magna Charta concerns the principle that the authors perhaps took most for granted, the idea that the university's primary task is to attain universal knowledge, which it produces, examines and hands down through teaching and research. It is the academy's collective and ever-increasing uncertainty about knowledge that has been the most insidious force in undermining the sort of vision put forward in Bologna. As was argued in Chapter 7, postmodern thought, with its challenge to the notion of disinterested inquiry in the quest for objective knowledge, has been particularly undermining. But even if one rejects the extreme relativism of postmodernism, the growth of specialisation in universities has also been undermining. Partly because the university project over the past century or so has been so successful in the creation of new knowledge, specialisation has increased and increased to a point that colleagues even within the same faculty can no longer discuss their areas of expertise without misunderstanding.

As Bauman (2000) argues, universities are now characterised by a form of multivocalism; standards vary within departments still more across universities, so it has become impossible to defend any particular hierarchy of subjects in the contemporary university today, let alone any notion of authoritative knowledge. And there are also now many alternative sources of authority over knowledge – television, the Internet – and wherever claims to knowledge are made they are challenged. Not surprising then that as Smith and Webster (1997) note, intellectuals have lost confidence in their own activities and as a result there is no one available to speak for the university.

So, notwithstanding the efforts of the Magna Charta to define what a university is or at least should be, the truth is that society finds it hard to give a singular answer to the question: what are universities for? It seems that as an institution, the contemporary university is increasingly characterised by difference and by diversity rather than any single idea or even a set of principles. And it is this fact, this lack, that Rothblatt (1997) and many others argue is the central cause of the discontents of the contemporary university.

And education's discontents as a university-based discipline are no more than a particular case of this malaise, if an extreme one. If universities have no essential purpose, if there is no longer any means by which they can *insist* on their independence and if there is no longer any confidence in the knowledge that they provide, then why should governments take the university-based study of education seriously except where it has practical utility for their policies? If universities are willing to offer programmes of training that are, in significant ways, defined by government, if they are willing to focus primarily on applied, policy-relevant research, then they may continue to be seen as valuable. But we should not fool ourselves; any valuing that there is, is fundamentally utilitarian.

There is little opportunity (or, indeed, appetite) in education faculties today to achieve the lofty goals of the Magna Charta – to attain universal knowledge or to be a trustee of the European humanist tradition. Put like that, the very suggestion seems laughable.

And in the face of this massive undermining over the past quarter of a century, how have departments and faculties of education responded? They have been silent. Very few people will stand up and say, 'In the face of the current challenges, this is why education must be a university-based discipline; this is what the university *can* contribute that is distinctive, that is important'. Critiques abound (Labaree's 2004 account of the 'Ed School' in the USA is particularly depressing (Judge, 2006)) but alternative visions are few and far between. The only real exception is Clifford and Guthrie's (1988) now somewhat dated study of elite 'Ed Schools' in the USA. In their book, Clifford and Guthrie try to mount an argument for professional education, symbolised in the EdD, which they suggest should be seen as quite distinct from academic education. Indeed they argue that the academic thrust of elite universities actually undermines the professional focus of 'Ed Schools'. Although Clifford and Guthrie should be applauded for taking up the challenge of articulating a core purpose for the university based study of education (something that Labaree fails to do), in the end their thesis will not do: it is far too narrow in focus and ultimately too elitist to fulfil the task.

And so to the aim of the final section of this book; it is to begin to explore what it is that universities offer to the study of education; why it is distinctive, why it is important. This chapter addresses this question at the level of the university as a whole. Drawing particularly on the work of Barnett (1990, 2000, 2007) and Lay (2004), it is suggested that even in the complex world of the contemporary university, it is possible to identify something that is distinctive about universities in their commitment to the contestability of knowledge and to 'the maximisation of reason'. Chapter 11 then goes on to examine the implications of this re-visioning for education – for professional education, for knowledge mobilisation and for research.

## Locating the contemporary university: ideas and ideas

In thinking again about the purposes of the university, one obvious place to begin is with Cardinal Newman. It was Newman who first put forward the idea of an idea for universities, a suggestion that it still powerfully seductive. As Rothblatt (1997: 22) argues in characteristically acerbic manner:

> The emotional appeal of thinking of universities as embodying an idea cannot be overestimated in the age of the multiversity continually bombarded by wide and contradictory demands and commitments ... However elusive the idea of a university, the conception of a basic thrust is a relief, an attractive alternative to the accurate perhaps but also shapeless, relativistic and uninspiring description of the contemporary university as one-stop shopping.

In recent years any number of commentators (though, as we have seen, few educationalists) have tried to reassert their personal idea, their personal recipe for rescuing the university. Some have called for academics to reassert their professional prerogatives as experts in educational content (Levidow, 2002) or in learning (Bowden and Marton, 1998). Others have argued that the idea of the university should be formed around issues of social justice (McLean, 2006) or democracy (Fallis, 2007). Delanty (2001) calls for rethinking the idea of the university around the knowledge society, by which he means promoting the university as a space within that not just new forms of knowledge can be created, but more fundamentally new ways of knowing.

The difficulty with many of these different propositions is that they are partial; they may have something interesting to say about some aspects of contemporary universities but neglect others. Rothblatt (1997), for example, focuses most of his attention on the elite research-intensive universities. Others, such as Nussbaum (2010), Delbanco (2012) and Collini (2012) all want to prioritise the importance of the university-based study of the humanities, which they see as essential for the maintenance of democracy in society. The humanities, they argue, based as they are on the principles of liberal education, need protecting from the narrow utilitarianism that dominates our universities. But as we have already seen, contemporary universities are highly complex and highly diverse institutions. Some are research-intensive but many are not; most offer courses in the humanities, but they also offer many other sorts of courses as well, courses based on a wide variety of different principles and objectives, serving the needs of very different sorts of students. If there is to be an idea and basic thrust, then it needs to start from here, from where we are.

The reason for this complexity is because the contemporary university is, in reality, not the product of a single idea; rather, it is a conglomeration of earlier concepts and organisational forms, the product of centuries of societal challenge and institutional response with one idea being laid on top of another.

Fallis (2007), in his analysis of the multiversity, suggests that contemporary universities have at least four different ideas at their core, ideas that have different historical heritages and that are sometimes complementary and sometimes in conflict. There is the idea of the university as a place of undergraduate liberal education for the elite: Newman's idea. This contrasts sharply with the idea of the university as a place of graduate education and basic research derived from the work of Humboldt. An alternative, even older medieval vision is of the university as place of professional education; finally, there is the Scottish and American Land Grant universities' idea of the university as places that serve the needs of contemporary society with accessible education and applied research. As Fallis says, each of these ideas can be taken as an archetype; each is a recurring motif in writing and thinking about universities. We can perhaps gain a little more purchase on the challenges that need to be addressed in any re-visioning by looking at each of these different ideas, in turn.

### *Newman again*

If we begin with Cardinal Newman, we must admit that few authors have been as influential as he in shaping the discussion of the purposes of the university. For Newman, the university was an unashamedly elite institution; the job of the dons was to expose students to 'the best that has been thought and said in the world' (Arnold, 1869). The primary purpose of the university was personal education for undergraduates through the pursuit of pure judgement; the cultivated man who had experienced higher education was very different from the uneducated man … or woman. As was noted at the very beginning of this book, Newman himself was not particularly interested in professional education; indeed, he saw liberal education as an approach that stopped the intellect from being 'sacrificed to some particular or accidental purpose, some specific trade or profession'. As he explained in his 'Discourse 7: Knowledge Viewed in Relation to Professional Skill' (1853b), it was liberal education that was the best form of preparation for the professions.

Interestingly, there are strong echoes here of the aspirations of the University Day Training Schools established for teachers at the end of the nineteenth century – and, indeed, in the Robbins Report of 1963 – the idea of the 'education of the scholar who happens to want to be a teacher'. In his arguments Newman was deliberately challenging the utilitarians of his day. It is 'mental culture' rather than narrow training, he asserted, 'that is emphatically useful'.

Of course, Newman was not describing what he saw as the reality of the contemporary university; rather like today, he saw it increasingly in the grip of utilitarian schools of thought. His aim was to elevate personal liberal education in universities so that they could become the moral centre of modern culture (Rothblatt, 1997). But as Fallis (2007) points out, one key idea in liberal personal education not picked up by Newman was the philosophical tradition of Aristotle and Socrates. For Socrates, liberal education is achieved through sceptical questioning, through the application of reason and through dialogue. Those in the Socratic tradition argue that:

> All our knowledge, all our ways of seeing and of doing, both individual and collective, should be subjected to scrutiny of reason. Through civil dialogue, question-and-answer, give-and-take, true knowledge emerges. Students should challenge orthodoxy and tradition; students should not accept thoughts; rather, they should have responsibility for their thoughts … Socrates believed that to be free to exercise one's own thought was the essence of being human.
>
> (Fallis, 2007: 23–24)

In other words, Newman's emphasis on liberal education as education in the greatest that has been thought and known – if that is the aspiration alone – could be entirely conservative. By contrast, liberal education in the Socratic tradition is more critical; it involves learning to question, to challenge and, thereby, to develop one's own judgement. If personal liberal education is to be at least one strand within the idea of the contemporary university, then I would argue, as do others, such as Barnett (1990, 2000), that it needs to be conceptualised in this Socratic tradition rather than in that of Newman alone.

## *Humboldt and Berlin*

Cardinal Newman also had surprisingly little to say about the discovery of new knowledge. His university was for teaching and for students and, most emphatically, not for research. That strand of the contemporary university has a different heritage.

In 1810, some 40 years before Newman published his work, a group of German reformers led by Wilhelm von Humboldt adopted a radical new approach to the organisation and function of the university. Their ideas were influenced by the scientific revolution and the enlightenment. For them, the modern university was to be centrally concerned with research and the discovery of new knowledge; through this strand of its development, the university became intimately bound with rise of modernity.

Humboldt envisaged a university based on three principles: unity of research and teaching, freedom of teaching and academic self-governance. For Humboldt, teaching and research were an inseparable process. As Lay (2004) puts it, 'The ideal university aimed to increase the sum total of human knowledge through research. The pedagogic relationship between lecturer and student would be replaced with a sense of comradeship in the pursuit of scholarly excellence' (p. 48). In other words, teaching rather than simply communicating 'the best that has been thought and said' was to be a means of improving both lecturer and student. Through their teaching, professors would develop their students' independence of mind, not to fill them with facts; in so doing, they enhanced their own understanding as well.

Significantly, in Berlin University, which Humboldt helped to found, professors were not seen as generalists, responsible for teaching broadly based knowledge as they were in Newman's vision. Instead, there was to be a division of labour in a field of knowledge. Professors had to be free to follow their own specialist interests in their research and students also had be free in choosing what to study. 'Knowledge progresses through [a] perpetual conflict between reason and tradition. This dialectic requires that professors are free to study and to teach according to the dictates of their curiosity and their application of reason' (Fallis, 2007: 29).

In fact, as Lay (2004) notes, the emphasis given to pure scholarship was, in the end, to have a negative impact on the autonomy of the university. Applied research was and is far more costly than simple teaching and this obliged the universities to become increasingly reliant on government support. And, as we have already noted, the endless pursuit of new and more specialised knowledge has, in the modern age, been a double-edge sword in that it has helped to undermine the coherence of universities as communities.

### *Professions and the rise of modernity*

There are two other strands that are important in the contemporary university that are visible in its history as well. The first is to do with professional education, the oldest element in the European tradition; the second concerns the contribution of the university to the development of society through mass higher education.

In fact, the early interest in vocational education has its roots in the institutions of higher learning of the ancient world. The classical world had produced a highly developed system of education and research within which there was considerable rivalry between the various branches of learning, particularly between the rhetoricians who promoted the value of practical, career-enhancing knowledge and the philosophers, who believed learning should be undertaken to improve the students' moral and intellectual character. As Lay notes, 'The debate begun by the students of Isocrates (the rhetorician) and Plato (the philosopher) over the relative value of the vocational and general approaches to learning remains unresolved even today' (2004: 29).

The European medieval universities did not develop directly from their ancient world counterparts and were initially at least more focused on the teaching of rhetoric than philosophy. Bologna, with its focus on law and Paris, with its focus on theology, were the first real universities to emerge in the twelfth and thirteenth centuries. The dominant intellectual tradition in the early universities was the scholastic method of enquiry, which involved the application of logic to the minute examination of tendentious issues of theology or law. 'The teaching inspired by this method was essentially vocational: students studied primarily in the hope of advancing their careers in the priesthood or public administration' (Lay, 2004: 40). However, the rediscovery of works of the classical philosophers in the Renaissance encouraged humanist thinkers to suggest that education could also become a means of self-fulfilment and should be pursued for its own sake. 'The knowledge they were interested in was the more human-orientated wisdom of the classical world, which seemed to stand in such direct opposition to the otherworldly musings of the theologians' (Lay, 2004: 40). Initially resisted, by the sixteenth century, universities had accommodated the humanists, taking both general as well as the vocational branches of learning into themselves.

### *Scotland and universities of the modern world*

One of the many contrasts between the medieval universities and the ideas put forward by both Newman and Humboldt is that because of their interest in vocational education, they were routinely engaged with the real world, something that both Newman and Humboldt eschewed. A fourth important idea of a university – developed by the eighteenth-century Scottish universities and later, in the nineteenth century, London University and American Land Grant universities – was that universities, like their medieval counterparts, should be involved in society.

For much of the Enlightenment, Oxford and Cambridge turned their backs on the new knowledge that was emerging with the growth of science. Instead, they became 'bastions of gentlemanly privilege' (Fallis, 2007: 33). In Scotland, by contrast, one of the first homes of the Enlightenment, the universities moved quickly to embrace the new scientific learning; they also became more democratic. Pedagogy was reformed: general tutors who dealt with the entire curriculum were replaced with tutors in each discipline; lectures replaced tutorials; laboratory demonstrations were introduced, revolutionising scientific and medical education. Instruction was also in the vernacular (English) rather than Latin and the possibility of part-time study was introduced.

> As medieval universities responded to the social and economic needs of their time, so, too, did Scottish universities in the eighteenth century, offering avenues of opportunity to the growing middle-class and advancing knowledge in science and technology to propel the process of industrialisation.
>
> (Fallis, 2007: 33)

Over time, other systems became influenced by the Scottish model that stressed the idea that higher education is a national responsibility to be undertaken in the interests and well-being of the many. Such a vision was particularly influential in the establishment of London University. University College, which opened in 1827, was a thoroughly secular institution focused on practical subjects, although not exclusively so. It was followed in 1829 by the more religiously oriented Kings College. Both colleges had an emphasis on broad accessibility and the education of the professional middle classes and by 1836 they had come together to form the University of London. Significantly, the new university's charter allowed it to offer degrees to students studying at affiliated colleges that encouraged a similar model of higher education to spread rapidly across the city, to the major industrial centres of the UK and then across the Empire.

By the mid-nineteenth century, therefore, four different ideas of the university had been set out: Newman's university of personal liberal education for undergraduates; the medieval university of professional schools; the German university of graduate education, research and pure science; the Scottish university of undergraduate accessibility and applied sciences. Gradually, the university was being connected to the nation state, its economy and its culture. And it was these ideas, these four archetypes, that came together in the second half of the twentieth century to form the contemporary university, with all of its tensions and contradictions. And, as Fallis puts it:

> the tensions of the nineteenth and early twentieth centuries – between elite education and accessible education, between teaching and research, between withdrawal from the world and engagement, between knowledge valued for its own sake and knowledge valued for its utility, between specialised learning and generalised learning between the humanities and the science – are with us still.
>
> (Fallis, 2007: 34).

## Finding the contemporary university: now you see it, now you don't

The contemporary university, therefore, is no longer based on any single coherent idea, but on a range of different ideas, some of which are compatible and some less so, something that Clark Kerr (1963) observed over 50 years ago, when he first coined the term *multiversity*. But where does this leave the contemporary university? Given these different historically derived ideas, what might an inclusive contemporary vision of the university actually be?

One of the most comprehensive recent statements comes from the 1997 National Committee of Inquiry into Higher Education, chaired by Lord Dearing (Dearing, 1997). Mindful of history and of the complex and diverse nature of universities today, the Dearing Report suggested that a contemporary vision of the university might be expressed in these terms:

1 to inspire and enable individuals to develop their capabilities to the highest potential levels throughout life so that they grow intellectually, are well-equipped for work, can contribute effectively to society and achieve personal fulfilment;
2 to increase knowledge and understanding for their own sake and to foster their application to the benefit of the economy and society;
3 to serve the needs of an adaptable, sustainable, knowledge-based economy at local, regional and national levels;
4 to play a major role in shaping a democratic, civilized, inclusive society (para. 5.11)

Certainly, one can see here traces of each of the historical elements described above, but they are woven together in a form that recognises the complexity of the task. There is a concern with intellectual growth, but it is both for personal development *and* as preparation for the world of work; there is a recognition that research is central to the mission of universities, but Dearing argues that it can be pursued for its own sake *as well as* for more utilitarian ends by engaging with the real world; and there is a recognition that universities have a role in fostering a 'democratic, civilised inclusive society', *as well as* contributing to the economy. The echoes of Newman's elite personal education, of Humboldt's research-based university, of the mediaeval rhetoricians and of the fathers of the eighteenth-century Scottish universities with a civic mission are all here, apparently working together without tension or contradiction.

Although Dearing should perhaps be given top marks for rising to the challenge of writing a mission statement for the increasingly diverse set of activities and institutions that is higher education, in the end, it will not do, certainly not on its own. And the reason it will not do is that it does not face up to the challenges that we all have to confront in contemporary society concerning knowledge. In Dearing's world, knowledge is king; knowledge is unproblematic. Universities develop knowledge through their pure and applied research; they introduce students to knowledge for their personal and professional education; through their combined research and teaching functions, knowledge contributes both to the (knowledge-based) economy and to civil society. Yet, as we have seen repeatedly throughout this book, life is now more complex than that; the knowledge genie is out of the bottle and won't easily be put back in.

In sharp contrast to Dearing, Barnett, in his various explorations of the idea of higher education (Barnett, 1990, 2000, 2007), starts from this point; he starts from the recognition that the nature of knowledge in society is deeply contested, deeply problematic. As we saw in Chapter 7, Barnett argues that the contemporary world is characterised by what he calls supercomplexity, where we are bombarded every day with competing ways of interpreting the world. It is not that our frameworks for making sense of the world are dissolving as such; rather, that for any one framework that appears to be promising, there are any number of rival frameworks that could contend against it.

> Today's student has a tough time of it. For the present age is one of supercomplexity. It is an age in which it is reflectively, albeit intuitively, understood that there are neither end points nor beginning points; that is to say, there is dispute even of the descriptions of presenting situations. This is an age that is replete with multiplying and contradictory interpretations of the world; it is a world that is discursively open.
>
> (Barnett, 2007: 36–37)

And this is the world that our graduates enter; a world where they will face continual challenge and insecurity. In this world, Barnett suggests, it is not knowledge that will carry them forward, but their capacity to embrace multiple and conflicting frameworks and to offer their own interpretation, their own positive mode of being.

This has profound implications for universities. He argues:

> We should therefore lay to rest, although certainly with dignity, the notions of the university that speak of knowledge and truth and of disciplines and that hold to a secure sense of the university retaining a separateness from the world, the better to understand it ... The age now beckoning is one of varied opportunities of multiple clients, activities and networks pursued through manifold and even conflicting discourses. This is an elusive university, not easily captured in any kind of linguistic or symbolic text. Now you see it, now you don't.
>
> (Barnett, 2000: 21)

But where does that leave us in understanding the purposes of the university in the contemporary world? Barnett himself has approached this challenge from a number of different points of view over the years. In 1990, drawing inspiration from the work of Habermas, he argued that whatever the current challenges to the nature of knowledge, the essential nature of higher education is not compromised if it maintains its commitment to the pursuit of truth. However, following the work of Habermas, Barnett suggests that truth is not an end point. 'Rather, truth is the description we give to a particular kind of human transaction.' (1990: 59)

This transaction, Barnett suggests, is a conversation but not just any kind of conversation. Within such a conversation, participants can say what they want provided they are trying to get at the truth, provided they are sincere, that they mean what they say, that their contribution is internally coherent and is intelligible to the other participants in the discussion.

Participation in this sort of intellectual debate imposes certain demands: people have to be heard, people have to listen attentively and participants need to be able to understand the discussion. Participants also need to be sincere, coherent and committed. Most fundamentally of all, according to Barnett, is the willingness to expose one's viewpoint to the critical gaze of others.

> Intellectual debate is not cosy or permissive; it is critical, judgmental and stern. Higher education in this view of truth cannot simply be a matter of truths disseminated to students; it is a much tougher and more demanding process. Through it, the student emerges, able to begin to take up an informed position of his or her own or at least to have some awareness of what that involves.
>
> (Barnett, 1990: 60)

In his more recent work, Barnett (2007: 166) has explored this process of the will to learn more fully.

> Faced with epistemological and ontological uncertainty, the student creates her own new uncertainties and thrives on them ... Here there is epistemological courage in coming to believe in her beliefs, but there is also and fundamentally so, *ontological courage*. It is the belief in herself that will fuel her will to learn, to press herself into the day, bending those experiences to further her own learning projects. The student puts herself forward; she leaps forward. She even flies by herself. This is not fantasy. It is achieved day in and day out, even in mass higher education and even against the odds.

In Barnett's ideal university, therefore, the Enlightenment lives on, but it does so through a commitment to a *process* rather than an end point. Importantly, it is a process that can be applied to all of the diverse purposes of higher education outlined by Dearing: personal education, professional education and to research, whether it is pure or applied. The commitment to the pursuit of truth is something that is (or should be) imposed on academic staff just as much as on students; it is this discipline that ensures that academic communities move forward. But while such ideals are still possible, Barnett is only too well aware that in the contemporary university, they are increasingly difficult to sustain; they are increasingly compromised, crowded out for both staff and students by marketisation, by neo-liberalism and by ever more invasive accountability frameworks.

Interestingly, there are important parallels between Barnett's focus on the *processes* underlying the practice of higher education and that of Lay (2004). In his prizewinning essay reflecting on the Bologna Magna Charta Universitatum (the document with which we opened this chapter), Lay argues that the process underlying all of higher education, in all of its diverse manifestations is or at least should be, on 'the maximisation of reason'.

> The fundamental importance of the protection and exploitation of reason is also an assumption in the Magna Charta. The teaching and research functions specified by the principles are clear examples of reason in use. The pursuit of the humanist mission identified in the document as the central role of the university is, in fact, simply that the major function of the university is intrinsically linked to the role of reason in society. A statement of the fundamental function of the true university must therefore reflect this relationship in a manner that can be presented as a direct answer to society's recurrent questions on the purpose of the university.
>
> (Lay, 2004: 104)

In an interesting parallel with Barnett's arguments, it is the *process* of the maximisation of reason that Lay argues is educative and it is just as relevant to today, in a world of uncertainty, as it was in less complex times. It is also the maximisation of reason that drives us on in our research even though we know that our findings, our truths, are always provisional, always temporary.

Lay goes on to argue that clearly stating that the essential purpose of universities in our society concerns the maximisation of reason would be politically important for universities in that it would clarify in a direct and easily understood manner the essential mission of the university and underline the benefits this mission offers to the society that supports it. Moreover, he suggests that the overall goal of maximising the influence of reason in society provides a defensible position from which to confront the social forces seeking to undermine the essential character of the university.

Significantly for the field of education, Lay argues that the maximisation of reason is an equally defensible goal for university-based vocational as well as general education. In sharp contrast to the arguments of Nussbaum (2010) or Fallis (2007), Lay makes the case that it is not only the humanities that are important. The humanities may well need defending in contemporary society, but not because they have a privileged position in the maintenance of our democracy.

> Vocational learning provides a means by which reason can be used for the direct betterment of humankind through the provision of practical skills – an outcome in direct accordance with the tenet of maximisation of reason. General education, on the other hand, employs reason primarily for the

> betterment of individuals; individuals who, through their positive actions, can then radiate these advantages outward through society. Thus, neither form of teaching is contrary to the primary purpose of the university; indeed, both vocational and general learning should be pursued in tandem if the university is to function at its fullest potential.
>
> (Lay, 2004: 106)

Finally, Lay argues that if universities are to survive in the contemporary world, they need to build more effective links between themselves and the institutions of civil society; they must leave the ivory tower, asking themselves what they can contribute rather than what society can contribute to them. That means that universities need to exercise leadership. If they are to be valued in society, he suggests that they must increasingly direct themselves not only to other academics, but to the general population as well; this would imply that they must be more proactive than at present, demonstrating in practice what the maximisation of reason can contribute to society.

## A note on vocational education and the development of *phronesis*: the missing fourth element

I would certainly agree with Lay in his assertion that universities need to build more effective links with civil society and they need to demonstrate their value as institutions devoted to the pursuit of reason. That is an issue that is discussed more fully in the next chapter, but before doing that, it is important to comment on his description of the role of the university in relation to vocational education. For while his arguments about the universities and the maximisation of reason are persuasive in relation to the majority of their work, in relation to vocational or professional education, he significantly understates the complexity and significance of the university's contribution. We can gain some insight into those complexities by looking again at the different forms of knowledge that make up the discipline of education; once again Aristotle is helpful.

So Lay is correct when he argues that universities can contribute to the betterment of humankind through the provision of practical skills – what Aristotle would describe as *techne*. They may also, through vocationally oriented research, contribute to scientific or other forms of rationally based insight into educational processes: *episteme*. And certain dimensions of vocational education (particularly the philosophy of education and other humanities-based insights) are not intended to be narrowly practical at all. Rather, they are part of what Aristotle would describe as *sophia*: theoretical or philosophical wisdom of a general kind (there are links here with Newman's conception of liberal education). All of these different elements are there in certain forms of professional education. But where university-based professional education (and particularly initial teacher education) goes a step further is that it aims draw on these different forms of knowledge (different forms of reason) and, in the light of them, supports its students in the development of *phronesis*, practical wisdom. As was argued in Chapter 1, *phronesis* involves the capacity to act truthfully and with reason in practical matters; it therefore involves a strong ethical dimension.

Practical wisdom, in Aristotle's terms, is derived from experience and is a core part of many professional programmes, including those in education.

> Practical wisdom, it is not a discrete skill, but is embedded in who we are, individually and as a community ... It requires an act which is more akin to 'perception' (i.e., immediate grasp of the concrete and particular) than to the application of general rules.
>
> (Oancea and Furlong, 2007: 127)

When university-based teacher educators are involved in supervising students in their professional practice, this is what they are doing; they are supporting them in the development of practical wisdom, in the development of *phronesis.* That involves students holistically bringing together skills (*techne*), scientifically based insight (*episteme*) and rationally based principles into *a particular concrete situation*; and they must do that in a way that is not only morally justifiable, but also in a way that is valid for them as a person. It is because this dimension of professional education is so personal that it is so demanding on both student and lecturer.

Interestingly, historically, it is this moral dimension of professional education that was seen as the most important. This was particularly so in religiously based teacher education of the nineteenth century and in normal school movement of the nineteenth and early twentieth centuries. As we saw in Chapter 2, right up until the 1950s, most teacher training colleges were small, isolated strongly moral communities. Their pedagogy was primarily charismatic, with small numbers of students overseen by their particular tutor, who gave demonstration lessons in school and then oversaw their emerging practice.

In the historical period since, this aspect of the professional education of teachers has been silenced; it has been lost amongst the louder voices firstly of rationally based scientific knowledge and in the contemporary period of the importance of skills. It is also rarely articulated in the university more widely even though it is a key element in all forms of supervised professional education, particularly in the caring fields such as medicine, nursing and social work. But when one looks at the work of teacher educators today, as we did in Chapters 4 and 5, we see that a significant part of their task continues to be the development of *phronesis*, helping their students develop practical wisdom. But in the best university-based schemes, it is very different from the 1950s.

Today university-based teacher educators are not merely charismatic, though some may well be; they do not merely act as models, though they sometimes do. What is distinctive about this particular group of staff is that they are supporting their students in the development of practical wisdom while at the same time being members of *a university*. As such, they have access to other forms of professional knowledge based on theory, on research. And they are part of an institution based on the principle of the maximisation of reason, an institution that insists that they subject their own knowledge, their skills and their values to critical scrutiny.

Given that this part of university professional education is so important but currently so silenced, there is an urgent need on the part of departments and faculties of education and other professionally oriented disciplines to recognise it, to articulate it and to value it. Not to do so, not to recognise the importance of practical wisdom and the contribution that universities can make to fostering it in their professional programmes means that in today's technical rationalist world, it can too easily be marginalised or even expunged from professional education altogether.

## Conclusion

> The real university is a state of mind. It is that great heritage of rational thought that has been brought down to us through the centuries which does not exist at any specific location. It is a state of mind which is regenerated throughout the centuries by a body of people who traditionally carry the title of professor, but even that title is not part of the real university. *The real University is nothing less than the continuing body of reason itself.*
>
> In addition to this state of mind, 'reason', there's a legal entity which is unfortunately called by the same name but which is quite another thing. This is a nonprofit corporation, a branch of the state with a specific address. It owns property, is capable of paying salaries, of receiving money and of responding to legislative pressures in the process. But this second university, the legal corporation, cannot teach, does not generate new knowledge or evaluate ideas. It is not the real university at all. It is just a church building, the setting, the location at which conditions have been made favorable for the real church to exist.
>
> Confusion continually occurs in people who fail to see this difference and think that control of the church buildings implies control of the church. They see professors as employees of the second university who should abandon reason when told to and take orders with no backtalk, the same way employees do in other corporations.
>
> (Pirsig, 1974: 65)

The contemporary university as an institution (Pirsig's second university) is highly complex, diverse and even contradictory. Born in mediaeval Europe, it has evolved through history, each age laying more and different expectations on it. By the middle of the twentieth century, it had grown into Clark Kerr's multiversity, what Rothblatt (2010) calls 'The house of many mansions'. But while in the 1960s, it might have been just possible for the multiversity to maintain its coherence, to hold the ring through its shared commitment to the development of new knowledge and to the care of students, in recent times that has been much more difficult to achieve. As Fallis argues, 'The multiversity is a great unwieldy bundle. Our age brings centrifugal forces as never before and the bonds that hold together the multiversity are weakening, especially under the relentless pressures of constrained finances' (Fallis, 2007: 335).

In these circumstances, defining what is distinctive about universities becomes ever more challenging but ever more important. But what this chapter has tried to show is that underlying the diversity, the differences and the contradictions that characterises the contemporary university, it is possible still to identify Pirsig's first university, the ideal of the enlightenment project. Whatever its surface form, whether large or small, old or new, whether research-intensive or primarily focused on teaching and whether that teaching is primarily academic or vocational, at its heart, this first university remains committed to 'the maximisation of reason'. The difficulty, as we have seen repeatedly in this book, is that while many people inside and outside the university world might recognise and, indeed, affirm this principle, in practice it is a principle that is increasingly difficult to sustain. The maximisation of reason may not be quite dead, but, especially in an applied field like education, it is increasingly silenced, crowded out by more utilitarian voices.

But Pirsig is right; it is important not to confuse the two forms of what a university actually is, not to confuse its essential idea with what it has become in the modern world: just a church building. The aim of the next and final chapter of this book is to explore how the maximisation of reason may be reinserted into the study of education; how, in contemporary form, it may be used to look again, to revision our teaching, our knowledge mobilisation activities and our research so that it does indeed live up to that first vision of what a university really is.

# 11 'Re-tooling' the discipline of education

In a classic paper on the impact of new technologies on education, Green and Bigum (1998) talked about the need to re-tool schooling in the face of the challenges brought about by the digital revolution. Re-tooling was a metaphor that they borrowed from Kuhn when looking at crises caused by paradigm shifts in science. In Kuhn's words:

> As long as the tools a paradigm supplies continue to prove capable of solving the problems it defines, science moves fastest and penetrates more deeply through confident employment of those tools. The reason is clear. As in manufacture, so in science – re-tooling is an extravagance to be reserved for the occasion that demands it. The significance of crises is the indication they provide that an occasion for re-tooling has arrived.
>
> (Kuhn, 1962: 76, quoted in Green and Bigum, 1998)

I, too, want to commandeer this metaphor in that it seems to me that the discipline of education as a whole is in crisis. It is at a turning point; so much so that the occasion for re-tooling has arrived.

In the previous chapter I tried to set out, at a generalised level, what the essential purposes of higher education in the modern world are. They concern 'the maximisation of reason'. It is this principle, I suggested, that is still at the heart of the idea of a university; it is this principle that can and should be applied to all of our research and to all forms of teaching, be they general or, as is more often the case in education, vocational. Like Barnett's student, even in the face of epistemological and ontological uncertainty, we want our students to be able to take up an informed position of their own; we want them to fly.

The maximisation of reason, then, is the essential purpose that marks the university out as a unique institution in society, even today. Other institutions – schools, think tanks, businesses, political parties, religious institutions – may, at times, engage in activities that have things in common with universities. They, too, may sometimes undertake research; they may critically assess evidence; they may engage in robust debate. But whereas now, these activities do happen on a wide scale within civil society, they are not the essential purposes of these institutions. Schools, businesses and most other institutions can and do continue to function perfectly well without making the maximisation of reason a core activity. What is distinctive about the university is that that is its very essence. In my view, if a university is not adopting that as its guiding principle in most of its activities, then it is not really worthy of the name.

But, as we have also seen, there are many different factors that are, today, making it increasingly hard for departments and faculties of education to realise this principle in their work. As I have indicated throughout this book, many of education's current difficulties are not of its own making. In some senses, the challenges faced by education are not fundamentally different from those faced by the whole of higher education today: the ever-growing elaboration of subspecialisms that fragments the academic community; the crisis of confidence in knowledge brought about by the 'postmodern turn'. And, most particularly, the marketisation of higher education with its multiple consequences: the development of managerialism; the casualisation of staffing; the increasing importance of externally defined utilitarian teaching and research. And in the face of these and many other challenges, the growing lack of self-confidence in higher education, the lack of any individual willing to stand up and say what the core purposes of the university actually are.

But, as I have also tried to make clear, education is a particularly extreme case of this more general university malaise. Education's difficulties go back right to the beginning of the nineteenth century, with the first intervention of the state into the professional education of teachers. Teacher education, both for initial preparation and for continuing professional development, has always been central to discipline of education within our universities; but it has always been far too important to governments simply to be left to the universities themselves to determine. As a result, apart from a brief period in the post-Robbins (1963) era, government intervention in teacher education has always been a major factor in the shaping of the field. Governments have, in different degrees, shaped the structure of provision, the curriculum and the entry and exit requirements of teacher education programmes. And this, in turn, has had major implications for the staff recruited to teach such courses, the professional and research interests that they develop, as well as the overall culture of most departments and faculties of education.

In all of these different ways, therefore, government intervention has been a major factor in the shaping of the discipline. And in recent years that intervention has become ever more invasive with the rise of simplistic neo-liberal policies that identify teacher quality as the only important variable in raising school achievement. As we saw in Chapter 8, as a result of these theories, teacher education is now at the epicentre of global policy change; departments and faculties of education increasingly find themselves having to live with the consequences.

Given these many challenges, it would not seem to be an exaggeration to say that the university-based discipline of education is in crisis. But the depth of the crisis is not one that many recognise. This is because it is much more profound than having to deal with the consequences of the latest government interventions

we begin to theorise it in order to make sense of it. For Hirst, though, the issue is not whether teachers naturally engage in theorising their practice; they do. Rather, the issue is whether the theories they espouse are good theories; whether they have been justified and developed by being exposed to the critical scrutiny of others; whether they are based on a consideration of evidence from research and from practice elsewhere; whether they have been interrogated in terms of the values and assumptions on which they are based.

It is when theories of teaching are developed in this rational way, they become what Hirst (1996) calls practical theories. As in other applied disciplines, such as engineering or clinical medicine, practical theories, he suggests, stand halfway between the world of practice and the world of research, disciplinary theory and other forms of knowledge. They remain practical; they are derived from practice and can help teachers in forming judgements about what to do in particular situations, but at the same time, they are based on some form of critical, rational reflection. Therefore, they are of crucial importance if the teaching profession is to develop and improve.

But Hirst does not go far enough. Like Hoyle's notion of extended professionality, the development of practical theories as described by Hirst is an exclusively intellectual exercise. It therefore stops short of what Aristotle highlighted in his notion of *phronesis*: the development of practical wisdom. As we saw in the previous chapter, for Aristotle, *phronesis* is the capability of acting truthfully and with reason in matters of deliberation. Practical wisdom emerges from practice but not simply from the application of skills; it involves the ability to reflect and achieve good ends as defined in the community. Technique has to be balanced by judgement; it therefore has a strong ethical dimension.

Being exposed to the best that is known about teaching and learning how to assess evidence and address the values implicit in different courses of action, learning how to utilise such knowledge to inform practical judgements, fostering the abilities and dispositions needed to develop morally justifiable practical wisdom in one's own work, all of these, then, are critical to effective professional education in a modern world. Without all of this and, above all, without developing the disposition necessary to acquire practical wisdom in relation to one's own practice, professional education becomes a narrow form of apprenticeship where current practices are simply reproduced.

But two questions remain. Firstly, why is it necessary for all teachers, individually, to develop practical wisdom in these ways? What is wrong with a centrally driven agenda? The answer is to be found in the forms of education needed in contemporary society. When we ask questions such as: what does it mean to prepare young people for learning in an uncertain world? Or: What forms of education are needed in a world where there are increasing uncertainties in relation to technology, in relation to knowledge and in relation to a society with ever increasing international mobility, diversity of values and cultural conflict? When we ask these sorts of questions, it becomes clear that the implications for teaching and learning are profound. More than ever before, we need to educate young people to think critically about knowledge and about values, to recognise differences in interpretation, to develop the skills needed to form their own judgements. And if that is true for our students, then it is also essential that all teachers develop similar aptitudes, skills and dispositions, constantly reflecting on their practice, systematically engaging with evidence, with critique and development.

As New Labour discovered rather late in the day (see Chapter 8), not all educational change can be mandated from the centre. Targets alone, however forcefully driven, will not achieve all that is needed for effective education in a rapidly changing world. Individual teachers themselves need to be engaged; they all need opportunities to look at good practice elsewhere and to expose their ideas, beliefs, practices and values to critical scrutiny. In short, they need opportunities to develop practical wisdom both through their initial training and through their further professional development.

The second question is to ask why universities must have a role in this process. Can't groups of schools simply do this for themselves? And the answer is that, of course, school to school, teacher to teacher, collaboration is an essential part of the process. We now have extensive research evidence showing that is true (Showers and Joyce, 1996; Cordingly *et al.*, 2003). But in addition to that, universities are in a unique position to make a distinctive contribution through a particular group of higher education staff – professional teacher educators. By the nature of their appointments, such staff are specialists in practical theory; they themselves have developed forms of practical wisdom in relation to teaching and learning. In the best current schemes, professional teacher educators, most of whom have, in the past, themselves been highly successful practitioners, have regular and direct involvement in schools. In this way, they are continually exposed to a wide range of different forms of practice.

At the same time, because they are based within universities, they have ready access to other forms of professional knowledge – to research, to other examples of what works, to disciplinary theory. Most importantly, they are based in an institution – the university – that is predicated on the principles of the maximisation of reason; they are part of a culture that expects to challenge, to debate, to interrogate taken-for-granted assumptions and values by exposing them to critical scrutiny. Professional teacher educators within universities are therefore uniquely well placed to work with practitioners to help them form a bridge for themselves between their own practical experience and other forms of professional knowledge. This is a key ingredient in the development of practical wisdom.

Such an approach to professional education has major implications for the university sector. It means that universities must maintain their commitment to the maximisation of reason in all their teaching. That, in turn, means that those at the forefront of teacher education cannot be casualised. Every lecturer needs to be a participant in a scholarly culture, able to contribute to the 'conversations at the forefront of their discipline' (Furlong, 1996). And, in turn, that means universities must support and expect all of their lecturers to undertake some form of personal research and/or scholarship – the essential ingredient for maintaining that scholarly culture.

But such a reassertion of the role of the university must not be seen as a justification for going back to the past, where universities remain distant from the world of practice. We urgently need forms of professional education that are more than instrumental, that debate ends as well as means. But if we have learned anything from the past 20 years of 'the turn to the practical', it is that we also need high quality practical training that is relevant to the needs of individuals, of schools and to the nation. The university must be a key contributor to the professional education of the future, but not as it was in the past. Schools need to be key contributors too; that is where the action is. It is practising teachers who know this school, this curriculum and these students. Far more than before, we therefore need universities and schools to work in forms of complementary partnership (Furlong *et al.*, 2000), where each contributes from its own strengths, its own essential purposes, where neither is in the lead, but where each institution learns from the other. Developing these sorts of partnerships is highly challenging for both schools and universities but is essential if we are to develop forms of professional education and, indeed, forms of schooling relevant to the twenty-first century.

Significantly, it is this vision of teacher education, with both strong university engagement as well as strong clinical experience in schools, that has recently been endorsed by the OECD in their review of the lessons for the USA that come about as a result of the most recent round of PISA results (OECD, 2011). As in other OECD documents, they lay great emphasis on the need to raise the entrance standards of teacher education programmes to make them comparable to other professions. In addition though they suggest that 'top performing countries' (Finland, Singapore, Shanghai) show some further common characteristics:

- Across the board, the best-performing countries are working to move their initial teacher education programmes towards a model based less on preparing academics and more on preparing professionals in clinical settings, in which they get into schools earlier, spend more time there and get more and better support in the process. In Finland, this includes both extensive course work on how to teach – with a strong emphasis on using research based on state-of-the-art practice – and at least a full year of clinical experience in a school associated with the university. These model schools are intended to develop and pilot innovative practices and foster research on learning and teaching.
- They put more emphasis on developing the capacity of teachers in training to diagnose student problems swiftly and accurately.
- They are working to develop the prospective teacher's capacity to draw from a wide repertoire of possible solutions that are particularly appropriate to the diagnosis.
- They put more emphasis on the specific instructional techniques that are appropriate for the subjects that the prospective teacher will teach. Because teacher education in Finland is a shared responsibility between the teacher education faculty and the academic-subject faculty, there is substantial attention to subject-specific pedagogy for prospective teachers.

- Some countries, notably Shanghai-China and Finland, provide teachers with the research skills needed to enable them to improve their practice in a highly disciplined way. In Finland, teachers are encouraged to contribute to the knowledge base on effective teaching practices throughout their career, with candidates not only expected to become familiar with the knowledge base in education and human development, but also required to write a research-based thesis as the final requirement for the masters degree. The Chinese, too, emphasise giving prospective teachers the skills they will need for action research and their method for improving their education system over time relies on research performed by teachers. China is also able to enlist teachers trained in this way as leaders of efforts organised by their ministries to systematically introduce and try out new ideas for improving their education systems.
- Part of the motivation for relocating teacher education programmes (from teachers' colleges) to the university has been to make sure that the preparation of teachers in the subjects they will teach is comparable to that of people who will go on to be professionals in other arenas. In most of these countries, people who are going on to be elementary or primary school teachers are required to declare whether they will specialise in either mathematics and science or their native language and social studies and they are required to attain a high level of substantive knowledge in the specialty they will teach. (OECD 2011:236)

In sharp contrast to current developments in England, the OECD vision therefore lays emphasis on both university based work and clinical school experience, on both research and professional practice. Such an approach is also in sharp contrast to the line of arguments put forward in Scotland by the Donaldson Report (2011). Though positive in many ways, Donaldson focuses only on the *personal* education of prospective teachers by insisting that they spend more time in other university departments; his recommendations therefore potentially weaken rather than strengthen the role of the university in professional education itself.

Much has been learned in England and Wales in the past decades about the best ways of developing the sorts of collaborative partnerships advocated by the OECD, partnerships where there is genuine joint ownership of profession learning, where there is mutual respect for the different contributions that schools and universities can make. In other parts of the UK and, indeed, internationally, those lessons have yet to be learned. Too often universities cling to their control of the system, misguidedly arguing that they can do it all. They can't. But even in England and Wales, genuine partnerships of this sort are still few and far between. Too often front line teacher educators have been casualised; too often they are on teaching-only contracts, not expected or encouraged to undertake research or scholarship, no longer full participants in the scholarly culture of their universities. Too often, instead of critical engagement, instead of the development of practical wisdom, the heavy hand of bureaucracy reduces professional learning to checklists, to standards and to performance targets. Too often universities themselves have let this happen. But as the best schemes in England and Wales have shown, it is possible to be both practically relevant and critically engaged, even against the odds of reductionist government directives.

The reason I have spent so long outlining the contribution of universities in professional education is because it is so central to the discipline as a whole. In a changing university world and in a hostile policy context, those involved in education need, yet again, to win the argument that universities have a central role here. It is an argument that as the OECD shows, has already been won in a number of very high performing school systems around the world; in recent months, Ireland has also signed up to a similar approach (Sahlberg *et al.*, 2012). That argument now needs to be won in the UK. If it is lost – and there is a chance that in England it might be – then this would have a profound effect in undermining the discipline as a whole. That is why it is so important. Universities do have a vital contribution to make to professional learning; it is perhaps more modest than was thought in the past – they can't do it all, they must work collaboratively – but their contribution is nonetheless critical. All of those with a stake in the field need to make that clear.

## Re-tooling for new forms of knowledge mobilisation

As we saw in earlier chapters, research is now a major dimension of the discipline of education, with nearly 1,700 active researchers returned to the previous RAE and an annual budget of probably in the region of £80,000,000. We also noted that notwithstanding Geoff Whitty's (2006) plea for the importance of education in addition to education*al* research – that is, research that studies the field of education for its own sake rather than simply for its use value – the vast majority of researchers do see their work as applied in some sense. They do want to make a difference; they do want to change the educational world, as well as understand it.

The moral position underlying a great deal of educational research is therefore a laudable one; for many of us, it is what drives us forward. However, the major weakness of this dominant ethic is that, in reality, the majority of educational research is not seen as making much impact on either policy or practice at all. It might contribute to the courses that we teach and that is important, but beyond that and with a few notable exceptions, its impact is not recognised or valued.

Of course, demonstrating the impact of any form of social research is very challenging, as those involved in preparing for the UK's 2014 REF can testify. As Carol Weiss (1979) pointed out over 30 years ago, most research does not have a direct impact on either policy or practice; rather, it works indirectly and over the long period, changing our assumptions about the world, changing the questions that need to be asked. This she characterised as 'knowledge creep', a process that may take as long as 20 years. So, demonstrating impact, convincing educational publics that research is important and has use value is very difficult to do.

And it is clear that, for the most part, education has not managed to do that effectively. This is a major problem for a discipline that characterises its research as primarily applied; it is a problem both inside and outside the university. Inside the academy, educational research is seen as weaker, as of lower status, precisely because it is applied rather than pure; outside of the academy it is considered largely academic, largely irrelevant to the day-to-day practices of schools, colleges and universities. This apparent lack of impact, I would argue, is a major flaw in the defence of the discipline; a flaw that urgently needs to be addressed.

In recent years the perception that educational research is remote, academic and therefore largely irrelevant have been exacerbated by the growing significance in educational policy circles of the arguments but forward by Gibbons and others (Gibbons *et al.*, 1994; Nowotny *et al.*, 2003) in relation to Mode 2 knowledge production. Their broad thesis is that universities, for so long the home of science, are no longer the only places in modern societies where knowledge is produced. Rather, the growing demand for specialist knowledge in our increasingly technical society and the expansion of the numbers of potential knowledge producers (as a result of the massification of higher education) means that, in many sectors of society, conditions are now set for the emergence of a new model of knowledge production, what they call Mode 2. Mode 2 research is, in principle, very different from Mode 1.

> In Mode 1 (which, for many, is identical with what is meant by science), problems are set and solved in a context governed by the largely academic interests of a specific community. By contrast, Mode 2 knowledge is carried out in a context of application. Mode 1 is hierarchical and tends to preserve its form, while Mode 2 is more heterarchical and transient … In comparison with Mode 1, Mode 2 is more socially accountable and reflexive. It includes wider, more temporary and heterogeneous sets of practitioners collaborating on a problem defined in a specific and localised context.
>
> (Gibbons *et al.*, 1994: 3)

Significantly, they argue, the outcomes of Mode 2 research are quite different from those produced in Mode 1. The knowledge produced will be more transitory, more context-specific, more frequently located within individuals themselves and their particular working context than in scientific journals. In short, it is, at least in part, embedded knowledge.

These arguments have, of course, been widely debated and critiqued. For example, Barnett (2000) makes an important point when he argues that although these ideas are a useful starting point, the straightforward distinction between knowledge inside and outside the university is simplistic and unhelpful. Increasingly, he argues, there are knowledges that intermingle in complex ways. Nevertheless, over the past 20 years, Gibbons *et al.*'s thesis has been powerfully influential in government policy, both scientific policy and educational policy. In education it is well captured in the highly influential paper by David Hargreaves (1999), 'The Knowledge-Creating School'. In that paper Hargreaves argues that, given the general view that educational research provides too little practical support to teachers and policymakers, the alternative is to make practitioners themselves the major source of knowledge creation.

The characteristics of knowledge-creating schools include a high volume of internal debate and professional networking, regular opportunities for reflection, enquiry and dialogue and a culture of no-blame experimentation and challenge. Knowledge creation, he suggests, may stem from involvement in initial teacher education or from schools themselves undertaking research. School-based research consortia, he argues, are particularly effective because they are collective rather than isolated enterprises.

And in England, in particular, it is precisely these sorts of initiatives that have been supported by governments in recent years. For example, the National College of School Leadership, which has been highly influential in the management and leadership of school systems, has had few formal links with the educational-research system in the UK. The primary emphasis of their work is to encourage schools themselves to work collaboratively together, supporting each other in creating and sharing knowledge rather than working in collaboration with universities in any systematic way. The same has been true in much of the TDA's strategy for continuing professional development. Increasingly, it has been schools themselves that have been seen as bodies that should create and disseminate good practice and these ideas are set to move further with the current policy development envisioned by the governments' new 'Teaching Schools' initiative (DfE, 2011a, 2011b, 2011c).

In other words a worrying number of government initiatives in education now explicity exclude universities as contributors to new developments in policy and practice. If university based educationalists believe that they do have something to say to professionals and to policy makers then they urgently need to find ways of connecting far more effectively than they have done in the past with their various publics. In short, it needs to re-tool by developing more effective strategies for 'knowledge mobilisation'.

I have borrowed the term knowledge mobilisation from the work of Levin and colleagues (Levin, 2011; Levin *et al.*, 2012). As he argues, there are a whole range of alternative phrases that are currently used to describe some of these processes – knowledge transfer, knowledge brokering, knowledge exchange. The term knowledge mobilisation, though, is perhaps more inclusive than most; it is also deliberately intended to be nonhierarchical.

> Knowledge mobilization is … getting the right information to the right people in the right format at the right time, so as to influence decision-making. Knowledge mobilization includes dissemination, knowledge transfer and knowledge translation.
>
> (Levin, 2011: 12)

There is potentially a wide range of different models available for knowledge mobilisation, some of which are already in use. However, it is clear that there is no one single or simple answer. Each model has its own strengths, weaknesses and challenges; each is only partial.

The strategy for knowledge mobilisation that has the longest pedigree in education is action research. Although Dewey did not use the term himself, it is clear that action research owes much to the pragmatist philosophy that he and others brought to educational thinking in the first part of the twentieth century (Hammersley, 2004). During the past 30 years, action research has become well established in the field of education and, in the UK, is particularly associated with the work of Stenhouse and his followers (Stenhouse, 1970, 1981; Elliott, 1978, 1985; Carr and Kemmis, 1986). More recently, it has been given a new twist by being reconceptualised as practitioner enquiry (Groundwater-Smith and Sachs, 2002; Campbell and Groundwater-Smith, 2007; Groundwater-Smith and Mockler, 2008). However, action research is, in fact, a much older tradition and much more varied (Lewin, 1948; Hodgkinson, 1957; Wallace, 1987); it is a broad church with many different interpretations and, indeed, disagreements about its core principles.

Nevertheless, there is agreement in the literature that action research is *situational*; it implies a commitment to diagnosing problems in specific contexts and attempting to solve them in those contexts. In most, though not all, interpretations (e.g. Halsey, 1972), there is also agreement that action research should be *collaborative* and *participatory*, with practitioners themselves having an active role in the research. Finally, in most interpretations action research is *self-evaluative*. Because the ultimate aim is to improve practice in some way, the context under study is continuously evaluated and practice, as well as the research design, constantly modified as the project moves forward.

But despite its popularity, there are often weaknesses and limitations with action research as a form of knowledge mobilisation. As I and my colleague Jane Salisbury (Furlong and Salisbury, 2005) noted in our evaluation of the English Best Practice Research Scholarship scheme (BPRS), which funded teachers to undertake action-research projects in their own schools, action-research projects do not always systematically build on what is known. As a result, they too often reinvent the wheel in what they were trying to do. In addition, although powerful as a form of personal professional development, all too often such research remains just that: personal.

Too many of the otherwise excellent projects that we saw were not effective in making their own findings public so that others could engage with them, critique them and build on them in relation to further research. In the best examples of action research that we saw, most of which were linked systematically with universities (which, once again, was not mandatory in this particular government scheme), these difficulties were overcome to some degree; there was evidence of more systematic engagement with the existing literature and with making findings public. But even here there were limitations to what could be achieved through this model of knowledge mobilisation. Individual practitioners are not professional researchers; therefore, they have neither the training nor the resources to carry out much of the research that is needed in a large-scale public education system.

While practitioner enquiry is appropriate for some forms of small-scale largely qualitative research and while it is potentially a highly effective strategy for encouraging serious engagement with and utilisation of existing research, it is not, nor is intended to be, a substitute for large-scale professional research. That sort of research needs to develop other sorts of strategies to ensure knowledge mobilisation.

In the UK over the past 20 years, we have had the benefit of a significant amount of experimentation with different forms of knowledge mobilisation for large-scale projects through the TLRP programme. User engagement was a central principle of all TLRP projects and reflections on that process were a key theme in one seminar series funded by the programme (Edwards *et al.*, 2007). As Edwards *et al.* note, 'The TLRP was the first large-scale systematic attempt to get to grips with aspects of Mode 2 knowledge production in educational research by making user engagement a requirement of funding'.

In their review of the different projects, Edwards *et al.* identify three major strategies that were utilised in this programme. Firstly, there were what they called university-led projects, where groups of users acted as co-researchers, advising on research design, on instruments and helped with data collection and dissemination. A second approach was what Edwards *et al.* call design experiments where materials or other interventions, developed by university-based research teams, were tested and developed in classrooms by teachers in cycles of iteration. As Edwards *et al.* note, this model of research revealed a number of productive tensions. For example:

> it was essential that classroom practitioners saw the time they spent on the research as worthwhile for their pupils; equally, it was important that they really did engage with the developments being tested. Also, boundaries between professional researchers and practitioner researchers became blurred, adding to tensions for the university-based researchers between being responsive to changes affecting practitioner communities while remaining faithful to the research designs.
>
> (Edwards *et al.*, 2007: 651)

The final strategy involved working with practitioners in order to create new concepts for new practices. This sort of research was different from the previous strategy in that researchers were not working with practitioners to *test* ways of working, but to generate fresh ways of explaining what was going on in both existing and emerging practices within relatively long-term partnerships.

Edwards et al. suggest that all of the participants left these projects with an enhanced capacity to contribute to their knowledge fields. It also led to research products that were socially robust and therefore more likely to have enhanced value in the worlds of policy and practice.

But action research and designing user engagement into research projects are not the only ways of enhancing knowledge mobilisation. Another strategy involves the use of mediators or knowledge brokers. In her recent research in

Canada, Cooper (2012) documents a wide range of such mediators working in education. There are government bodies such as ministry research branches and funding agencies; not-for-profit agencies such as some think tanks and university research centres; there are for-profit organisations such as textbook and test producers; and there are membership groups such as trade unions and other professional associations. All of these different sorts of groups, she argues, may engage in forms of research knowledge mediation, raising awareness, brokering linkages, providing policy sheets and fact sheets, all with a view to influencing policy.

Increasingly, it would seem that it is these mediating institutions that are key carriers of research messages to policymakers. Rather than direct linear relationships, researchers need to develop a network of relationships with these bodies. Not surprising, then, that one key capability that Edwards et al. advocate is the development amongst researchers of the key skill of know-who; it is just as important, they suggest, as know-what, know-why and know-how.

A final strategy for knowledge mobilisation is more radical than any of the above in that it involves thinking again about the institutional structures for supporting educational research. It might be argued that conventional university departments and faculties are not the most appropriate organisational form to ensure that universities continue to provide high quality research-based knowledge that is relevant and accessible to the educational system.

An interesting recent initiative (constitutionally, that is) has been Futurelab (http://www.futurelab.org.uk/). Initially based in Bristol (2001–2010) and overseen by NESTA (National Endowment for Science, Technology and the Arts), Futurelab was a charitable organisation devoted to research and development in the field of new technologies and learning. Working in partnership with a range of others, Futurelab's task was to: incubate new ideas, taking them from the lab to the classroom; support the design and use of innovative learning tools; communicate the latest thinking and practice in educational technology; and provide the space for experimentation and exchange of ideas between the creative, technology and education sectors. In short, it was involved both in basic and applied research and in knowledge mobilisation.

In order to achieve these ends, Futurelab was set up with a particularly interesting constitution. It had strong links with Bristol University but was not part of it, it had core government funding with close links with the Department for Education and it had close links with industry, both hard- and software manufacturers and the creative industries. All three groups – university, government and industry – were key partners with Futurelab but not in charge of it. Close links to government meant that research remained close to current policy agenda; close links to the university ensured high quality independent research; close links to industry meant access to the latest technical developments and opportunities for commercial exploitation. However, all research, even when funded by industry, was widely disseminated; it was all in the public domain.

It is not that Futurelab is necessarily a model for the future of all or, indeed, any other research institutes in the field of education. Nevertheless, its highly successful ten-year story does raise questions as to whether, in a rapidly changing world, we need to rethink the shape and constitution of at least some of our university-based activities.

Interestingly, similar questions have been floated recently by the English government, with its proposals for University Training Schools (DfE, 2010), where designated schools will serve both as sites for teacher education and for research and development. At the time of writing, two such schools have been proposed by the Institute of Education and the University of Birmingham. The difficulty, though, for most universities is that the initiative is, at present, linked to the government's controversial Free School initiative; therefore, universities have to set up an entirely new Free School in order for it to become designated as a University Training School. Were these two distinct policies to be uncoupled, I am sure that we would see many more new and different sorts of institutional arrangements begin to develop.

If educational research is to establish its legitimacy more effectively than at present, if it wants to convince its various publics that the university-based discipline of education has something important to contribute to the development of educational policy and practice, then it has to take knowledge mobilisation far more seriously than in the past. A discipline that defines itself, that prides itself on being applied but then fails to engage effectively with either policymakers or practitioners in much of its work is not credible. But saying it is needed does not mean that it is easily achieved. There is no single or simple answer to knowledge mobilisation; all of the strategies described above and probably many more are probably needed. But if educational research on any scale is going to survive in today's harsh economic climate, knowledge mobilisation must become a far more important issue for all educational researchers and research managers today.

## Re-tooling for research

The final area where education needs to re-tool is in relation to research or, I should say more precisely, research and scholarship, for I do not want to confine my comments to any particular genre of research or, indeed, only to the sort of research that might be entered into the REF. But, as I have tried to emphasise throughout this book, the engagement by academic staff in broadly based research and scholarship is central to what a university is. This is because the maximisation of reason must underpin all of its teaching activities if a university is to be worthy of its name.

It is not that all academic staff always need to be leading empirical researchers themselves; they don't. It is not that they all need to be publishing in leading international journals; they don't. But if academic staff are to engage in teaching and supervision that is to be truly based on the principle of the maximisation of reason, then they themselves need to be participants in conversations at the forefront of their specialist areas; they need to be full participants in a scholarly culture that supports the same principles in relation to their own work. This was the principle established by Humboldt in the University of Berlin in the early nineteenth century. Humboldt realised that university teaching was a two-way educative process, educative for both students and for their lecturers.

But how can deans and heads of departments ensure that there is such a scholarly culture amongst all of their staff? I would argue that the best way is to support, to encourage and to expect all academic staff to undertake personal research and scholarship of their own. Without that, how can we expect them to embrace the maximisation of reason as a core principle in their teaching?

But, as we have seen throughout this book, this principle of ensuring that all staff have the time, the opportunity and the support needed to develop as researchers and scholars is a principle that is just as often marked by its absence as by its affirmation. The figures outlined in Chapter 4 were startling: only one-third of all academics in education being entered for the 2008 RAE; only one-quarter holding a doctorate as their highest qualification; over a third of all academic staff on part-time, mainly hourly paid contracts.

On all of these indices, the position of academic staff in education is significantly worse than in any other social science discipline, implying that a far greater proportion of education's staff are *not* currently part of such a scholarly culture. In other words, since it fully joined the university sector, education has been sold short; in many cases, it has sold itself short.

Research-based teaching is not something that governments, particularly in England and Wales, expect or demand in many of the professional courses that they purchase from universities. Personal research and scholarship is not something that governments (across the UK) demand from all the staff that are employed delivering those courses. But these are things that deans and heads of departments can and should expect from all of their staff and in all of their teaching. Many universities – and not just the research elite universities – do manage to achieve this in their work. If education as a *university*-based discipline is to have any chance to arguing that it has something distinctive and important to contribute, then it is essential that all universities do the same.

So much for the general importance of research. But there are other sorts of re-tooling needed as well if educational research is to survive and thrive. We also need re-tooling in relation to methods, to theories and in relation to the topics that are studied.

In relation to research methods, things have improved substantially in the past decade or so. As we saw in Chapter 6, there is good evidence (from the ESRC, from the report of the last RAE panel) that the methodological quality of educational research is now strong. If it ever was true, there is now confidence that the criticisms of very low quality that were levelled at the discipline at the end of the 1990 are no longer valid.

Why has this happened? There have been a number of reasons. There have been several major investments in education with a particular focus on research-methods training and capacity development, especially the TLRP and the Scottish Applied Educational Research Scheme (AERS). In addition, over the past decade, the ESRC has invested some £28,000,000 in the National Centre for Research Methods, which offers intermediate- and advanced-methods training and development for the whole social science research community.

And lead bodies such as BERA have also had a role to play by offering training courses and master classes. But probably the biggest impetus to methodological improvement has been the very substantial increase in research funding during the New Labour period; research funding that was largely awarded by competitive tendering. Research funding is now contracting, but, nevertheless, we might expect research quality to continue to improve in the coming years as the ESRC's 21 Doctoral Training Centres begin to have an impact through the 600 studentships funded each year and through their other outreach activities.

But as positive as this story is, there is still more to be done. Although the quality of our best research is as good as in any other comparable discipline, there is still a long tail of average- and poor-quality work, as any large conference programme will demonstrate. And although things have improved substantially, there is still far too little quantitative research capacity within the discipline. It is not right that the discipline representing such a major field should still be so dominated by small-scale (often untheorised) qualitative research studies. And, finally, there is a need for more considered epistemological work in relation to mixed-methods research.

Mixed methods has increasingly emerged as an important strategy in research design. As such, it represents a considerable step forward from the paradigm wars of 20 or 30 years ago, where such designs would have been unthinkable. But, at present, it would seem that the rapprochement between different research traditions has only been possible by sidestepping many of the thorny epistemological differences that underlie them. One of the many challenges of the development of more interdisciplinary work, which we will consider below, is that it becomes increasingly important to employ multiple research methods. If education is to take its full part in this increasingly important area of work, it will need to face up to these difficult theoretical questions.

We also need to look again at the theories that underpin our work. In my book with Martin Lawn (Furlong and Lawn, 2010), we looked at the past and current roles of the disciplines of education – sociology, psychology, history, economics, etc. in educational research. It was not that we thought that these were the only or even the most important theoretical frameworks available in education; there are any number of others – poststructuralism, sociocultural theory, feminism and many, many more. Our argument, though, was that these original disciplines were still important because they were still generative of educational research in a whole variety of methodological and theoretical ways. We also thought that with the development of a more market-driven economy in higher education, there was a real danger that these important perspectives would be squeezed out from research and scholarship as they have been from much of our teaching.

What we discovered was that in most but not all cases, the disciplines of education were alive and well but usually lived out on voluntary bases in conferences, in journals and in learned societies. What we did not find beyond the Institute of Education was their representation in formal courses and in designated lectureships and professorships. They do, therefore, remain vibrant but highly specialised subareas of activity.

Given this profile, it seems that the disciplines need to be opened up in a number of different ways. In comparison with 20 years ago, most disciplines of education are now cut off from their parent disciplines of sociology or philosophy or history, etc. This is a problem in that in education, most of these disciplinary-based communities are very small. For example, Oancea and Bridges (2010) estimate that there are fewer than 100 academics working in education departments in the UK who publish in the field of philosophy of education; Crozier (2010) estimates that there are about 200 education academics publishing in psychology; numbers of sociologists and historians, economists and geographers are likely to be even smaller. We also know that many of these disciplinary specialists work in relative isolation in their own institutions, perhaps inevitable given the lack of disciplinary-based teaching that is available in many university departments of education.

As a result, there is a real danger that these small communities lack the size to support lively debate about theories, methods and epistemologies; without being more outgoing, there is a real danger that they will atrophy. If this is true of the established disciplines, it is even more true of other theoretical perspectives employed in education; they are likely to be even more isolated.

The second opening up needed is between disciplines of education to more applied work. Given the reality of current political economy of educational research, if they are to survive, all theoretical perspectives need to make their case as important contributors to applied work. It is increasingly difficult to sustain an argument that their contribution is only in terms of pure research.

A final opening up concerns the relationship between different theoretical perspectives themselves. What is increasingly clear – particularly in applied work – is that however powerful the contribution of the disciplines and other theoretical perspectives are in the framing of educational problems, any such framing is, in itself, inevitably only partial. The strength of theoretical perspectives – their ability to frame educational issues in ways that can promote rigourous analysis – is also often their weakness, in that they can limit the questions that we can ask about complex educational issues. Limited questions give limited answers.

This brings us neatly to the final challenge for re-tooling in educational research and that concerns the topics that we study, our research agenda. Partly because of the nature of teaching in education and its consequent impact on the staff recruited, the vast majority of research is focused on the school population. In recent years higher education has started to emerge as an important topic for research as well, although in many institutions this takes place as much outside departments and faculties of education as inside them.

However, if the discipline of education is to have a secure position university of the future, then it rapidly needs to broaden its research ag Issues of teaching and learning in the school system are important to study, in the modern world, educational questions are emerging in an ever-increasi range of contexts. It is now widely accepted that there are important educatio questions that need to be asked in relation to climate change, social equality, the economy, world poverty and social change, particularly the fact that we have a rapidly aging society. However, it is salutary to reflect that, although there is wide recognition that there are educational dimensions involved in all of these major issues, few governments or other funding bodies would turn to university departments and faculties of education to contribute to research and advanced teaching in relation to them. Not surprising if so much of education's research and expertise remains so firmly rooted in the compulsory British school system.

If education is to maintain its position in the university system, there is an urgent need to re-tool itself to broaden its research agenda. But here there is a link with the earlier discussion of theory and method. None of the issues identified above are purely educational ones. Developing a research profile in them will therefore demand that educational researchers become much more collaborative than in the past. That will demand new approaches to theory and new approaches to research methods and it will demand increasing attention to the epistemological complexities underlying interdisciplinary and multidisciplinary work. There is growing evidence that key funding and policy bodies – the European Union, the ESRC and the Department for International Development (DfID) – now recognise that in addressing key policy issues, interdisciplinary teams are essential. For many educationalists, this will be highly challenging, but it will be essential if education as a discipline is not to be squeezed out from the key research agenda of the future.

## Conclusion

Planning and writing this book over the past few years has been something of a rollercoaster. When I first thought of the need for such a book in about 2008, England was still under a New Labour government and the implications of the financial crash were not clear. Although not without its problems, particularly its excessive managerialism, New Labour did invest substantially in higher education generally and in teacher education in particular and more money was spent on educational research than ever before. Little did I know that when I actually came to begin work on the book, shortly after the 2010 election, how much would change and how rapidly.

Today the outlook for universities in the UK and particularly in England seems profoundly uncertain as we move towards a largely market-based system of provision with an end to government subsidies for most university teaching. The encouragement of private, for-profit universities is also unsettling. Other uncertainties that affect the whole of the higher education arise because of the consequences of the recession; the substantial contraction in research funding is particularly significant here. But the position of departments and faculties of education in England is particularly bleak, where the prospect of the School Direct model of initial teacher education is about to destabilise the system even further. As I have indicated before, the size and shape of the university-based discipline of education could look very different in England in five years' time from what it does today.

But in the light of these seismic changes, how should departments and faculties of education respond? Given that so many of the challenges faced by education are beyond its control – the ever-increasing marketisation of higher education, the impact of neo-liberal policies on teacher education and on research management – what, if anything, can be done? Clearly, there are political answers here that, though vitally important, are beyond the remit of this book.

My aim in this book has been to argue that before any political strategies are adopted, we need to be much clearer than we have been in the past as to what the purpose of the university-based study of education actually is. Those closest to the discipline need to be much more aware than they often have been about where the discipline comes from, about its current strengths and weaknesses and about the forces that help currently to shape it. But most important of all is to understand its essential purposes, to understand how the discipline of education has something important and unique to contribute to the advancement of the field both practically and intellectually.

It has been a long journey since the Cross Commission of 1888 first encouraged the engagement of the universities with the education of teachers; 125 years since the discipline of education gained its first foothold in the university system. Much has been achieved, especially in the past quarter of a century. Today education is a major part of the university sector. At best, its teaching is both academically rigorous as well as practically relevant; its research, particularly that which is entered for national research assessment, can stand shoulder to shoulder with the very best in the social sciences.

Overall, its teaching and its research has had a major impact on our understanding of education wherever it takes place; it has also contributed substantially to its improvement. I personally believe that even in England, the future contribution of our universities to teaching and research in education will be a positive one. Despite the fact that educational policymaking is currently in the grip of hostile ideologies, growing international evidence (from Singapore, from Finland, from Shanghai) reaffirms the vital contribution that universities can and must make to the development of our educational institutions and practices.

These are messages that are already understood in the rest of the UK, particularly in Scotland, but they are messages that will, I believe, eventually be understood even in England. In the short-term the challenges may be severe, but in those circumstances the best thing we can do is to be clear about what our essential purposes are and do our very best to stick to those principles, come what may. In the longer term that will be in the best interests of the discipline of education and in the best interests of learners everywhere.

# Appendix

## Tables from Chapter 4

*Table 4.1* Full- and part-time staffing in 10 UK university faculties and departments of education (2010/11)

| *University type* | | *Russell Group* | | *Other pre-1992* | | | *Ex-polytechnics* | | *'Recent'* | | |
|---|---|---|---|---|---|---|---|---|---|---|---|
| Institution | | 1 | 2 | 3 (IOE) | 4 | 5 | 6 | 7 | 8 | 9 | 10 |
| Teaching and res | f/t | 27 | 31 | 154 | 39 | 41 | 74 | 75 | 75 | 23 | 36 |
| | p/t | 1 | 12 | 89 | 10 | 1 | 5 | 32 | 45 | 2 | 17 |
| Teaching only | f/t | 10 | 2 | – | 3 | 17 | – | – | – | – | |
| | p/t | 3 | 9 | 5 | 9 | 2 | 4 | – | – | 21 | |
| Teaching only | Hourly | 121 | 6 | 111 | 122 | Not available | 37 | 122 | 146 | 25 | 33 |
| Research | f/t | 12 | 10 | 64 | – | 6 | 1 | 4 | – | – | – |
| | p/t | 1 | 7 | 78 | 5 | 1 | 1 | 8 | – | – | 1 |

*Table 4.2* Staff entered for the RAE in 2008 in 10 UK faculties and departments of education

| *University type* | *Russell Group* | | *Other pre-1992* | | | *Ex-polytechnics* | | *'Recent'* | | |
|---|---|---|---|---|---|---|---|---|---|---|
| Institution | 1 | 2 | 3 (IOE) | 4 | 5 | 6 | 7 | 8 | 9 | 10 |
| Teaching and research staff employed 2007/8* | 24 | 41 | 178 | 36 | 138 | 60 | 88 | 87 | 26 | 32 |
| Staff entered 2008 RAE ** | 19 | 43 | 218 | 9 | 54 | 7 | 15 | 27 | 9 | 4 |
| 'Research intensity ratio' | 0.77 | 1.05 | 1.22 | 0.25 | 0.39 | 0.15 | 0.17 | 0.31 | 0.34 | 0.12 |

*Numbers include FTE staff reported to HESA staffing survey 2007–8
** Figures taken from RAE (2008a) results (http://www.rae.ac.uk/)

*Table 4.3* Student numbers (new enrolments) on principal undergraduate courses in 10 UK faculties and departments of education in 2010/11

| *University type* | *Institution* | | *Foundation degree* | | *BA(Ed) QTS primary* | | *Other undergrad without QTS* | |
|---|---|---|---|---|---|---|---|---|
| | | | home | o/s | home | o/s | home | o/s |
| Russell Group | 1 | f/t | | | | | | |
| | | p/t | | | | | | |
| | 2 | f/t | | | | | | |
| | | p/t | | | | | | |
| Other pre-1992 | 3 (IOE) | f/t | 49 | | | | 1 | |
| | | p/t | 2 | | | | 79 | 4 |
| | 4 | f/t | 48 | | 55 | | 47 | |
| | | p/t | | | | | | |
| | 5 | f/t | | | 43 | | | |
| | | p/t | | | | | | |
| Ex-polytechnics | 6 | f/t | | | 19 | | 28 | |
| | | p/t | 30 | 19 | | | | |
| | 7 | f/t | 15 | | 168 | | 75 | |
| | | p/t | | | | | | |
| 'Recent' | 8 | f/t | 151 | | 313 | | 340 | |
| | | p/t | | | | | 5 | |
| | 9 | f/t | 10 | | | | 95 | |
| | | p/t | | | | | 21 | |
| | 10 | f/t | 155 | 19 | 140 | | 38 | 32 |
| | | p/t | | | | | 1 | |

*Table 4.4* Student numbers (new enrolments) on PGCE* programmes in 10 UK faculties and departments of education in 2010/11

| *University type* | *Institution* | | *PGCE primary + KS 2/3* | | *PGCE secondary* | | *PGCE PCET* | |
|---|---|---|---|---|---|---|---|---|
| | | | home | o/s | home | o/s | home | o/s |
| Russell Group | 1 | f/t | | | 173 | | | |
| | | p/t | | | | | | |
| | 2 | f/t | | | 240 | | | |
| | | p/t | | | | | | |
| Other pre-1992 | 3 (IOE) | f/t | 221 | 1 | 822 | 12 | 79 | 141 |
| | | p/t | 60 | 1 | 57 | | | |
| | 4 | f/t | 59 | | 189 | 4 | | |
| | | p/t | | | | | | |
| | 5 | f/t | 130 | 20 | 464 | 15 | | |
| | | p/t | | | | | | |
| Ex-polytechnics | 6 | f/t | | | 139 | | 150 | |
| | | p/t | | | | | 514 | |
| | 7 | f/t | 79 | | 110 | | 139 | |
| | | p/t | | | | | 419 | |
| 'Recent' | 8 | f/t | 238 | | 189 | 3 | | |
| | | p/t | | | | | | |
| | 9 | f/t | 255 | 1 | 335 | 1 | | |
| | | p/t | | | | | 61 | |
| | 10 | f/t | 146 | | 17 | | | |
| | | p/t | 1 | | | | | |

*PGDE in Scotland

*Table 4.5* Student numbers (new enrolments) on principal higher degree programmes in 10 UK faculties and departments of education in 2010/11

| *University type* | *Institution* | | *Professional masters – MEd etc.** | | *Other masters – MSc, MPhil etc.* | | *PhD* | | *EdD* | |
|---|---|---|---|---|---|---|---|---|---|---|
| | | | home | o/s | home | o/s | home | o/s | home | o/s |
| Russell Group | 1 | f/t | 42 | 6 | | | 5 | | 24 | |
| | | p/t | 183 | 2 | | | 2 | | | |
| | 2 | f/t | 40 | 37 | 10 | 37 | 8 | 10 | 1 | 2 |
| | | p/t | 70 | 25 | 11 | 25 | 2 | 3 | 10 | 30 |
| Other pre-1992 | 3 (IOE) | f/t | 27 | 10 | 191 | 163 | 24 | 31 | | |
| | | p/t | 118 | 2 | 1501 | 163 | 51 | 4 | 41 | 11 |
| | 4 | f/t | | | | 9 | 2 | 7 | | |
| | | p/t | 122 | | 117 | | 3 | | 19 | |
| | 5 | f/t | | | | | 11 | 12 | 3 | 1 |
| | | p/t | 450 | | 5 | | 23 | | 33 | |
| Ex-polytechnics | 6 | f/t | | | | | | 2 | | |
| | | p/t | 266 | | | | 4 | 3 | 16 | |
| | 7 | f/t | | | | | | | | |
| | | p/t | 237 | 12 | | | 4 | 3 | 11 | 2 |
| 'Recent' | 8 | f/t | 31 | 32 | | | 6 | 1 | | |
| | | p/t | 10 | 11 | | | 8 | 1 | 7 | 9 |
| | 9 | f/t | | | | | | | | |
| | | p/t | 93 | | 9 | | 2 | | | |
| | 10 | f/t | | | | | | 1 | | |
| | | p/t | 69 | | | | 4 | | | |

*Includes Chartered Teacher Programme in Scotland

# References


Alexander, R. (1984) Innovation and continuity in the initial teacher education curriculum, in R. Alexander, M. Craft and J. Lynch (eds) *Change in Teacher Education: Context and Provision Since Robbins*. Austin: Holt, Rinehart and Winston.

Allen, R. (2010) Replicating Swedish Free School reforms in England, *Research in Public Policy*, Centre for Market and Public Organisation Issue 10, 4–7.

Altbach, P. (2010) *Trends in Global Higher Education: Tracking an Academic Revolution*. Boston: Centre for International Higher Education, Boston College.

Arnold, M. (1869) Culture and anarchy, in R. Super (ed.) (1965) *The Complete Prose Works of Matthew Arnold*, vol. V. Ann Arbor: The University of Michigan Press, 1960–1977.

Australian Research Council (2010) *ERA 2012 Journal List*. Available online: http://www.arc.gov.au/era/era_2012/era_journal_list.htm (last accessed 11 October 2012).

Bailey, C. (1984) *Beyond the Present and the Particular: A Theory of Liberal Education*. London: Routledge.

Ball, S. (2003) The teacher's soul and the terrors of performativity, *Journal of Education Policy*, 18(2), 215–228.

Barnett, R. (1990) *The Idea of Higher Education*. Buckingham: Open University Press.

Barnett, R. (2000) *Realizing the University in an Age of Super-Complexity*. Buckingham: Open University Press.

Barnett, R. (2007) *A Will to Learn: Being a Student in an Age of Uncertainty*. Maidenhead: Open University Press.

Bauman, Z. (2000) *Liquid Modernity*. Cambridge: Polity Press.

BBC (2010) *Schools spending 'will not rise in real terms'*. Available online: http://www.bbc.co.uk/news/education-11983026 (last accessed 11 October 2012).

Becher, T. (1989) *Academic Tribes and Territories: Intellectual Enquiry and the Cultures of Disciplines*. Buckingham: Open University Press.

Becher, T. and Trowler, P. (2000) *Academic Tribes and Territories: Intellectual Enquiry and the Cultures of Disciplines*. 2nd edn. Buckingham: Open University Press.

Bell, A. (1981) Structure, knowledge and relationships in teacher education, *British Journal of Sociology of Education*, 2(1), 3–23.

Benton, P. (ed.) (1990) *The Oxford Internship Scheme*. London: Calouste Gulbenkian Foundation.
BERA/UCET (2012) *Prospects for Education Research in Education Departments in Higher Education Institutions in the UK*. London: BERA/UCET. Available online: http://www.bera.ac.uk/news/bera-ucet-report (last accessed 11 October 2012).
Berliner, D. (2002) Educational research: the hardest science of all, *Educational Researcher*, 31(8), 18–20.
Bernstein, B. (1971) *Class, Codes and Control: Towards a Theory of Educational Transmissions* (2nd edn, vol. 3). London: Routledge and Kegan Paul.
BIS (2011) *The Government's Response to Lord Browne's Review*. London: BIS.
Blair, T. (1996) *Speech Given at Ruskin College, Oxford*, 16 December 1996.
Blunkett, D. (2000) Influence or irrelevance: can social science improve government? *Research Intelligence* 71, 12–21.
Bochel, H. (2011) Conservative approaches to social policy since 1997, in H. Bochel (ed.) *The Conservative Party and Social Policy*. Bristol: The Policy Press
Bologna Process (2007–10) *Doctoral Education: Key issues*. Available online: http://www.ond.vlaanderen.be/hogeronderwijs/bologna/actionlines/doctoral_education_key_issues.htm (last accessed 11 October 2012).
Bowden, J. and Marton, F. (1998) *The University of Learning: Beyond Quality and Competence in Higher Education*. London: Kogan Page.
Bowe, R. and Ball, S. with Gold, A. (1992) *Reforming Education and Changing Schools: Case Studies in Policy Sociology*. London: Routledge.
Brew, A. and Lucas, L. (eds) (2009) *Academic Research and Researchers*. Buckingham: Society for Research in Higher Education/Open University Press.
Bridges, D. (2006) The disciplines and discipline of educational research, *Journal of Philosophy of Education*, 40(2), 259–272.
Brown, R. (2010) *Higher Education and the Market*. London: Routledge.
Browne Report (2010) *Securing a Sustainable Future for Higher Education. Independent Review of Higher Education (the Browne Report)*. London: BIS.
Burn, K., Childs, A. and McNicholl, J. (2007) The potential and challenges for student teachers' learning of subject specific pedagogical knowledge within secondary school subject departments, *The Curriculum Journal*, 18(4), 429–446.
Burton, D. and Goodman, R. (2011) The Masters in Teaching and Learning: a revolution in teacher education or a bright light quickly extinguished?, *Journal of Education for Teaching*, 37(1), 51–56.
Cabinet Office (2011) *Open Public Services* (White Paper). London: Cabinet Office.
Cameron, D. (2010) *The Big Society*. London: Office of the British Prime Minister. Available online: http://www.number10.gov.uk/news/big-society-speech/ (last accessed 11 October 2012).
Campbell, A. and Groundwater-Smith, S. (2007) *An Ethical Approach to Practitioner Research: Dealing with Issues and Dilemmas in Action Research*. New York: Routledge.
Campbell, A. and Groundwater-Smith, S. (eds) (2010) *Action Research in Education*. Los Angeles: Sage Publications.
Campbell, A., McNamara, O., Furlong, J., Howson, J. and Lewis, S. (2005) *The National Partnership Project Evaluation: Final Report to the TTA*. Liverpool: Liverpool Hope University.

Carr, W. (2006) Education without theory, *British Journal of Educational Studies*, 54(2), 136–159.

Carr, W. (2007) *Educational Research In The 21st Century: Confronting The Postmodern Challenge*, unpublished paper.

Carr, W. and Kemmis, S. (1986) *Becoming Critical: Education, Knowledge and Action Research*. London: Falmer.

Centre for Market and Public Organization (2011) *Delivering Better Public Services*. Bristol: Centre for Market and Public Organization. Available online: http://www.bristol.ac.uk/cmpo/publications/bulletin/winter11/better services.pdf (last accessed 11 October 2012).

Chomsky, N. (1999) *Profit Over People: Neo-liberalism and Global Order*. New York: Seven Stories Press.

Christie, D. (2006) The Standard for Chartered Teacher in Scotland: A New Context for the Assessment and Professional Development of Teachers, *Studies in Educational Evaluation*, 32, 53–72.

Clark, B. (1998) Creating entrepreneurial universities: organizational pathways of transformation, *Higher Education*, 38(3), 373–374.

Clifford, G. and Guthrie, G. (1988) *Ed School: A Brief for Professional Education*. Chicago: University of Chicago Press.

Cochran-Smith, M. (2005) The new teacher education: for better or for worse? *Educational Researcher*, 34(6), 181–206.

Cochran-Smith, M. (2008) The new teacher education in the United States: directions forward, *Teachers and Teaching: Theory and Practice*, 14(4), 271–282. Reprinted in J. Furlong, M. Cochran-Smith and M. Brennan (eds) (2008) *Policy and Politics in Teacher Education: International Perspectives*. London: Routledge.

Cochran-Smith, M. and Lytle, S. (2009) *Inquiry as Stance: Practitioner Research in the Next Generation*. New York: Teachers' College Press.

Cochran-Smith, M., Piazza, P. and Power, C. (forthcoming) The politics of accountability: assessing teacher education in the US, *The Educational Forum*.

Collini, S. (2012) *What Are Universties For?* London: Penguin Books.

Cooper, A. (2012) *Research Mediation in Education: A Cross-case Analysis of 44 Knowledge Mobilization intermediaries across Canada*. Paper presented at AERA 2012, Vancouver, Canada.

Cordingley, P., Bell, M., Rundell, B., Evans, D. and Curtis, A. (2003) *The Impact of Collaborative CPD on Classroom Teaching and Learn*ing: *An Eppi Systematic Review*. Available online: http://eppi.ioe.ac.uk/cms/Default.aspx?tabid=136 (last accessed 11 October 2012).

Crook, D. (1995) Universities, teacher training and the legacy of McNair, 1944–94, *History of Education*, 24(3), 231–245.

Crook, D. (1997) Challenge, response and dilution: a revisionist view of the Emergency Training Scheme for Teachers, 1945–1951, *Cambridge Journal of Education*, 27(3), 379–389.

Crook, D. (2002) Educational studies and teacher education, *British Journal of Educational Studies*, 50(1), 57–75.

Cross Commission (1888) *Final Report of the Royal Commission on the Working of the Elementary Education Acts, England and Wales (1888) (Cross Commission Final Report)*. London: HMSO.

Crozier, W. R. (2010) The psychology of education: achievements and challenges, in J. Furlong and M. Lawn (eds) *The Disciplines of Education. Their Role in the Future of Education Research*. London: Routledge.

Cunningham, P. (1992) Teachers' professional image and the press 1950–1990, *History of Education*, 21(1), 37–56.

Dale, R. (1999) Specifying globalisation effects on national policy: focus on the mechanisms, *Journal of Education Policy*, 14, 1–17.

Davies, C. and Eynon, R. (2012) *Teenagers and Technology*. London: Routledge.

DCSF (2008) *Being the Best for our Children: Releasing Talent for Teaching And Learning*. London: DCSF.

Dearing, R. (1997) *National Committee of Inquiry into Higher Education (The Dearing Report)*. London: HMSO.

Deem, R., Hilyard, S. and Reid, M. (2007) *Knowledge, Higher Education and the New Managerialism: The Changing Management of UK Universities*. Oxford: Oxford University Press.

Deem, R. and Lucas, L. (2007) Research and teaching cultures in two contrasting UK policy contexts: academic life in education departments in five English and Scottish universities, *Higher Education*, 54(1), 115–133.

Delanty, G. (2001) *Challenging Knowledge: The University in the Knowledge Society*. Buckingham: Society for Research in Higher Education/Open University Press.

Delbanco, A. (2012) *College: What It Was, Is and Should Be*. Princeton: Princeton University Press.

Demeritt, D. (2000) The new social contract for science: accountability, relevance and value in UK and US science and research policy, *Antipode*, 32(3), 308–329.

Deng, Z. and Luke, A. (2008) Subject matter: defining and theorizing school subjects, in M. Connelly, M. F. He and J. Phillion (eds) *The Sage Handbook of Curriculum and Instruction*, Los Angeles: Sage Publications, 66–87.

DENI (2011) *An Inspection Report on the PGCE Programme, with a Focus on Literacy and Numeracy, Queen's University Belfast Inspected: June 2010*. Belfast: Education and Training Inspectorate.

Dent, H. (1977) *The Training of Teachers in England and Wales, 1800–1975*. London: Hodder and Stoughton.

DES (1984) *Initial Teacher Training: Approval of Courses (Circular 3/84)*. London: DES.

DfE (2010) *The Importance of Teaching* (White Paper), London: DfE.

DfE (2011a) *Training our Next Generation of Outstanding Teachers: A Discussion Paper*. London: DfE.

DfE (2011b) *Training our Next Generation of Teachers: Implementation Plan*. London: DfE.

DfE (2011c) *Teachers' Standards Effective from 1 September 2012*. London: DfE.

DfEE (1997) *Circular 10/97*. London: DfEE.

DfEE (1998a) *The Learning Age (Green Paper)*. London: DfEE

DfEE (1998b) *Teachers: Meeting the Challenge of Change (Green Paper)*. London, DfEE.

DfEE (2001) *Schools: Building on Success (Green Paper)*. London: DfEE.

DfES (2003) *Every Child Matters (Green Paper)*. London: HMSO.

DfES (2006) *Primary National Strategy: Primary Frameworks for Literacy and Mathematics.* London, DfES.

DfES/TTA (2002) *Qualifying to Teach (Professional Standards for Qualified Teacher Status and Requirements for Initial Teacher Training).* London: DfES/TTA.

Donaldson, G. (2011) *Teaching Scotland's Future.* Edinburgh: The Scottish Government.

Eason, T. (1971) Main subject courses, in J. Tibble (ed.) *The Future of Teacher Education.* London: Routledge and Kegan Paul.

Edwards, A. (1997) *Evidence-based Teaching.* Paper given at Standing Conference for Studies in Education Conference: What Teaches Need to Know: the research basis of teaching, Van Milder College, Durham, June.

Edwards, A. (2010) *Being an Expert Professional Practitioner: The Relational Turn in Expertise.* Dordrecht, Springer.

Edwards, A., Sebba, J. and Rickinson, M. (2007) Working with users: some implications for educational research, *British Educational Research Journal,* 33(5), 647–661.

Elliott, J. (1978) What is action-research in schools? *Journal of Curriculum Studies,* 10(4), 355–357.

Elliott, J. (1985) Educational action research, in J. Nisbet and S. Nisbet (eds) *Research Policy and Practice,* London: Kogan Page.

Ellis, V., McNicholl, J. and Pendry, A. (forthcoming) Institutional conceptualisations of teacher education as academic work in England, *Teaching and Teacher Education.*

Estyn (2011) *Annual Report 2009–10.* Cardiff: Estyn.

European Commission (2005) *European Universities: Enhancing Europe's Research Base.* Luxembourg: Office for Official Publications of the European Communities.

European Commission (2006) *Delivering the Modernization Agenda for the Universities.* Brussels: European Commission.

Fallis, G. (2007) *Multiversities, Ideas and Democracy.* Toronto: University of Toronto Press.

Farry, S. (2011) *Northern Ireland Assembly Report (Hansard) Reports 11–12,* 28 November 2011. Available online: http://www.niassembly.gov.uk/Assembly-Business/Official-Report/Reports-11-12/28-November-2011/#a2 (last accessed 11 October 2012).

Feuer, M. J., Towne. L. and Shavelson, R. J. (2002) Scientific culture and educational research, *Educational Researcher,* 31(8), 4–14.

Fiske, J. (1987) *Television Culture.* London: Routledge.

Furlong, J. (1996) Do student teachers need higher education? in J. Furlong and R. Smith (eds) *The Role of Higher Education in Initial Teacher Training.* London: Kogan Page.

Furlong, J. (1998) *Inaugural Lecture. Educational Research: Meeting the Challenge of Change.* Bristol: Graduate School of Education, University of Bristol.

Furlong, J. (2004) BERA at 30: have we come of age?, *British Educational Research Journal,* 30(3), 343–358.

Furlong, J. (2005) New Labour and teacher education: the end of an era?, *Oxford Review of Education,* 31(1), 119–134.

Furlong, J. (2011a) The English Masters in Teaching and Learning: a new arena for practitioner inquiry? In N. Mockler and J. Sachs (eds) *Completing the Circle: Practitioner Inquiry for and with Teachers and Students. A Festschrift in Honour of Susan Groundwater-Smith.* New York: Springer.

Furlong, J. (2011b) Universities and the discipline of education: understanding the impact of the United Kingdom's Research Assessment Exercise, *Power and Education*, 3(1), 18–30.

Furlong, J. (2013) Globalisation, neo-liberalism and the reform of teacher education in England, *The Educational Forum* (forthcoming).

Furlong, J., Barton, L., Miles, S., Whiting, C. and Whitty, G. (2000) *Teacher Education in Transition: Re-forming Teacher Professionalism?* Buckingham: Open University Press.

Furlong, J. and Davies, C. (2012) Young people, new technologies and learning at home: taking context seriously, *Oxford Review of Education,* 38(1), 45–62.

Furlong, J., Hagger, H., Butcher, C. and Howson, J. (2006) *Review of Initial Teacher Training in Wales.* National Assembly for Wales (The Furlong Report). Oxford: University of Oxford Department of Education. Available online: http://wales.gov.uk/docrepos/40382/4038232/4038211/40382121/itt-provision-wales-e.pdf?lang=en (last accessed 11 October 2012).

Furlong, J., Hirst, P. H., Pocklington, K. and Miles, S. (1998) *Initial Teacher Training and the Role of the School.* Milton Keynes: Open University Press.

Furlong, J. and Lawn, M. (eds) (2010) *The Disciplines of Education: Their Role in the Future of Education Research.* London: Routledge.

Furlong, J. and Oancea, A. (2006) Assessing quality in applied and practice-based research in education: a framework for discussion, *Review of Australian Research in Education, No 6: Counterpoints on the Quality and Impact of Educational Research*, 85–100.

Furlong, J. and Salisbury, J. (2005) The Best Practice Research Scholarship Scheme: an evaluation, *Research Papers in Education*, 20(1), 45–83.

Gardner, P. (1998) Classroom teachers and educational change 1876/1996, *Journal of Education for Teaching*, 24(1), 33–50.

Gardner, P. and Cunningham, P. (1998) Teacher trainers and educational change in Britain, 1876–1996: a flawed and deficient history? *Journal of Education for Teaching*, 24(3), 231–255.

General Teaching Council for Scotland (2006) *Standards for Initial Teacher Education.* Available online: http://www.gtcs.org.uk/web/FILES/the-standards/the-standard-for-initial-teacher-education.pdf (last accessed 11 October 2012).

Gibb, N. (2010a) Speech to the Reform Conference, July 2010 London: DfE. Available online: http://www.education.gov.uk/inthenews/speeches/a0061473/nick-gibb-to-the-reform-conference. (last accessed 11 October 2012).

Gibb, N. (2010b) So Who is Nick Gibb? *Guardian Newspaper*, 17 May 2010. Available online: http://www.guardian.co.uk/education/2010/may/18/nick-gibb-schools-minister-teachers (last accessed 11 October 2012).

Gibbons, M., Limoges, C. and Nowotny, H. (1994) *The New Production of Knowledge: The Dynamics of Science and Research in Contemporary Societies.* London: Sage.

Giddens, A. (1990) *The Consequences of Modernity.* Stanford: Stanford University Press.

Giddens, A. (2000) *The Third Way and its Critics*. Cambridge, Polity Press.

Gorard, S. (2002) *How Do We Overcome the Methodological Schism (Or Can There Be a 'Compleat' Researcher)?* Cardiff: Cardiff University School of Social Sciences. Occasional Paper 47.

Gove, M. (2010) *Michael Gove to the National College Annual Conference*, Birmingham, June 2010.

Gove, M. (2011) *Speech to Cambridge University*, November 2011. Available online: http://www.education.gov.uk/inthenews/speeches/a00200373/michael-gove-to-cambridge-university (last accessed 11 October 2012).

Gove, M. (2012) *Speech to the National College Annual Conference, June 2012*. Available online: http://www.education.gov.uk/inthenews/speeches/a00210308/michael-gove-at-the-national-college-annual-conference (last accessed 11 October 2012).

Green, B. (2011) Knowledge, the future and education(al) research: a new-millennial challenge, in A. Lee, N. Johnson, R. Parkes, G. Martin and D. Maher (eds) *The National Educational Research Futures Summit Final Report*. Sydney: University of Technology.

Green, B. and Bigum, C. (1998) Re-tooling schooling? Information technology, cultural change and the future(s) of Australian education, in J. Smyth, R. Hattam and M. Lawson (eds) *Schooling for a Fair Go*. Annadale: Federation Press.

Groundwater-Smith, S. and Mockler, N. (2008) *Teacher Professional Learning in an Age of Compliance: Mind the Gap*. Rotterdam: Springer.

Groundwater-Smith, S. and Sachs, J. (2002) The activist professional and the reinstatement of trust, *Cambridge Journal of Education*, 32(3), 341–358.

GTCNI (2007) *Teaching: The Reflective Profession Incorporating the Northern Ireland Teacher Competences*. Available online: http://www.gtcni.org.uk/uploads/docs/GTCNI_Comp_Bmrk%20%20Aug%2007.pdf (last accessed 11 October 2012).

Guardian (2012) Thousands of vocational qualifications to be stripped out of GCSE league tables. London: Guardian Newspapers. Available online: http://www.guardian.co.uk/education/2012/jan/31/vocational-qualifications-stripped-league-tables (last accessed 11 October 2012).

Hagger, H. and McIntyre, D. (2006) *Learning Teaching from Teachers: Realising the Potential of School Based Teacher Education*. Buckingham: Open University Press.

Halsey, A. H. (1972) *Educational Priority Volume 1: Educational Priority Area Problems and Policies*. London: HMSO.

Hammersley, M. (1997) Educational research and teaching: a response to David Hargreaves' TTA lecture, *British Educational Research Journal*, 23(4), 405–420.

Hammersley, M. (2004) Action research: a contradiction in terms? *Oxford Review of Education*, 30(2), 165–181.

Hargreaves, D. (1996) *Teaching as a Research-based Profession: Possibilities and Prospects. The Teacher Training Agency Annual Lecture 1996*. London: TTA.

Hargreaves, D. (1999) The knowledge creating school, *British Journal of Educational Studies*, 47(2), 122–44.

Hargreaves, D. (2006) *Education Epidemic: Transforming Secondary Schools Through Innovation Networks*. London: Demos.

Harvey, D. (1989) *The Conditions of Postmodernity: An Enquiry Into the Conditions of Cultural Change*. Oxford: Blackwell.

Hayhoe, R. and Li, J. (2010) The idea of a normal university in the 21st century, *Frontiers of Education in China,* 5(1), 74–103.

Hazelhurst, S., Morris, B. and William, W. (2010) Supplementary report: national financial implications of RAE 2008 outcomes. Appendix 1 to *BERA/UCET Review of the Impacts of the RAE 2008 on Education Research in UK Higher Education Institutions.* Macclesfield: BERA/UCET.

HEFCE (2009) *PhD Study Trends and Profiles, 1996–97 to 2004–05.* Bristol: HEFCE.

HEFCE (2012) *Research Excellence Framework (REF) 2014.* Bristol: HEFCE.

Held, D. and McGrew, A. (2005) *The Global Transformation Reader: An Introduction to the Globalization Debate* (3rd edn). Cambridge: Polity Press.

Henkel, M. (2000) *Academic Identities: Policy Change in Higher Education.* London and Philadelphia: Jessica Kingsley Publishers.

Henkel, M. (2005) Academic identity and autonomy in a changing policy environment, *Higher Education*, 49(1–2), 155–176.

HESA (2011) *Students by Subject of Study, First Year Indicator, Mode of Study and Level of Study 2009/10.* Available online: http://www.hesa.ac.uk/content/view/1897/706/ (last accessed 11 October 2012).

Hillage, J., Pearson, R., Anderson, A. and Tamkin, P. (1998) *Excellence in Research on Schools.* London: DfEE.

Hillgate Group (1989) *Learning to Teach.* London: The Claridge Press.

Hirst, P. (1966) Educational theory, in J. W. Tibble (ed.) *The Study of Education.* London: Routledge and Kegan Paul.

Hirst, P. (1996) The demands of professional practice and preparation for teachers, in J. Furlong and R. Smith (eds) *The Role of Higher Education in Initial Teacher Training.* London: Kogan Page.

Hirst, P. and Thompson, G. (1996) *Globalization in Question: The International Economy and The Possibilities of Governance.* Cambridge: Polity Press.

HMIE (2010) *Report on the Aspect Review of Initial Teacher Education.* Edinburgh: Her Majesty's Inspectorate for Education (Scotland). Available online: http://www.hmie.gov.uk/documents/publication/arite (last accessed 11 October 2012).

Hodgkinson, H. L. (1957) Action Research: a critique, *Journal of Educational Sociology*, 33, 137–153.

Hofstetter, R. and Schneuwly, B. (2002) Institutionalisation of educational sciences and the dynamics of their development, *European Educational Research Journal*, 1(1), 1–24.

Hood, C. (1995) The 'New Public Management' in the 1980s: variations on a theme' in *Accounting Organisations and Society*, 20(3), 93–109.

Hoyle, E. (1974) Professionality, professionalism and control in teaching, *London Education Review,* 3(2), 13–19.

Hoyle, E. (1982) The professionalisation of teachers: a paradox, *British Journal of Educational Studies*, 30(2), 161–171.

Hoyle, E. and John, P. (1995) *Professional Knowledge and Professional Practice.* London, Cassell.

Hughes, O. (2003) *Public Management and Administration: An introduction.* Basingstoke: Palgrave Macmillan.

Institute for Effective Education (2009/10) *Annual Report*, 2009/10. York: University of York.

James, E. (1972) *Teacher Education and Training (The James Report)*. London: HMSO.

Judge, H. (2006) Book review of *The Trouble with Ed Schools* by David Labaree, *American Journal of Education*, 12(3), 256–462.

Judge, H., Lemosse, M., Paine, L. and Sedlak, M. (1994) *The University and the Teachers: France, the United States, England*. Wallingford: Triangle Books.

Keep, E., Mayhew, K. and Payne, J. (2006) From skills revolution to productivity miracle – not as simple as it sounds, *Oxford Review of Economic Policy*, 22(4), 539–559.

Keiner, K. (2010) Disciplines of education: the value of disciplinary observation, in J. Furlong and M. Lawn (eds) *The Disciplines of Education: Their Role in the Future of Education Research*. London: Routledge.

Kennedy, M. (1997) The connection between research and practice, *Educational Researcher*, Oct, 4–12.

Kerr, C. (1963) *The Uses of the University*. MA: Harvard University Press.

Kuhn, T. S. (1962) *The Structure of Scientific Revolutions* (1st edn). Chicago: University of Chicago Press.

Labaree, D. (2004) *The Trouble with Ed Schools*. Yale: Yale University Press.

Lauder, H., Brown, P., Dillabough, J. -A. and Halsey, A. H. (2007) The prospects for education: individualisation, globalisation and social change, in H. Lauder, P. Brown, J. -A. Dillabough and A. H. Halsey (eds) *Education, Globalisation and Social Change*. Oxford: Oxford University Press.

Lawlor, S. (1990) *Teachers Mistaught: Training Theories or Education in Subjects?* London: Centre for Policy Studies.

Lawn, M., Deary, I., Bartholomew, D. and Brett, C. (2010) Embedding the new science of research: the organised culture of Scottish educational research in the mid-twentieth century, *Paedagogica Historica*, 2010, 1–25, iFirst Article.

Lay, S. (2004) *The Interpretation of the Magna Charta Universitatum and its Principles*. Bologna: Bologna University Press.

Lee, A. (2010) *What Counts as Educational Research? Some Questions of Boundaries and Limits*. Paper presented at The National Educational Research Futures Summit University of Technology, Sydney February 25–26.

Levidow, L. (2002) Marketizing higher education: neo-liberal strategies and counter-strategies, in K. Robins and F. Webster (eds) *The Virtual University? Knowledge, Markets and Management*. Oxford, UK: Oxford University Press.

Levin, B. (2011) Mobilising research knowledge in education, *London Review of Education*, 9(1), 15–26.

Levin, B., Qi, J. and Edelstein, H. (2012) *The Impact of University Research in Education: International Perspectives on Knowledge Mobilization*. Bristol: Policy Press.

Lewin, K. (1948) *Resolving Social Conflicts*. New York: Harper Row.

Lo, Y. and Macaro, E. (2012) The medium of instruction and classroom interaction: evidence from Hong Kong secondary schools, *International Journal of Bilingual Education and Bilingualism*, 15(1), 29–52.

Lofthouse, M. (2009) *The Role of the Churches in Teacher Training, 1914–1945*. Oxford: University of Oxford Department of Education.

Lucas, L. (2006) *The Research Game in Academic Life*. Buckingham: Society for Research into Higher Education/Open University Press.

Luke, A. (2003) After the marketplace: evidence, social science and educational research, *Australian Educational Researcher*, 30(2), 87–107.

MacLure, M. (2003) *Discourse in Educational and Social Research*. Milton Keynes: Open University Press.

Magna Charta Universitatum (1988) *Magna Charta Universitatum*, Bologna: Observatory of the Magna Charta.

Maguire, M. and Weiner, G. (1994) The place of women in teacher education: discourses of power, *Educational Review*, 46(2), 121–139.

Mahony, P. and Hextall, I. (2000) *Reconstructing Teaching: Standards, Performance and Accountability*. London: Routledge/Falmer.

Marginson, S. (1993) *Education and Public Policy in Australia*. Cambridge: Cambridge University Press.

Marginson, S. (2009) The academic professions in the global era, in J. Enders and E. deWeert (eds) *The Changing Face of Academic Life: Analytical and Comparative Perspectives*. London: Palgrave.

Marginson, S. and Considine, M. (2000) The enterprise university: power, governance and reinvention in Australia, *Higher Education*, 46(4), 543–544.

McIntyre, D. (2006) Partnership in ITE in Scotland and England: can we learn again from research and from experience? *Scottish Educational Review*, 37, 5–19.

McKinsey (2007) *How the World's Best Performing School systems Come Out on Top*. McKinsey and Company. Available online: http://www.mckinsey.com/clientservice/socialsector/resources/pdf/Worlds_School_Systems_Final.pdf (last accessed 11 October 2012).

McKinsey (2010) *How the World's Most Improved School Systems Keep Getting Better*. McKinsey and Company. Available online: http://mckinseyonsociety.com/how-the-worlds-most-improved-school-systems-keep-getting-better/ (last accessed 11 October 2012).

McLean, M. (2006) *Pedagogy and the University: Critical Theory and Practice*. London and New York: Continuum.

McNair, A. D. (1944) *Teachers and Youth Leaders: Report of the Committee Appointed by the President of the Board of Education to Consider the Supply, Recruitment and Training of Teachers and Youth Leaders* (The McNair Report). London: HMSO.

Menter, I. (2011) Four 'academic sub-tribes' but one territory? Teacher educators and teacher education in Scotland, *Journal of Education for Teaching*, 37(3), 293–308.

Menter, I., Brisard, E. and Smith, I. (2006) Making teachers in Britain: professional knowledge for initial teacher education in England and Scotland, *Educational Philosophy and Theory*, 38(3), 269–286.

Menter, I. and Hulme, M. (2008) Is small beautiful? Policy-making in teacher education in Scotland, in J. Furlong, M. Cochran-Smith and M. Brennan (eds) *Politics and Policy in Teacher Education: International Perspectives*. London: Routledge.

Menter, I. and Hulme, M. (2012) Teacher education in Scotland – riding out the recession?, *Educational Research*, 54(2), 149–160.

Millett, A. (1997) *Speech to TTA Research Conference, 5.12.97.* London: TTA.

Mills, D., Jepson, A., Coxon, T., Easterby-Smith, M., Hawkins, P. and Spencer, J. (2006) *Demographic Review of the Social Sciences. Commissioned by the Economic and Social Research Council.* Swindon: ESRC.

Mockler, N. and Sachs, J. (eds) (2010). *Rethinking Educational Practice Through Reflexive Inquiry: Essays in Honour of Susan Groundwater-Smith.* Rotterdam: Springer.

Moon, R. (1998) *The English Exception? International Perspectives on the Initial Education and Training of Teachers, UCET Occasional Paper No. 11.* London: UCET.

Murray, J. and Male, T. (2005) Becoming a Teacher Educator: evidence from the field, *Teaching and Teacher Education,* 21(2), 125–142.

Mutton, T., Burn, K. and Hagger, H. (2011) Learning to plan, planning to learn: the developing expertise of beginning teachers, *Teachers and Teaching: Theory and Practice,* 17 (4), 399–416.

Neave, G. (1988) On the cultivation of quality efficiency and enterprise: an overview of recent trends in higher education in Western Europe 1986–1998, *European Journal of Education,* 23(1 & 2), 7–23.

Newman, J.H. (1853a) *Newman Reader – Idea of a University – Discourse 5: Knowledge its own ends.* Available online: http://www.newmanreader.org/works/idea/discourse5.html (last accessed 11 October 2012).

Newman, J.H. (1853b) *Newman Reader – Idea of a University Discourse 7. Knowledge Viewed in Relation to Professional Skill.* Available online: www.newmanreader.org/works/idea/discourse7.html (last accessed 11 October 2012).

Newman, J. (2001) *Modernising Governance: New Labour, Policy and Society.* London: Sage.

Newsom, J. (1963) *Half Our Future (Newsom Report).* London: HMSO.

Nisbet, J. (2002) Educational research: the birth of a discipline, *European Educational Research Journal,* 1(1), 37–44.

Nisbet, J. (2005) What is educational research? Changing perspectives through the 20th century, *Research Papers in Education,* 20(1), 25–44.

Nowotny, H., Scott, P. and Gibbons, M. (2003) 'Mode 2' revisited: the new production of knowledge, *Minerva,* 41(3), 179–194.

Nunes, T. and Bryant, P. (2006) *Improving Literacy by Teaching Morphemes.* London: Routledge.

Nunes, T., Bryant, P., Evans, D., Bell, D. and Barros, R. (2012) Teaching children how to include the inversion principle in their reasoning about quantitative relations, *Educational Studies Mathematics,* 79(3), 371–388.

Nussbaum, M. (2010) *Not For Profit: Why Democracy Needs the Humanities.* Princeton: University Press.

O'Hear, A. (1988) *Who Teaches the Teachers?* London: Social Affairs Unit.

Oancea, A. (2006) *Procrustes or Proteus? Towards a Philosophical Dimension of Research Assessment.* British Educational Research Association Conference. In: *Symposium on Philosophy and Action Research* (symposium with Wilfred Carr, John Elliott and Richard Pring), BERA conference, University of Warwick, 2006.

Oancea, A. (2010) *The Impacts of RAE 2008 on Education Research in the UK: Main Report.* Macclesfield: UCET/BERA.

Oancea, A. and Bridges, D. (2010) Philosophy of education in the UK: the historical and contemporary tradition, in J. Furlong and M. Lawn (eds) *The Disciplines of Education. Their Role in the Future of Education Research.* London: Routledge.
Oancea, A. and Furlong, J. (2007) Expressions of excellence and the assessment of applied and practice-based research, in J. Furlong and A. Oancea (eds) *Research Papers in Education*, 22(2), 213–228.
OECD (1995) *Educational Research and Development: Trends, Issues and Challenges.* Paris: OECD.
OECD (2005) *Teachers Matter: Attracting, Developing and Retaining Effective Teachers.* Paris: OECD.
OECD (2011) *Lessons from PISA for the United States: Strong Performers and Successful Reformers in Education.* Available online: http://www.oecd.org/dataoecd/32/50/46623978.pdf (last accessed 11 October 2012).
Ofsted (2011) *The Annual Report of Her Majesty's Chief Inspector of Education, Children's Services and Skills 2010/11.* London: Ofsted.
Parlett, M. and Hamilton, D. (1972) Evaluation as illumination: a new approach to the study of innovatory programmes, in D. Hamilton, D. Jenkins, C. King, B. MacDonald and M. Parlett (eds) *Beyond the Numbers Game: A Reader in Educational Evaluation*. London: Macmillan Education, 6 –22.
Patrick, H. (1986) From Cross to CATE: the universities and teacher education over the past century, *Oxford Review of Education*, 12(3), 243–261.
Pelikan, J. (1992) *The Idea of the University: A Re-examination.* New Haven: Yale University Press.
Phillips, M. (1926) University department or two-year college? *The Forum of Education*, 4.
Pirsig, R. M. (1974) *Zen and the Art of Motorcycle Maintenance: An Inquiry into Values.* New York: William Morrow and Co.
Plowden, B. (1967) *Children and their Primary Schools. A Report of the Central Advisory Council for Education (England) (The Plowden report).* London: Her Majesty's Stationery Office.
Polanyi, M. (1966) *The Tacit Dimension.* Garden City, NY: Anchor Books.
Power, S. and Whitty, G. (1999) New Labour's education policy: first, second or third way?, *Journal of Education Policy,* 14(5), 535–546.
Pratt, J. (1997) *The Polytechnic Experiment 1965–1992.* Buckingham: Society for Research into Higher Education/Open University Press.
Pring, R., Hayward, G., Hodgson, A., Johnson, J., Keep, E., Oancea, A., Rees, G., Spours, K. and Wilde, S. (2009) *Education for All: The Future of Education and Training For 14–19-year-olds.* London: Routledge.
QAA (2008) *The Framework for Higher Education Qualifications in England and Wales and Northern Ireland.* London: QAA. Available online: http://www.vitae.ac.uk/policy-practice/1689/Quality-Assurance-Agency-QAA.html (last accessed 11 October 2012).
RAE (2008a) *Research Assessment Exercise.* Available online: http://www.rae.ac.uk/ (last accessed 11 October 2012).
RAE (2008b) *Sub-Panel 45 Education: Subject Overview Report.* Available online: http://www.rae.ac.uk/pubs/2009/ov/ (last accessed 11 October 2012).
Readings, B. (1996) *The University in Ruins.* MA: Harvard University Press.

Richardson, W. (2002) Educational studies in the United Kingdom, 1940–2002, *British Journal of Educational Studies*, 50(1), 3–56.

Rizvi, F. and Lingard, R. (2009) *Globalizing Education Policy*. London: Routledge.

Robbins, L. C. (1963) *Higher Education (The Robbins Report)*. London: HMSO.

Robertson, S. (2007) Remaking the world: neo-liberalism and the transformation of education and teachers' labour, in L. Weis and M. Compton (eds) *The Global Assault on Teachers, Teaching and their Unions*. New York: Palgrave.

Rothblatt, S. (1997) *The Modern University and its Discontents: The Fate of Newman's Legacies in Britain and America*. Cambridge: Cambridge University Press.

Rothblatt, S. (2010) Gaining a commanding voice, in J. Furlong and M. Lawn (eds) *Disciplines of Education: Their Role in the Future of Education Research*. London: Routledge.

Ryle, G. (1949) *The Concept of Mind*. Chicago: University of Chicago Press.

Sahlberg, P., Furlong, J. and Munn, P. (2012) *Report of the International Review Panel on the Structure of Initial Teacher Education Provision in Ireland: Review Conducted on Behalf of the Department of Education and Skills*. Dublin: Higher Education Authority of Ireland.

Schön, D.A. (1983) *The Reflective Practitioner*. New York: Basic Books.

Schwab, J. (1978) *Science, Curriculum and Liberal Education: Selected Essays* (eds I. Wesbury and N. Wilkof). Chicago: Chicago University Press.

Scott, S., Sylva, K., Doolan, M., Price, J., Jacobs, B., Crook, C. and Landau, S. (2012). Randomized controlled trial of parent groups for child antisocial behaviour targeting multiple risk factors: the SPOKES project, *The Journal of Child Psychology and Psychiatry*, 51, 48–57.

Scottish Funding Council (2010) *Intake Targets for the Controlled Subjects in Higher Education Institutions for Academic year 2010–11*. Available online: http://www.sfc.ac.uk/web/FILES/CircularsSFC0510/sfc0510.pdf (last accessed 11 October 2012).

Sector Skills Council for Life Long Learning (2007) *New Overarching Professional Standards for Teachers, Tutors and Trainers in the Lifelong Learning Sector*. London: Life Long Learning, UK.

Shattock, M. (ed.) (2009) *Entrepreneurialism in Universities and the Knowledge Economy: Diversification and Organisational Change in European Higher Education*. Maidenhead: Open University Press.

Showers, B. and Joyce, B. (1996) The evolution of peer coaching, *Educational Leadership*, March, 12–16.

Simon, B. (1974) *The Politics of Educational Reform, 1920–1940*. London: Lawrence Wishart.

Slaughter, S. and Leslie, L. (1999) *Academic Capitalism: Politics, Policies and the Entrepreneurial University*. Baltimore: The Johns Hopkins University Press.

Slavin, R. (2002) Evidence-based education policies: transforming educational practice and research, *Educational Researcher*, 31(7), 15–21.

Smith, A. and Webster, F. (eds) (1997) *The Post Modern University*. Buckingham: Open University Press.

Smithers, A. and Robinson, P. (2011) *The Good Teacher Training Guide, 2011*. Buckingham: University of Buckingham.

SFRE (2010) *Strategic Forum for Educational Research*. Available online: http://www.sfre.ac.uk/ (last accessed 11 October 2012).

Stenhouse, L. (1970) *The Humanities Research Project: An Introduction*. London: Heinemann.

Stenhouse, L. (1981) What counts as educational research?, *British Journal of Educational Studies*, 29, 103–114.

Stiglitz, J. E. (2002) *Globalisation and its Discontents*. New York: Penguin.

Sutherland, S. (1997) *Teacher Education and Training: A Study (Sutherland Report)*. London: HMSO.

Sylva, K., Melhuish, E., Sammons, P., Siraj-Blatchford, I. & Taggart, B. (2011) Pre-school quality and educational outcomes at age 11: low quality has little benefit, *Journal of Early Childhood Research*, 9(2) 109-124.

Taylor, C., Connoly, M., Power, S. and Rees, G. (2007) *Formative Evaluation of the Applied Educational Research Scheme (AERS)*. Edinburgh: Scottish Government Social Research. Available online: http://www.scotland.gov.uk/Resource/Doc/208243/0055238.pdf (last accessed 11 October 2012).

Taylor, W. (ed.) (1969) Towards a policy for the education of teachers: proceedings of the twentieth symposium of the Colston Research Society held in the University of Bristol, April 1st to 5th, 1968. *Colston Papers No. 20*. London: Butterworth.

Taylor, W. (1988) Robbins and the education of teachers, *Oxford Review of Education*, 14(1), 49–58.

TDA (2007) *Guidance to Accompany the Requirements for Initial Teacher Training*. London: TDA.

TDA (2009) *The National Framework for Masters in Teaching and Learning*. London: TDA.

Telegraph (2012a) GCSEs scrapped as Michael Gove accuses exam boards of 'dumbing down. Available online: http://www.telegraph.co.uk/education/educationnews/9346476/GCSEs-scrapped-as-Michael-Gove-accuses-exam-boards-of-dumbing-down.html (last accessed 11 October 2012).

Telegraph (2012b) Top graduates to get £25,000 to teach in tough schools. Available online: http://www.telegraph.co.uk/education/educationnews/9330113/Top-graduates-to-get-25000-to-teach-in-tough-schools.html (last accessed 11 October 2012).

Tibble, J. W. (ed.) (1966) *The Study of Education*. London: Routledge and Kegan Paul.

TLRP (2009) *Teaching and Learning Research Programme*. Available online: http://www.tlrp.org/ (last accessed 11 October 2012).

Torrance, H. (2008) *Overview of ESRC Research in Education*. Swindon: ESRC.

Wagner, P., Wittrock, B. and Whitley, R. (eds) (1993) *Discourses on Society: The Shaping of the Social Science Disciplines*. Dordrecht: Kluwer.

Wallace, M. (1987) A historical review of action research: some implications for the education of teachers in their managerial role, *Journal of Education for Teaching*, 13(2), 97–115.

Watson, A. (2009) *Key Understandings in Mathematics Learning. A Review Commissioned by the Nuffield Foundation. Paper 6: Algebraic Reasoning*. London: Nuffield Foundation.

Weiss, C. (1979) Knowledge creep and decision accretion, *Knowledge: Creation, Diffusion and Utilisation*, 1(3), 381–404.

Welsh Government (2011) *Revised Professional Standards for Education Practitioners in Wales: Circular 020/2011.* Cardiff: Welsh Government.

Welsh Government (2012) *Another Step Forwards for the Teaching Masters.* Available online: http://wales.gov.uk/newsroom/educationandskills/2012/120417teachingmasters/?lang=en (last accessed 11 October 2012).

Whitty, G. (2006) Education(al) research and education policy making: is conflict inevitable? *British Educational Research Journal,* 32(2), 159–176.

Wilkin, M. (1996) *Initial Teacher Training: The Dialogue of Ideology and Culture.* London: Falmer Press.

Woodhead, C. (1998) Academia gone to seed, *New Statesman,* 26 March 1998, 51–52.

Yates, L. (2004) *What Does Good Education Research Look Like? Situating a Field and Its Practices.* Maidenhead: Open University Press.

Young, M. (1971) *Knowledge and Control.* London: Routledge.

Young, M. (2008) *Bringing Knowledge Back In.* London: Routledge.

# Index

Please note that page references to non-textual content such as illustrations will be in *italics*, while the letter 'n' will follow references to Notes.